The attention to detail that Jonathan require careful study on your part. But passage and what many have said about beautifully portrays a consistent and powerful justification that "goes all the way," not only to save, but to form the basis for sanctification centered on our union with Christ. His insights inspired me, and I know they will do the same for you in this very important book.

DR. DANIEL KUIPER, ACADEMIC DEAN AND PROFESSOR OF BIBLICAL THEOLOGY
ALL NATIONS SEMINARY, JUAREZ, MEXICO

One of my haunting memories from my early years as a pastor is the time I was asked by a college student about what the Bible means when it says we have died to sin and now live to God. We were on a chartered bus heading toward a Bible conference. This young man was serious about victory over sin and about correct theology. I tried to put on a confident face as I muddled my way through an explanation that didn't ring true for me experientially and just plain sounded confusing as it came out of my mouth. I could tell by the young man's expression that everything I had said was clear as mud. How many times since then have I sat through—and even led—confusing Bible studies on this topic of the "sinful nature" and death to sin! What a breath of fresh air this book has been to me! What clear sense it makes of the passages! I…will continue to endorse *Dead Men Rising* as a must read for those I know who are serious about the theology and practice of the new life and sanctification!

RAY MEUNICH, PASTOR, FELLOWSHIP CHURCH, COLLEGE STATION, TX

I highly endorse this fresh look at Romans 6. *Dead Men Rising* challenged my thinking about what I had been taught all my life. Very seldom does something new come along that better matches the whole of Scripture and thus influences me to change my perspective. Not only does Williams' approach help me in my personal walk with Christ, but as a counselor and pastor it will help those I minister to in their journey toward Christlikeness. *Dead Men Rising* is an inspiration for our journey of sanctification and can help keep us from the stumbling block of self-dependence and performance. I trust that God will powerfully use this book.

GREG VAN NADA, NATIONAL CAMPUS DIRECTOR, GCM CHURCHES

This excellent exposition of Romans 6 is probably the best I've read. The research is obvious and the conclusions worth serious consideration. I heartily encourage all to study and consider Jonathan's contribution.

HERSCHEL MARTINDALE, VETERAN PASTOR AND FORMER DIRECTOR
EUROPEAN MISSIONS FOR GREAT COMMISSION CHURCHES

I have known Jonathan Williams for three decades, and I have always appreciated his clarity of thought in teaching the Word of God. *Dead Men Rising* is another phenomenal example of Jonathan's careful and sharp exposition of the Scriptures. This explanation of Romans 6:1-14 is a must read for anyone who wants to understand what it means to be dead to sin and alive to God.

JOHN HOPLER, NATIONAL DIRECTOR, GREAT COMMISSION CHURCHES

In *Dead Men Rising*, Williams describes Romans 6 as the simple, straightforward, yet powerful teaching I'm now convinced Paul intended it to be. Williams' careful exposition of the passage, along with comparisons of similar texts in other Pauline epistles, give the reader a settled confidence that Romans 6 is not a bewildering claim about an inner man that died to sin but still sins. Rather, Romans 6 is a passage about real, eternal truths outside of myself that were accomplished in Christ (not in me), and which opens the door for a sanctifying power through the Spirit that Paul addresses later. If you really want to understand the message from Romans about life-change, this book might be indispensible.

JOHN MEYER, PASTOR, SUMMITVIEW COMMUNITY CHURCH, LOVELAND, CO

In this penetrating commentary, Pastor Williams investigates not only the theological implications of this daunting and curious passage, but its impact on the Christian life. Exegetically accurate, systematically coherent, and practically relevant, this treatment of justification and sanctification gives a sound rejoinder to the age-old dilemma of reconciling my position in Christ with the relentless struggles in my daily walk. I commend this work, to galvanize and refresh the weary and pessimistic soul!

MARK MARLEY, BIBLE EXPOSITOR, GRACE COMMUNITY CHURCH, SAN ANTONIO TX

Joining God in the renewal of all things requires that we understand how to appropriate God's grace in the redemption of our own lives, for the greatest obstacle to mission is ourselves. Jonathan Williams, in *Dead Man Rising*, shares the fruit of his lifelong quest to discern what it means to be dead to sin and alive to Christ. His biblical exposition of Romans 6:1-14 avoids common double-talk and gives us an interpretation that is true to life and scripture. This book will help the Church become mature, fully human, and fully alive, like Christ.

JR WOODWARD, CO-FOUNDER OF KAIROS LA & THE ECCLESIA NETWORK
AUTHOR, CREATING A MISSIONAL CULTURE

JONATHAN WILLIAMS

DEAD MEN RISING

THE *Death* OF *Sin,* THE *Rise* OF *Grace*

Dead Men Rising
The Death of Sin, The Rise of Grace
© 2012 by Jonathan Williams

Published by
Deep River Books
Sisters, Oregon
http://www.deepriverbooks.com

ISBN–13: 9781937756062
ISBN–10: 1937756068

Library of Congress: 2012938769

Printed in the USA

Cover design by Jason Enterline

DEDICATION

I would like to dedicate this book to two people.

First, I dedicate it to my wife, Kathy, who asked me to commit to one day a week and do nothing but write. I made the commitment, and her encouragement kept me going. Thank you for being for me!

Second, I dedicate it to Dr. J. Sidlow Baxter, now with the Lord. I met Dr. Baxter many years ago and sat under his teaching when I was in high school. His godly example and especially his insights on Romans 6 pointed me in the right direction. I look forward to thanking you in eternity.

TABLE OF CONTENTS

PART 1

DEAD MEN

The Contradictory Reality

THE PASTOR WAS DESPERATE. For years he had ministered effectively in his teaching ministry, but as he looked within his heart, he saw the ugliness of sin's stain. It's not that he was cherishing secret sin. He wanted victory, complete victory, and he wanted to please God in body and soul. He wanted to be an example to his flock and lead them in the righteous ways of God. But how could he lead them when he couldn't lead himself?

Finally, he had had enough. He could no longer maintain the status quo of his life. Late one night he took a train to its last stop on the edge of the city. He walked into the country and found an isolated place where he could cry out to God for deliverance from inward sin. He fell to his knees beneath a tree and prayed for hours, asking God for the blessing that would take away the power of sin in his life.

During those hours, no greater devotion could be found in the world. This man surrendered everything he was and everything he had to God, and after long hours of prayer that followed many months of anxiety about sin and temptation in his heart, he collapsed to the ground from exhaustion. And then it happened. Ecstasy filled his soul. He had never felt anything like this before in his life. He cried out to the Lord, "I believe, Lord, I believe. You have cleansed me from all inner sin and sanctified me. You have given me power over sin. I am a holy man."

Filled with joy, the young pastor made his way back into the city, knowing that his struggles with sin were behind him since his sin nature was now made powerless by the cross of Christ. But as days turned into weeks, he discovered sinful desires resurfacing from deep within. How could this be? Had he not surrendered his all to Christ? Had not Christ filled him with the Spirit and made his old sinful nature inoperative by faith?

He sought the counsel of an experienced teacher in such matters who assured him that what he was feeling was not inward sin but just the temptations of the evil one. But after awhile, he could no longer accept that explanation.

Yes, the evil one may have been tempting him, but he could not ignore the sinful desires, thoughts, and motives coming from within.

Again and again the young pastor sought the Lord, sometimes in all-night vigils, claiming the crucifixion of the old sin nature by faith, and many times he felt that he had gained complete victory only to lapse back into the sad reality that it was not so. He still struggled mightily with the power of sin in his soul.

Finally, he could bear it no longer. The pastor asked for a leave of absence, sought refuge in a place of rest, and searched for relief from the spiritual, mental, emotional, and theological anguish that filled his soul.

❋ ❋ ❋

Sin is the "contradictory reality." Sin is the great contradiction for every Christian. For that matter, sin is the greatest contradiction in the world! It promises life but brings death. It promises pleasure but brings pain. It prods us to give it a try, like a friend inviting us to a good time, but then it becomes our master.

Our good, all-powerful and holy God created the world. He intended it to be the expression of His glory and the perfect environment for our life. Yet, sin surrounds us in His world. Atrocities in distant lands or this morning's enraged driver signaling obscenities remind us daily that sin still parades through God's good creation.

But I don't want to talk about sin "out there," whether it's sin strutting across the world or across the street. I want to talk about sin "in here"—sin in my heart and sin in your heart. Sin is the greatest contradiction in a Christian. We who follow Jesus make amazing claims: We are born again, justified, redeemed, filled with the Holy Spirit, and hoping for His return and a new world where righteousness dwells. Yet, in spite of these amazing truths, we still struggle with sin in this life. How can this be?

All the apostles point to this ongoing struggle, this contradictory reality. Paul exhorted the believers in Rome, "Do not let sin reign in your mortal body so that you obey its lusts" (Romans 6:12). To the Corinthians he said, "Become sober-minded as you ought, and stop sinning" (1 Corinthians 15:34). With great earnestness, he warned the Galatians to walk by the Spirit lest they fall to the lusts of the flesh (Galatians 5:17–19).

Peter spoke of sin's war upon the believer: "Abstain from fleshly lusts which wage war against the soul" (1 Peter 2:1). James warned against the perils of temptation rising from within (James 1:13–16), and John wrote to his followers so that they would not sin, but knowing that they probably would, he added that the Savior would be there for them like a great defense attorney (1 John 2:1–2).

I doubt that many of us need reminders of our sinful tendencies which, frankly, can become more than tendencies. They sometimes prevail against us. We don't need Bible verses to tell us the obvious—though at one level Christ has saved us from our sins, on another level, we are still a work-in-progress, dealing with sinful desires and habits. It seems a contradiction, a sinning Christian; yet it is reality, the contradictory reality. And it is the greatest cause of sorrow in the life of the Christian and the greatest obstacle to the advance of the kingdom in the world.

Did you understand that? Do you agree with what I just stated—that sin is the greatest obstacle to the advance of the kingdom in the world? What about the need to raise funds for mission projects? It is greater. What about the need to learn and apply church growth and management principles? It is greater. What about the development of leaders for the church? It is greater. The greatest obstacle to the advance of the kingdom is our sin.

If Christians consistently lived with righteousness, our money, leadership, principles, strategies, and a hundred other things would multiply their effect; joy would abound; and the kingdom would advance more rapidly. Can anything be more urgent than prevailing against sin in our lives? Can anything be more urgent than the church being a holy church?

My lifelong ambition has been to live a Christ-pleasing life. In this quest, I have discovered the greatest obstacle to full fruitfulness: Me!

It has not been the sin or issues of other leaders with whom I have served. It has not been the never-ending cries of people in need because they made yet another stupid choice. It has not been family issues or the annoying idiosyncrasies of friends. It has not been trying circumstances like a church that won't grow, or a job I don't care to have, or even the trauma of watching a loved one die. As difficult as all these things have been, I have been my greatest obstacle.

In my struggles with sin I have received counsel, prayed, been prayed over, fasted, studied the Word, and claimed promises. All have helped greatly. In my study of the Word, I have examined many passages that provided great insight and encouragement. But I have most often turned to one passage for clues to solve the mystery of sin *in me*. The passage is Romans chapters six through eight.

I am not the first to look at its majestic and piercing words. Pastors, preachers, laypeople, and great theologians have examined this text for centuries and pointed to it as "the answer." John Stott, speaking of these chapters and Romans 5, said,

> They are without doubt among the greatest and most glorious chapters of the whole New Testament. They portray our Christian privilege, the privileges of those whom God has "made new," those whom He has "justified," that is, declared righteous and accepted in Christ. The earlier chapters of the Epistle are devoted to the need and the way of justification. They are concerned to make it plain that all men are sinners under the just judgment of God, and can be justified solely through the redemption which is in Christ Jesus—by grace alone, through faith alone. Now, at this point, having set forth the need and explained the way of justification, Paul goes on to describe its fruits, the results of justification in a life of sonship and obedience on earth and a glorious hereafter in heaven.[1]

For decades, I followed the lead of others and made pilgrimages to this greatest of Paul's epistles that held within it the answer to the struggles of my soul. It is a great passage, no doubt, and arguably the apex of Paul's greatest letter, but I have encountered a problem. The interpretations I have received from sermons, seminars, and studies have most often failed on two accounts. On the one hand, they never matched my experience. On the other, they didn't seem to cohere with the rest of Scripture.

Yes, I know the warning: "Don't let your experience interpret Scripture for you. Don't put your experience above the Word of God." I agree. Experiences can deceive. Yet, when I read in Romans 6 that I have died to sin, and then I hear that I must claim the truth that I am dead to sin and victory will be mine, I have to confess, my experience has not matched that interpretation of Romans 6.

Maybe I'm the problem. Maybe I'm the exception. Maybe I'm not claiming the verse hard enough or accurately enough or "something" enough. But deep down, I know this is not true. I hear, or I read, that my death to sin is effective only when I consider or "reckon" it so. I say to myself what I've heard others say: *The reason you have problems with sin is you do not* consider *yourself dead to sin as Scripture says (Romans 6:11), and when you do not, sin raises its ugly self within you and overcomes you.*

So they say.

I'm sorry. The Bible may say *I* am dead to sin, but sin sure doesn't seem dead inside me! And I who am supposedly dead to sin find myself sometimes attracted or entertained by sin's impulses. But I thought Paul said I was dead to all that? Sin is like one of those bad guys in a horror movie you just can't quite kill. No matter what you do, he always seems to come back and cause more problems. "I thought we killed him," the actors scream as he reappears—alive, well, and chasing them.

But this isn't a movie, or a bad dream. It is reality, the contradictory reality. Others have told me the same. And many who have not confided to me have failure etched on their faces. I have seen it and so have you.

Maybe Paul meant something else. After all, he did tell the Roman Christians not to let sin *reign* in their bodies just a few sentences after he said they had died to sin. How can sin reign in our lives if we died to it? If we died to it, shouldn't it be dead to us? When Herod the Great was alive, he spread his misery throughout the land of Judea. But when he died, his reign came to an end. No more Herod. He didn't partially die. He wasn't incapacitated. He didn't rise again and kill more family members, or Jews, or whoever was on his list for that day. He was dead and gone, thankfully, and no longer capable of afflicting the world with his insanity.

Some have resorted to semantic trickery in hopes of alleviating the problem. I have heard: "The Bible says you are dead to sin but it never says sin is dead to you. Sin didn't die. You died, and you have to claim *your* death to sin, otherwise sin will overpower you." But this is just playing with words and Scripture doesn't even support such a distinction.

In Romans 7:1–5, Paul uses the husband-wife relationship to teach a lesson about our relationship with sin. We are the wife, sin is the husband, and the Law keeps us in union with sin. In his analogy, Paul says that *the husband dies* and because he dies we (the wife) also die to the Law that bound us to him and are therefore free to unite with another—the resurrected Christ. Based on this analogy, we can scripturally say that we died to sin *because sin (the husband) first died to us.*

Galatians 6:14 reinforces this way of thinking, although Paul is speaking of the world system: "But may it never be that I would boast, except in the cross of our Lord Jesus Christ, through which the world has been crucified to me, and I to the world."

It's not a one-way street. When one dies, the other dies. No, semantic trickery doesn't help, and eventually, even without these verses we will know it is only a semantic trick because we will experience the attempts of sin to reign in our lives. Thus, we have Paul's exhortation: "Do not let sin reign in your mortal bodies!"

How can this be? How can Paul exhort us not to let sin reign if we died to sin and sin died to us? That leads to the second issue: the biblical issue. What did Paul mean?

Great men and women of the faith have proposed two theories to explain this contradictory reality and provide a remedy for God's people. Theory number one is the Eradication Theory. Some believe John Wesley to be the architect of the view that sought to take Romans 6:6 (and similar passages) at face value.[2] Here is what Romans 6:6 says: "Knowing this, that our old self was crucified with Him, in order that our body of sin might be done away with, so that we would no longer be slaves to sin."

"If the Bible says we are dead to sin," Wesley might say, "then we are dead to sin. If our old man was crucified with Christ, then he must be dead. We must take God's Word as it clearly states and conform our experience to it rather than it to our experience." And so John Wesley and his brother Charles and many other great brothers and sisters of our faith, devised a "second blessing" theology where, in a crisis experience, the believer could have his sin nature eradicated with the result that the believer could say that he was indeed dead to sin. Hear it in Wesley's own words:

> Inward sin is then totally destroyed; the root of pride, self-will, anger, love of the world, is then taken out of the heart...The carnal mind, and the heart bent to backsliding, are entirely extirpated.[3]

And this theology, naturally, found its way into the great hymns of Charles Wesley and come to us through the Methodist hymnbook.

Enter my soul, extirpate sin,
Cast out the cursed seed.
Speak the second time: Be clean!
Take away my inbred sin.[4]

Our churches today could use the fresh air of holiness and victory over sin within us, as the Wesleys were so diligent to promote. Yet, is this teaching biblical? Is it true that a "second blessing" will take away inbred sin, our old nature?[5]

Some will argue that Wesley did not teach this although he opened the door for others to draw this conclusion. Melvin E. Deiter, in *Five Views on Sanctification*, presents the Wesleyan perspective and says that Wesley had a much more balanced view of sanctification as a process followed by a crisis followed by more process. He says this about Wesley's belief:

> Although other theological traditions of his day believed that this struggle against an innate, inward rebellion was a normal and even a necessary element of the Christian's quest for the holy life, Wesley believed that the whole gospel, in promise and command, indicated otherwise. He believed that there was freedom from the dominion of sin for every Christian, even under these unhappy inner struggles, and that God's grace was always moving the believer to a life of greater peace, happiness, and love. There was a remedy for the sickness of systemic sinfulness, namely, entire sanctification—a personal, definitive work of God's sanctifying grace by which the war within oneself might cease and the heart be fully released from rebellion into wholehearted love for God and others. This relationship of perfect love could be accomplished, not by excellence of any moral achievements, but by the same faith in the merits of Christ's sacrifice for sin that initially had brought justification and the new life in Christ.[6]

Deiter then quotes Wesley's description of this entire sanctification experience. It was a "total death to sin and an entire renewal in the image of God."[7] I am not a Wesleyan historian, and I may not grasp the nuances of his thinking or even his theological development through the years, but "total death to sin and an entire renewal in the image of God" sounds very much like an eradication of something inside the believer!

But it wasn't Wesley only or even Wesley primarily that promoted this eradication view of sin within the believer. Deiter presents a gracious but revealing account of the heirs to Wesley's theology, revivalists and camp meeting preachers within and beyond the boundaries of Methodism, who hardened his teaching into the eradication theology.

> The American revival context, especially as the movement grew, seemed to expedite the ease with which eradication could move from a simple analogy that was useful to describe the extent of the promised release from sin to become, rather, a concept in holiness teaching that created the impression for many hearers that sin was a substance that could be excised from the heart in the grace of the sanctifying moment. The use of eradication terminology became pervasive. It tended to narrow the focus of the popular theology of the movement and of the holiness churches, shaped as they were by the preaching of their evangelists, who presented sanctification teaching almost exclusively within special revivals or camp meetings held for the promotion of the doctrine.[8]

This eradication teaching met up with the "baptism of the Holy Spirit" movement in the early 1900s. "The initial phase of the Pentecostal revival in the early 1900s was very much influenced by the Wesleyan holiness doctrine of a 'second blessing' and came out of the same American revivalist context. A few went to the extreme of the saying that this 'second definite work' took out sin, 'root and branch,' to the point that individuals were not able to sin anymore."[9]

A variation of this teaching is surfacing in our day. It, too, speaks of the eradication of the sin nature but points to "the moment of conversion" as the time when it happens. The proponents of this view teach that unbelievers have an old, sin nature completely in rebellion to God. But when they come to Christ, the old nature is slain and a new nature is given so that they are completely righteous in their soul and spirit. Believers also have only one nature, but it is a divine nature, righteous and holy.[10]

When one asks the obvious question, "Well, then, where are these sinful impulses coming from?" they will reply, "From your flesh. God dealt with your old nature decisively on the cross, but He has given His Spirit to help you overcome the lusts of the flesh."

I will speak to this viewpoint throughout the book, but for now I hope it is sufficient to quote one verse to show the biblical problem with this teaching. In Galatians 5:24, Paul says that those who belong to Christ Jesus "have crucified the flesh with its passions and desires." According to this verse, it's not just the old sin nature that got the nails, the flesh received them, too. And if the flesh was crucified because of my union with Christ,[11] then where are my sinful desires coming from?

A second viewpoint has largely usurped Wesley's Eradication Theory in evangelical theology. If we are honest, we must admit that it emerged from personal as much as scriptural reflection. I say personal reflection because many "second blessing" adherents had to admit that even after their "crisis experience" or "baptism-with-the-Spirit experience," they still found sinful impulses at work within them. Sin in them wasn't as dead as they thought! And so they traversed the well-marked path of Romans 6, trying to make sense of it and trying to match their experience with God's truth. Many have called this the Suppression or Counteraction Theory.

One prominent strand of theology that has sometimes promoted this viewpoint is known as the Keswick Theology movement. This is sometimes called the Higher Life Movement and has been greatly used of God to promote holiness, service, and missions in the world. Dr. J. Robertson McQuilkin has ably presented the basic ideas of Higher Life Theology[12], although he also states there is no *official* theological statement and teachers at Keswick conferences have presented a broad range of theological ideas. Nevertheless, many speakers inside and outside this movement have promoted this Suppression or Counteraction Theory.

One of the presuppositions of this viewpoint is that "the Christian life is a battleground between one's old nature and one's new nature. The 'old man' and 'new man' of biblical analogy are taken to indicate an old nature, which one has by birth, and a new nature, which is imparted at the new birth."[13] In addition, "the 'old nature' is generally considered to be incapable of improvement, though not all hold this position."[14] The sinful nature, the old man, remains in us and is active as long as we live in this mortal body. Yet, through an inward co-crucifixion with Christ, it is rendered inoperative. It is not destroyed but made weak.

This viewpoint focuses on the Greek word *katargethe*/καταργηθη in Romans 6:6—"that the body of sin might be *destroyed*" (KJV, RSV)—and provides alternate renderings. Some translations, influenced by the Suppression Theory, have softened the "might be destroyed" to "done away with" (NASB, NIV, NKJV), "brought to nothing" (ESV), or "abolished" (HCSB).

Paraphrases have had a field day with it—"a decisive end" (MSF), "might lose its power in our lives" (NLT), "might be made ineffective" (AMP), and "might be broken" (Phillips).

The proponents of the Suppression view say that Christ did not literally destroy the body of sin (sinful nature) but rendered it powerless, weakened it, or dealt it a severe blow. As we do our part by faith—that is, as we claim our co-crucifixion with Christ of the old man or old self (6:6a) based on Paul's admonition in Romans 6:11 to consider (reckon or make real) our co-death with Christ—we enforce the *rendering powerless/doing away with/bringing to nothing/abolishing* the body of sin with the happy result that we finally experience Romans 6:6c and are no longer slaves to sin. [15] Sounds good!

I followed this viewpoint for years. But I have come to believe that though it is a "well meant alternative" [16] to the Eradication Theory, it too has its deficiencies both experientially and scripturally. Experientially, many have claimed their co-crucifixion with Christ countless times (I among them) but have found the sinful impulses hardly weakened, made nothing, or broken. They resurfaced as strong as ever! Scripturally, we have to admit that crucifixion doesn't lead only to weakening, being ineffective, or broken. It leads to death. And Paul clearly says "we died" to sin, not "we were weakened" to sin.

I will deal with this in much greater detail in the chapters to come, but for now, as you can see, the argument revolves around a few key phrases in Romans 6. These phrases are:

- Dead to sin – 6:2, 11
- Old man – 6:6
- Body of sin – 6:6

- Slaves to sin – 6:6
- Freed from sin – 6:7

What do these mean, and what did Paul mean in the whole passage? That is what this book is about. It is a journey through Romans 6:1–14 and a new look at an old problem—and a contemporary one—the problem of sin within us. As you read this book and discover Paul's way of thinking, you will find answers to questions that have long puzzled and exasperated Christians who want to be faithful to the Word but honest with the condition of their soul. You will resolve biblical dilemmas, and something much more important will take place. You will draw near with confidence to the crucified, risen, enthroned, and Spirit-empowering Lord who will enable you to live in a way pleasing to God. Joy will abound, and the kingdom will advance in your life and in the world around you.

Having now explained the primary issues before us, I believe it appropriate to tell people what this book is not about. First, this is not a "how to" book. It is not, for example, a "seven-step formula" for overcoming sin. Such formulas, steps, or principles can be good, and I even have a seven-step formula of my own that I use and teach—seven practical steps to overcome sin in our lives. But that's not what this book is about.

Second, this is not a book that identifies specific sins like anger or lust with practical guidelines for defeating them in our lives. Books like that fill the shelves of our Christian bookstores. As I carefully look through bookstores today, I find a book on just about every subject imaginable—why people commit this sin or that sin, the root causes of these sins, practical ways to avoid them, and helpful steps to grow in righteousness.

I am grateful for those books. Some of them have helped me. We have to be honest and admit that sin in humanity is creative. It is like a mutating virus that changes its composition and makes its lethal attack in new forms. To counteract the mutations of sin within us, we need practical helps, steps, or "how-to's"—strategies to fight the war against sin. Like a wise military leader, we need to recognize that different enemies require different weapons and strategies.

But this is not that kind of book. This book probes deeper, and I believe it is time for such a book. It delves into the text of Romans 6 to find the solid bedrock upon which we can build our strategies to fight battles with sin.

Third, this book does not deal with institutional sin. Sin is not only like a mutating virus showing up in new guises inside the believer, sin is also like a weed that will grow incessantly and wrap its tendrils around every facet of life including our families, our communities, our schools, and our governments.

Where sin remains unchecked by the truth, it entrenches itself in the institutions of our society and culture. Sin is not content to remain in the human heart. It will dominate the world. In our own country we have suffered from the sin of slavery and racism.

I read a heart-wrenching book by Gary Haugen[17] where he speaks of the injustices of the world. One of these injustices is the lawlessness that two-thirds of the world lives under. Two out of every three people in the world live in a society ruled by power or greed rather than the rule of law. Sin becomes entrenched in cultures, and to walk against it is to walk in danger of one's own life. But even as we learn and respond to these corporate expressions of sin, we must still acknowledge that their root is in human hearts, and the primary weapon is to learn what God did through Christ on the cross to deal with sin once for all.

Finally, this book will not examine every verse or concept related to holiness. For example, I have very little to say in this book about the power of the Holy Spirit. How can one write a book on overcoming sin and not write about the Spirit? The answer is: Paul says nothing about the Holy Spirit in these verses, although, of course, understanding his broader thought, the work of the Holy Spirit is everywhere assumed. He does speak about the Spirit later in Romans 8, but Paul has other issues to deal with first, and I have followed Paul's lead, focusing on what he discusses.

In the same way, I have little to say about Galatians 5:16–25, the believer's struggle with the flesh, or even how to define "the flesh." I realize this could cause frustration for some, especially those who hold to the variation of the Eradication Theory that states that an old nature was crucified with Christ upon conversion but our continuing struggle with sin is because of the flesh. For this reason, I did provide an appendix to give a brief overview of the biblical teaching on the flesh.[18] For this book, however, I decided to focus on the issues Paul presents in Romans 6:1–14, the meaning of the key phrases I listed earlier, and *Paul's* application of his theology in 6:11–14.

Having told you what the book is not about, maybe I should tell you what it is about. First, the book focuses on these five phrases that I will list again:

- Dead to sin – 6:2, 11
- Old man – 6:6
- Body of sin – 6:6
- Slaves to sin – 6:6
- Freed from sin – 6:7

But as we shall see, the definitions of these terms and our experience of them (such as being dead to sin and the crucifixion of the old man) is based on our union with Jesus Christ in His death and resurrection. We died to sin because we were crucified with Him. Everything is with Him or in Him.

This is a book about learning what it means to have been united with Christ when He died and rose and what that means for us today. I hope you find that promising and exciting, because Jesus, in His death and resurrection, accomplished the greatest feat in the history of the world, and I hope to show every believer how we are part of that greatest achievement.

Second, this book is not just about overcoming sin, i.e., saying no to sin's desires. It is not even about only keeping sin in its place so that it doesn't rule over us. That is important but negative. This book is positive. It is about growing in righteousness. It is about living in resurrection power. It is about presenting ourselves to God as people who are alive from the dead and becoming fully conformed to His image in our character and conduct so that when people see us, they see Christ shining through us.

Third, throughout the book I will refer to justification and sanctification in the following way: justification is the work of God through Christ by which He declares us righteous or fit to stand before Him. Sanctification is the work of God through Christ by which He makes us righteous in our character and in our conduct. The former declares us righteous before God. The latter changes us and makes us like Christ. The former is a once-for-all, one-time event. The latter is a work-in-process. I realize that in some passages the New Testament writers use the word sanctification in both ways, our "once-for-all" being set apart for God and the daily process by which we change and become like Jesus Christ.[19] But in this book, I will use sanctification only in the latter sense.

Dead Men Rising has two parts to it. Part One focuses on Romans 6:1–10 and the meanings of the key phrases. Chapters one through six deal with these phrases.

In chapter one, I lay out Paul's questions and answers in Romans 6:1–2. Unfortunately, Paul's questions and answers are different from ours. We approach Romans 6 with our moral questions. While the passage deals with moral issues and our sanctification, Paul was first addressing other issues. If we are going to find victory over sin, we must first understand the issues Paul was addressing.

Chapter two deals with the first of the several key phrases in Romans 6:1–7, "dead to sin." What does it mean for the believer to be dead to sin? In this chapter, I explain that it can only mean what it meant to Christ, since Christ died to sin and we died with Him. I examine two parallel passages in 2 Corinthians 5:14–21 and Galatians 2:14–21 for guidance in interpreting Romans 6.

If Paul meant one thing in 2 Corinthians 5 and Galatians 2, could he have meant something else in Romans 6?

In chapter three, I examine key concepts in Romans 6 such as our baptism with Christ and the phrases "once-for-all" and "death no longer is master over Him." I conclude that Romans 6 is saying the same thing as the 2 Corinthians 5 and Galatians 2 passages. I convincingly prove what it means to be dead to sin (and what it does not mean!) with its implications for holy living.

Chapter four is where the fun escalates. What did Paul mean when he said, "your old man was crucified with Christ"? What is the "old man"? Is it something inside us, an "old sin nature" so totally corrupt that it cannot be redeemed and must be reckoned dead? Or, did Paul mean something entirely different from what popular speakers say?

In chapter five, I propose a new meaning for "the body of sin." Other commentators have started on this interpretive path, only to stop short and not carry their thinking to its logical conclusion. This new interpretation unlocks the biblical puzzle that has confounded commentators and Christians for years.

"No longer slaves" and "freed from sin" are the final phrases in the opening verses of Romans 6 that have confounded many commentators. In chapter six, I explain the forensic intent of Paul's exposition, bring every phrase into harmony with the others, and match it all with Christian experience. I conclude this chapter with a compelling paraphrase of Romans 6:1–10 that brings out

Paul's intention, showing its simplicity and clarifying our understanding of it.

Chapter seven begins part two and the practical application of Paul's theology in Romans 6:11–14. In this chapter we look at Romans 6:11 and discover what Paul had in mind when he told believers to consider themselves to be dead to sin. As with the other chapters, we discover Paul's forensic emphasis and discover that considering ourselves dead to sin does not mean to make something happen, but to realize what is already true for those in Christ Jesus.

We have placed so much attention on Christ's death to sin and our death with Him that we have missed half of Paul's powerful statement in 6:10: "The life that He lives, He lives to God." In chapter eight, I examine what it means for Christ to be "alive to God" and what it means for holy living since we are to consider ourselves alive to God. Then we look at again at 6:11 where Paul says, "Consider yourselves to be…alive to God in Christ Jesus."

If we died to an old sin nature, why does Paul so quickly tell us not to let sin reign? In chapter nine, I stay consistent with my interpretation of dead to sin in the previous chapters and examine why Paul must tell us not to let sin reign in our mortal bodies. Practical helps and exhortations guide the believer to stay away from sin when it comes "knocking on our door."

In chapter ten, I continue examining 6:12–13 where Paul exhorts us not to present ourselves and our bodily members to sin but to present ourselves to God as those alive from the dead and our members as instruments of righteousness to Him. Additional practical helps consistent with the preceding verses will encourage the believer to come to God—no matter what is going on in life.

In chapter eleven, we arrive at the source of power for Christian living: grace. Paul says, "You are not under law but under grace" (6:14). In this chapter, I explain what it means to find the power for holy living by accessing the rich storehouses of grace available to every Christian.

Finally, in chapter twelve, we come to our journey's end where we summarize the book, think upon all that Christ has done for us, and present ourselves to Him for a life of experiencing grace and victory.

Are you ready to journey through this amazing passage of Scripture? I want to warn you: It will not always be easy. You may feel like giving up or you may raise your hands in exasperation at some of the things I will say in the first few chapters. Persevere. Treat this book like a hike in rugged country. Difficult areas will rise up to challenge us and great exertion of energy will be required. Yet some turns in the road will surprise us with breathtaking landscapes. Unspeakable beauty, like scenery that a camera cannot capture, will emerge before our eyes, speak life to our soul, and change us for the glory of God. When we get to the end, the journey will be worth it. We will be dead men rising!

INTRODUCTION ENDNOTES

[1] John Stott, *Men Made New* (Grand Rapids, Michigan: Baker Book House, 1988), 9–10.

[2] But we always must remember that "face value" often can mean "the way I see it at a particular moment," and the way we see it may be influenced by previous teaching, or upbringing, or a hundred other influences we bring to the text.

[3] Sermons, Volume I, 124 quoted by J. Sidlow Baxter, *A New Call to Holiness* (Grand Rapids, Michigan: Zondervan, 1973), 46.

[4] Ibid., 47.

[5] Stanley N. Gundry, editor, *Five Views on Sanctification* (Grand Rapids, Michigan: Zondervan, 1987). See pages 11–46 for an overview of the Wesleyan perspective. Wesley's statements quoted by Baxter certainly seem to promote the eradication theory. Regardless of who they should be attributed to, my purpose is to expose the fallacy of this way of thinking—that sin within the believer can be completely destroyed in this life.

[6] Melvin E. Dieter, "The Wesleyan Perspective" in *Five Views on Sanctification*, Gundry, editor, 17.

[7] Ibid., 17.

[8] Ibid., 41–42.

[9] Ibid., 50. In *Five Views of Sanctification*, Stanley Horton provides a definitive view of Pentecostalism on this issue and shows how most Pentecostal theologians in the early days of its movement up to our day have not embraced the eradication theory. See pages 103–135.

[10] For example, see Bill Gillham, *Lifetime Guarantee* (Eugene, Oregon: Harvest House, 1993) and Steve McVey, *Grace Walk* (Eugene, Oregon: Harvest House, 1995).

[11] The passage points to union with Christ, as in Romans 6, when Paul says, literally in the Greek, "those who are *of Christ Jesus*." Most translations render this "belong to." The point is that by virtue of our "belonging to Him" or being "of Him," we crucified the flesh.

[12] Dr. J. Robertson McQuilkin, "The Keswick Perspective" in *Five Views of Sanctification*, Gundry, editor, 151–183.

[13] Ibid., 157.

[14] Ibid.

[15] For example, "By faith we accept the fact that in Christ sin no longer has the mastery over us. Believers must not only recognize intellectually but embrace in full belief the truth that "our old self was crucified with him [Christ] so that the body of sin might be rendered powerless, that we should no longer be slaves to sin" (Rom. 6:6) and that sin is no longer our master because we are not under law but under grace (v. 14). Anthony Hoekema: "The Reformed Perspective" in *Five Views of Sanctification*, Gundry, editor, 65.

[16] A gracious title given by Dr. Baxter. See the chapter "A Well Meant Alternative" starting on page 57 of *A New Call to Holiness*.

[17] Gary Haugen, *Good News About Injustice* (Downers Grove, Illinois: IVP, 2009).

[18] See Appendix D, "What about the Flesh?"

[19] For example, in 1 Corinthians 1:2 and 6:11, Paul uses sanctification in a positional, once-for-all sense, and in 2 Corinthians 7:1, he speaks of perfecting holiness in the fear of God. In Hebrews 2:11 we are sanctified, but in 12:14 we are told to pursue sanctification.

CHAPTER ONE

SHALL WE CONTINUE IN SIN?

What shall we say then? Are we to continue in sin so that grace may increase? May it never be! How shall we who died to sin still live in it? Or do you not know that all of us who have been baptized into Christ Jesus have been baptized into His death?

ROMANS 6:1–3

ARE WE TO CONTINUE IN SIN that grace may increase? The question, no, even the thought is a misunderstanding at best and a mockery of the Gospel at worst. Paul slams the door in the face of such a suggestion with a blunt, "May it never be," or "God forbid![1]

He asks, "How shall we who died to sin still live in it? Or do you not know that all of us who have been baptized into Christ Jesus have been baptized into His death?" Did you catch Paul's logic? If we *died* to sin, how can we *live* in it? Death and life mix like oil and water. Both cannot be true at the same time. In the same way, continuing in sin is incongruous with being a Christian.

"We can't continue in sin," Paul reasons, because "we have died to it!" And with this passage, Paul introduces the phrase that has been at the heart of scholarly debate and anguished soul-searching for ordinary Christians who simply want to live for Christ: "We died to sin!"

"Don't you know this?" Paul asks. Paul seems to know something the Roman Christians knew at one time and forgot, or perhaps never grasped. They died to sin. If they died to sin, how is it possible they could continue in it?

But let's give the Roman Christians a break. They weren't quite like the Corinthians with all their moral and relational culpabilities! Yes, they had issues to work through, but Paul doesn't introduce this question because he is dealing with a major sin question in the Roman church. Instead, he was anticipating and answering the question of an opponent employing a teaching technique called diatribe[2] to build his case, rhetorically presenting the question to set up his answer for the Roman Christians who needed to grow in

29

their understanding of what Christ had done for them.[3]

Regardless of who or what prompted the questions—"Are we to continue in sin?" and "How shall we who died to sin still live in it?"—they are questions every Christian needs to ask although we ask them from a different angle.

Our angle is, "I am a follower of Jesus. I want to please Him. I want to advance in my faith, but I have these problems in my life that cause me to stumble. I want to believe I died to sin, but I find myself still living in it. I don't want to continue sinning. May it never be! God forbid! But I do. Can you help me?"

Our question is different from the approach Paul was taking in his letter and is a primary reason why so many get into trouble interpreting this passage. But if we will first listen to *Paul's* questions and answers, we will find clues to answer *our* question.[4] Let's dig in and discover what these verses were about when Paul wrote them.

PAUL'S QUESTIONS AND ANSWERS

The opening question in verse 1—"What shall we say then?" tells us that Paul is arriving at a conclusion for his readers. We might paraphrase it, "What shall we say then, in light of all I have just stated," or, "What conclusion can we make?" Unfortunately, many who listened to Paul's gospel of grace were coming to the wrong conclusion: "Let's continue in sin!"

Why would they come to this conclusion? What was Paul saying that would create the questions of 6:1–2? We have to go back to Romans 5:12–21 where Paul is comparing Adam and Christ.

Adam brought sin, condemnation, and death. Jesus brought obedience, righteousness, and life. The climax of the comparison is 5:18–19 where he says, "So then as through one transgression there resulted condemnation to all men, even so through one act of righteousness there resulted justification of life to all men. For as through the one man's disobedience the many were made sinners, even so through the obedience of the One the many will be made righteous."

But Paul knew that his succinct contrast between Adam and Christ would prompt an alert and devout first-century Jew to react and ask a question such as the following, "Brother Paul, not so fast! You have jumped from Adam to Jesus with hardly a reference to our nation's defining moment! What about Moses and the giving of the Law? What about the role of our people Israel? Where do we fit? You have all but skipped over us, the sons of Abraham, and

God's great gift of the Law in your presentation. Surely the Law is important in God's plan to bring salvation to the world."

Here is Paul's reply:[5] "The Law came in so that the transgression would increase; but where sin increased, grace abounded all the more, so that, as sin reigned in death, even so grace would reign through righteousness to eternal life through Jesus Christ our Lord" (5:20–21).

This answer was shocking to first-century Jews: "The Law came in so that transgression would increase, not diminish." But after getting over the initial shock, if Jews did not scoff at Paul or run him out of town (or flog him for blasphemy[6]), they would ask the next logical question: "Brother Paul, you have presented a bleak picture. If the giving of the Law of God did not help our people but only increased their sin, what hope do we have against sin?"

To this, Paul would reply, "Ah, I was hoping you would ask that. That's the perfect question. And here is the glorious answer. Our hope is in the grace of the Messiah. Yes, the Law came in[7] with the result that transgression increased, but where sin increased, the grace of the Messiah abounded all the more!"

Every Israelite familiar with his national history would know that God's giving of the Law did not meet with increased obedience. From Moses forward, the prophets lamented and cried out against Israel's sin.[8] Joshua challenged the people to put away the foreign gods and serve God only.[9] Samuel grieved over Israel's rejection of God as their king.[10] Isaiah described Israel as a body bruised and wounded from head to foot with sin.[11]

Jeremiah observed, "As a well keeps its waters fresh, so she keeps fresh her wickedness… Were they ashamed because of the abomination they have done? They were not even ashamed at all. They did not even know how to blush" (Jeremiah 6:7, 15). An honest first-century listener familiar with Israel's history would have to agree. Israel's history was often embarrassingly sinful.

In the opening phrase of Romans 5:20, Paul underscores his point by using a specific word for sin—"transgression"—the breaking of a known command.[12] What men once did in ignorance (sin) they now acted out in rebellion (transgression). The Law intensified sin. Sin became trespass. The Law, rather than delivering Israel from Adam's rebellion, revealed that Jews as well as Gentiles were their own Adam and in need of another kind of help.[13]

But this is where grace stepped in. In 5:21, he shows that rather than meet His people with further judgment, God sent the Anointed One and met them with grace. Sin increased, but grace abounded more. And grace did more than abound. Because of the Messianic death and resurrection, grace has begun *to reign*. Whereas sin reigned in death, now grace reigned: "As sin reigned in death, even so grace [reigns] through righteousness" (Romans 5:21).

But some were not quite ready to accept Paul's version of Israel's history and God's response to Israel's sin. There seemed to be a fundamental flaw in Paul's presentation. "If that's true," they reasoned, "If God met Israel's increased sin with abounding grace, then what keeps us from doing the same? Why not sin more (and enjoy it!), knowing that grace will come! If God met Israel's sin with grace, then won't He meet our increased sin with abounding grace? And if He does, your Jesus message isn't an answer to sin. If the Law increases sin, your gospel multiplies it." To put this in modern terms, if the Law didn't put the brakes to sin, but accelerated it, the gospel of grace fills the gas tank with high-performance fuel and presses the pedal to the metal!

To this Paul would say, "God forbid! May it never be! That is not the point of increased grace. If you think we (who have met the Messiah) shall continue in sin that grace might increase as it did in our nation's history, then you have missed the point of my gospel! What God did historically with Israel, meeting increased sin with overwhelming grace, was so that sin might be put away once for all! We shall not continue in sin that grace might abound because we died to sin. How shall we who died to sin still live in it? We died to sin because we who have been baptized into Messiah Jesus have been baptized into His death! And you can experience this same death to sin and resurrection to new life if you will embrace the Messiah."

OUR QUESTION AND PAUL'S ANSWERS

This was the debate of Paul's day and the reasoning underlying his questions in 6:1–2. But now, let's return to the question I asked at the beginning of the chapter, "Shall we continue in sin? Shall we who live in the twenty-first century indulge a sinful lifestyle knowing God has forgiven our sins and will give us grace?" We know the quick answer. Of course not—the abounding grace was a once-for-all, unrepeatable, historical response to Israel's rebellion. Its purpose was to do away with sin for all time through the climactic events of the death and resurrection of the Messiah. Even though God meets our daily failures with daily grace, we sense that His grace is not a free ticket to a life of sin without consequences but the means by which we escape the clutches of sin and find a new life.

The answer to our twenty-first century question begs to continue speaking and give a thorough explanation. Yet, Paul does not let this voice speak fully at this time (although he allows it a few words in 6:4–5 and 6:11–14) because he first wants to develop his theology of death to sin. To let this voice speak fully would be to look far down the path rather than make important observations about the terrain around us. But because we ask the question from an urgent appeal to find solutions for our sinful tendencies, I would like to give voice to our modern question again and provide a brief answer, even though we risk misunderstanding and have much ground to cover in our journey before we can fully appreciate Paul's answer.

"I am a follower of Jesus. I want to please Him. I want to advance in my faith, but I have these issues in my life that cause me to stumble. I want to believe I died to sin, but I find myself still living in it. I don't want to continue sinning. May it never be! God forbid! But I do. Can you help me?"

Yes, there is help, and the answer is in a word: Grace. Grace was the answer for the increased sin of ancient Israel. Grace is the answer for all who struggle with sin in their lives.

Paul introduces the remedy in 5:21, where he speaks of grace reigning. He concludes this section of his argument in 6:14 by saying, "For sin shall not be master over you, for you are not under law but under grace."

Grace fills Paul's letters from beginning to end. Look at these points of grace in Romans:

- Paul begins and ends with a blessing of grace – 1:7; 16:20, 24
- Paul found power and effectiveness for apostolic ministry because of grace – 1:5; 12:3; 15:15ff
- Justification is by grace – 3:24
- The promise to inherit the world comes by grace – 4:14–16
- Our justification was an introduction to grace – 5:2
- We stand in grace – 5:2
- The grace of God super-abounded over the transgression of Adam – 5:15, 17
- Inclusion in the elect people of God is by grace – 11:6

- Grace empowers us for ministry – 12:6ff

Grace is God's resource available to us for a myriad of reasons, *including our struggle with sin*. And, to use Paul's phrase in this chapter, we are "under grace."

What does it mean to be "under something"? You have probably seen one of the many movies about the life of Jesus. After Pilate pronounces the sentence of death, Jesus is marched to the place of execution. Roman soldiers surround Him. One of them precedes Jesus and carries a placard announcing His crime and the crimes of the others Rome will execute on that day. Jesus is to be executed for a crime against the state—the crime of insurrection against the authority of Caesar—and walks toward Golgotha under the placard that announces His guilt.

Paul has already used the "under" terminology. In 3:9, after speaking of Israel's special place in God's plan, he nevertheless concluded the following: "What then? Are we better than they are? Not at all; for we have already charged that both Jews and Greeks are all *under sin*" (italics mine).[14] All of us—Jew and Gentile—have a guilty sentence hanging over us. We were condemned criminals on our way to the place of execution, walking under a placard saying, "Guilty of the following sins: _____."

The first part of Romans 6:14 carries this idea. Paul says, "We are not under law." To be "under law" means that we are responsible to keep the Law's commands and accountable for violating those same commands. And, if we are under the Law's violations, we are under the Law's condemnation for our sins and a prisoner on the way to execution.

But Paul says, "Wait! God has lifted the guilty placard from your procession and put another in its place. Instead of a list of your crimes, the placard contains a list of God's grace to you." As we look more closely, we discover the procession is not sorrowful but joyful. Instead of spears and swords, scowls and mockery fencing us in, joyful exuberance, cheers of encouragement, and a flower-strewn path stretch before us. We are not on our way to an execution but an enthronement, our enthronement next to the Messiah. We are not under law/sin/guilt/death, but we are under grace/freedom/ justification/life.

God's life-giving love is the banner under which we stand, walk, and breathe every moment. We are under grace, and as we learn to live under grace, we will come to see that it is about a whole lot more than forgiveness! God does not release His grace to us only when we sin. God releases His grace to us every moment as we walk by faith and as we make progress on our journey with Him.

Grace is more than cleansing from sin. Grace is for healing, equipping, and empowerment to live a holy life! Grace is over us…behind us…in front of us… under us…and in us! God met Israel's increased sin with abounding grace, but He did it so that grace would replace the tyranny of sin's reign. To put it in Paul's words: "That, as *sin reigned* in death, even so *grace would reign* through righteousness to eternal life through Jesus Christ our Lord" (Romans 5:21, italics mine).

This is the solution Paul gives in Romans and throughout his letters for believers struggling with sin—grace. Consider these verses in his other letters:

1 Corinthians 15:10 – But by the grace of God I am what I am, and His grace toward me did not prove vain; but I labored even more than all of them, yet not I, but the grace of God with me.

2 Corinthians 1:12 – For our proud confidence is this: the testimony of our conscience, that in holiness and godly sincerity, not in fleshly wisdom but in the grace of God, we have conducted ourselves in the world, and especially toward you.

Galatians 6:18 – The grace of our Lord Jesus Christ be with your spirit, brethren. Amen.

Ephesians 2:7 – So that in the ages to come He might show the surpassing riches of His grace in kindness toward us in Christ Jesus.

Philippians 1:7 – For it is only right for me to feel this way about you all, because I have you in my heart, since both in my imprisonment and in the defense and confirmation of the gospel, you all are partakers of grace with me.

Colossians 4:6 – Let your speech always be with grace, as though seasoned with salt, so that you will know how you should respond to each person.

2 Thessalonians 1:12 – So that the name of our Lord Jesus will be glorified in you, and you in Him, according to the grace of our God and the Lord Jesus Christ.

2 Timothy 2:1 – You therefore, my son, be strong in the grace that is in Christ Jesus.

Titus 2:11–12 – For the grace of God has appeared, bringing salvation to all men, instructing us to deny ungodliness and worldly desires and to live sensibly, righteously and godly in the present age.

Grace. It was the historical solution for Israel's sin. It was the all-encompassing solution for the sin of the world, and it is the only solution for a life pleasing to God. As much as we would like to explore the depths of grace at this point, we have to wait until we arrive at 6:14. For now, we have to get back to the task at hand.

We have discovered the historical context of Paul's questions and answers in Romans 6:1–2 that so many have grappled with through the centuries. We have filled out Paul's answers in order to get a better grasp of the issues he was facing. We have also taken a bend in the road that has enabled us to catch a glimpse of our final destination. But to get to that final destination, we have to stay on the trail with many stops and starts along the way.

We leave this temporary and partial view of grace in order to pick up the pace on our journey. The trail leads us into difficult terrain. Many have stumbled on this ground. I am talking about Paul's statements that believers have died to sin. What did he mean by that statement and how can a correct understanding of it help us in our war against sin?

CHAPTER ONE ENDNOTES

[1] Translators render the Greek *me genoito* in a variety of creative ways: "By no means!" (NIV, ESV, RSV), "Of course not!" (NLT), "Certainly not!" (NKJV), "May it never be!" (NASB), and "God forbid!" (KJV).
A.T. Robertson translates it, "Horrible thought!" A.T. Robertson, *Word Pictures in the New Testament, Volume IV, Epistles of Paul* (Nashville, Tennessee: Broadman 1931), 361.

In his commentary on Romans, Lenski translates it "Perish the thought!" R.C.H. Lenski, *The Interpretation of St. Paul's Epistle to the Romans* (Minneapolis, Minnesota: Augsburg Publishing House, 1961), 388.

Hodge says it is "Paul's usual mode of expressing denial and abhorrence," Charles Hodge, *Commentary on the Epistle to the Romans* (Grand Rapids, Michigan: Eerdmans, 1976), 192.

[2] Diatribe employs fictional conversations and debates, rhetorical questions, and the use of *me genoito* in order to press home a point with creativity. Dennis E. Johnson states that Paul addresses "debating opponents whom he does not necessarily expect to be in the Roman Christian congregations to whom his epistle is addressed (e.g. 2:1–5, 17–24). He also anticipates, articulates, and answers the objections and false conclusions that have often been evoked by his gospel of grace (3:3–4, 5–6, 30–31; 6:1–2, 14–15; 7:5–7, 11–13; 9:11–14; 10:19; 11:1, 9–11)." Tipton & Waddington, editors, *Resurrection and Eschatology, Theology in Service of the Church* (Philipsburg, New Jersey: P&R Publishing, 2008), Dennis E. Johnson, *The Function of Romans 7:13–25 in Paul's Argument for the Law's Impotence and the Spirit's Power, and Its Bearing on the Identity of the Schizophrenic "I,"* 17.

[3] This is the viewpoint of Dunn: "Initially Paul resumes a modified diatribe style, but now not so much to argue with querulous fellow countrymen, more as a device for exhorting his Roman audiences." James D.G. Dunn, *Word Biblical Commentary, Vol. 38A, Romans 1–8* (Nashville, Tennessee, Thomas Nelson Publishers, 1988), 305.

[4] Dennis E. Johnson reminds us of the necessity of "a deliberate effort to focus our attention not, first of all, on the sorts of questions and concerns that the text evokes *in us* as we encounter it in the context of our own spiritual experience…but rather on the precise question…that Paul specifically tells us that he is answering," Johnson, 15.

[5] This is the fourth time Paul has broken off his main argument to deal with the question of the law. He only partially presents his view of the law in these brief digressions, leaving his full explanation of the role of the law to Romans 7. The previous references to the role of the law in God's plan are 3:1–8; 4:15; and 5:13–14.

[6] 2 Corinthians 11:24.

[7] The Greek for "came in" is *pareiserxomai,* which is used only here and in

Galatians 2:4 where it refers to people sneaking in to spy out the liberty Christians were experiencing through Christ. Moo calls for balance in understanding Paul's use of it. On the one hand, we should not think that Paul was saying that the Law snuck in with evil intent. It was God's good law with good purposes. Yet, the use of the term was to "relativize the role of the law in salvation history." He also states that the word was commonly used with negative connotations during the New Testament period. See Douglas Moo, *The Epistle to the Romans* (Grand Rapids, Michigan: Eerdmans, 1996), 346–47.

[8] "For I know that after my death you will act corruptly and turn away from the way which I have commanded you" (Deuteronomy 31:29).

[9] "Now, therefore, fear the LORD and serve Him in sincerity and truth; and put away the gods which your fathers served beyond the River and in Egypt, and serve the LORD. If it is disagreeable in your sight to serve the LORD, choose for yourselves today whom you will serve: whether the gods which your fathers served which were beyond the River, or the gods of the Amorites in whose land you are living; but as for me and my house, we will serve the LORD" (Joshua 24:14–15).

[10] "But the thing was displeasing in the sight of Samuel when they said, 'Give us a king to judge us.' And Samuel prayed to the LORD. The LORD said to Samuel, 'Listen to the voice of the people in regard to all that they say to you, for they have not rejected you, but they have rejected Me from being king over them'" (1 Samuel 8:6–7).

[11] "From the sole of the foot even to the head there is nothing sound in it, only bruises, welts and raw wounds, not pressed out or bandaged, nor softened with oil" (Isaiah 1:6).

[12] The Greek word is *paraptoma,* paratwma. Paul uses it prominently in 5:15–20 to describe Adam's breaking of God's command. He also uses it in reference to Israel's rebellion in 11:11–12 and in 2 Corinthians 5:19; Galatians 6:1; Ephesians 1:7; 2:1, 5; and Colossians 2:13.

[13] "Israel's failure is of a piece with the sin of humankind as a whole," Dunn, 306. "The law has the function of turning those it addresses into 'their own Adam,'" Moo, 348.

[14] See also Galatians 3:22.

HOW DEAD IS DEAD TO SIN?

May it never be! How shall we who died to sin still live in it?
ROMANS 6:2

HOW MANY TIMES HAVE I THOUGHT about being dead to sin? Only God knows. I've thought about it for theological reasons—I want to understand what Paul is talking about in Romans 6. But I've also thought about it for personal reasons—I've messed up again. I hate it and I want to live a godly life. If I am dead to sin, why do I keep doing this! What does this "dead to sin" thing mean? And how does it work? Actually, this is only one of five issues scholars and students of the Word have grappled with for centuries in the first few verses of Romans 6. I mentioned them in the introduction; here they are again.

- What does it mean to be dead to sin? (6:2)
- What is the "old man" who was crucified? (6:6)
- What is the "body of death" that was destroyed? (6:6)
- In what way are we no longer slaves to sin? (6:6)
- What does Paul mean when he says we have been freed from sin? (6:7)

We will deal with the last four in the following chapters, but for now, we will focus on the phrase "died to sin" in 6:2. Let's first review the context. Paul was answering his critics. They charged him with presenting a message of licentiousness: "If God met increased sin with increased grace, let's keep sinning to keep the grace flowing." To this Paul replied, "God forbid! How shall we who died to sin still live in it!" There is our phrase: "Died to sin." And so we ask what Paul meant when he said we have died to sin. This has been the subject of discussion, debate, sermons, and commentaries through the ages. Here's a sample of what some have said:

Dead to Sin Means That We Not Give in to the Cravings of Sin

Origen—"To obey the cravings of sin is to be alive to sin; but not to obey the cravings of sin or succumb to its will, this is to die to sin.... If then anyone, chastened by the death of Christ, who died for sinners, repents in all these things..., he is truly said to be dead to sin through the death of Christ."[1]

Luther—[Dead to sin means] "we do not yield to our sinful passions and sin, even though sin continues in us."[2]

Dead to Sin Means We Are Freed from the Fallenness and Control of Our Flesh

Witherington—"Paul is in essence saying that the believer is freed from domination by the fallenness of the flesh, the desire to sin, the desire to rebel or sin in the face of death. One must still live in one's body, but its fallenness no longer controls the believer."[3]

Dead to Sin Means a Breaking of the Will

Godet—"The death to sin of which the apostle speaks is a state...of the will, which continues only so long as it keeps itself under the control of the fact which produced it, and produces it constantly—the death of Jesus."[4]

"We conclude by saying that death to sin is...an absolute breaking of the will with it, with its instincts and aspirations, and that simply under the control of faith in Christ's death for sin."[5]

Dead to Sin Means That We Have "Seemingly" Died to Sinning

Newman/Nida—"We have died to sin" may be rendered as "we have died as far as sinning is concerned," or "if it is a matter of sinning, then we are dead," or "we have seemingly died; sin cannot move us." It may be necessary to introduce some such expression as "seemingly" in order to indicate clearly that the "dying" is to be understood metaphorically. In some languages, however, died to sin must be rendered as "dead from sin," that is to say, "dead, and in this way separated from the power of sin."[6]

Dead to Sin Means We Are Paralyzed to Sin

Govett—"God would show the justified, then, their crucifixion with Christ, as one with Him. He would teach them His mind about the justified; which is, that at once sin in them be paralyzed, and moving daily downward to death."[7]

A theme runs through these explanations: "Dead to sin" refers to being dead to the *experience of sinning*. Believers, in some way, are to live above sin or have power over sin because we are dead to sin. But I also get the impression, as I read these and similar statements, that they are attempting to explain something hard to explain and not true in their lives or in the lives of others. It's like the feeling you get when you're putting a puzzle together. You think you've found a long sought after piece, but when you try to snap it in place, you have to push a little harder than normal and down deep you know it's not quite the right fit.

All of us should commend and heed the exhortation to holy living these writers are promoting, but I believe they are reaching for something and just when it seems to be in their hand, its slippery nature enables it to elude their grasp. And because they can't quite get their arms around the concept of dead to sin, they commit logical and biblical fallacies. Let's examine these statements more closely.

Origen appears to be talking to both unbelievers and believers in his statement. Those who obey the cravings of sin are alive to sin. They do not know Christ. But when a person "repents in all these things" (becomes a follower of Christ) he is "truly said to be dead to sin." But does this mean that such a person will no longer have the "cravings of sin"? I truly repented of my sins at my conversion and I have on numerous occasions truly repented of failures in my Christian life, but failures have continued. Since this is the case for me (and all other Christians), does this mean that we are not dead to sin anymore? He also seems to say that when we resist sin, *at that moment* we die to sin—"not to obey sin's cravings is to die to sin." But Paul puts our death to sin in the past and unrelated to our success or failure in resisting sin.[8]

For Luther, dead to sin means that we do not yield to our passions. But when we do yield, are we no longer dead to sin? Yet Scripture is clear, those in Christ have died to sin. In a similar line of thinking, Godet equates dead to sin with the breaking of the will. But is our will ever completely broken? And if our will is in the process of breaking, are we in the process of dying to sin and not dead to sin? If we choose to be willful and disobey, do we nullify our "deadness to sin"? Have we "come back to life" in regard to sin?

Witherington says Christ has freed us from the domination of the flesh. Its fallenness no longer controls the believer. But could we say this to a Christian struggling with explosive anger, habitual lying, or…pornography?

I am amazed at the lengths to which other writers have gone to explain this phenomenon—a dead-to-sin man sinning. Newman and Nida insert the word "seemingly" in an effort to match the text with the obvious realities of the Christian life. But is that what Paul said? You *seemingly* died with Christ? And if he meant that, did Christ only seemingly die?

Govett makes the mistake of taking an analogy too far.[9] It is true that when a person is nailed to a wooden beam—crucified—he does not die immediately and can linger in pain and agony. But is that the condition of the believer? Are we still on the cross, in agony, with some supposed sinful nature inside us slowly dying, its life ebbing away? The text does not allow it. We were not only crucified with Christ; we died with Him. Christ is not still on the cross. He died and was buried, and we died and were buried with Him!

Again, these teachers are well-intentioned. I would not be surprised if, in the Judgment, their glory surpasses my own. But they have missed the mark on two counts: First, their statements do not match experience, and second, they have misunderstood Paul's intent.

Let me again address the experience issue. Would someone please tell me why, if I have died to sin, I am still tempted? I remember hearing a popular seminar speaker state, "If you prop a dead man up against a wall, a man who died from lung cancer after years of smoking, and offered him a cigarette, he would not respond because he is dead to it. In the same way you are dead to sin." H. P. Liddon made a similar statement in his commentary on Romans: "This is the motto of that life to which Baptism (ver. 3) introduces the Christian. This…[death] has presumably made the Christian as insensible to sin, as a dead man is to the objects of the world of sense. Obviously then the Christian cannot live in sin, as if it were the home or sphere of this moral life."[10]

Sounds good, but that sure hasn't been me! Although nicotine never was an issue in my life, plenty of other vices have presented themselves to me and they looked good. I, the "dead man in Christ," wanted them badly!

Let me present the issue another way. If my old sin nature in Adam has died, as some teach,[11] why do I still feel the urge to sin? Wait, I'm not being completely forthright. I confess. I experience more than urges. I have given in to temptation more times than I feel comfortable writing about. If I am dead to sin and its power in my life, why do I yield to it?

Let's revisit the two explanations I mentioned in the introduction. One is the Eradication theory and the other is the Suppression theory. Wesley expressed the Eradication theory in these words:"'I am crucified with Christ; nevertheless I live; yet not I, but Christ liveth in me'—words that manifestly describe a deliverance from inward as well as outward sin...'I live not' (my evil nature, the body of sin, is destroyed)."[12]

This destruction of inbred sin supposedly takes place at a "second blessing" experience after conversion. And while we honor Wesley's passion for holy living for himself and his followers (and would wish for a revival of such passion today), we have to ask: Does this really happen? Is sin completely destroyed in a believer's heart? The venerable Dr. J. Sidlow Baxter, now in the presence of God, questioned these interpretations of Romans 6. In his ministry, which covered the globe, Baxter stated, "I have yet to meet even an eradicationist who would seriously maintain that his or her supposedly once-for-all eradication-surgery had left an *utter* absence of all thoughts or desires less than the absolutely holy."[13]

In his work, Baxter told the story of another great preacher, H.A. Ironside. He was more than a great preacher. Like Wesley, he desired to live a holy life before God and man and diligently sought the second blessing in order to experience the destruction of "the old man" as Paul supposedly taught in Romans 6:6. Baxter reported:

> "If ever a young man sincerely handed himself over to Christ, and reverently 'claimed the blessing,' and intensively persevered to experience the eradication of inbred sin, he did. Yet at last, exhausted after years of painful trial and re-trial he knew that any further pretence was sheer hypocrisy; and at the same time he discovered that others around him who professed 'the blessing' were similarly heart-sick with secret agony of disillusionment."[14]

Even John Wesley questioned this teaching! Baxter quotes Wesley in a letter to his brother Charles concerning dying to sin: "I am at my wit's end with regard to...Christian perfection. Shall we go on asserting perfection against all the world? Or shall we quietly let it drop?"[15] It is noteworthy that he said, "All the world," meaning "shall we go on asserting perfection against all evidence to the contrary, evidence of sin in the life of believers everywhere?"

The other theory, much more widespread today, is that Christ did not completely destroy our sinful nature, but He enables us to suppress or counteract it as we acknowledge the crucifixion of our sinful nature in Christ. Our death to sin is effective when we reckon it dead by faith. Paul, we are told, gives this key in 6:11 where he says, "Consider yourselves to be dead to sin, but alive to God in Christ Jesus." The King James Version renders it, "Reckon ye also yourselves dead indeed unto sin."But is that what 6:11 is about?[16] Is my death to sin real only when I reckon it or consider it so?

Unfortunately, this is saying pretty much the same thing as Origen, who stated that "dead to sin" means not obeying the cravings of the flesh and Godet, who said that "dead to sin" means a breaking of the will. Believers must reckon it so, break the will, not give in—then we experience death to sin.

But if I imperfectly apply Romans 6:11 and do not "consider it so," if I yield an inch to a craving, or become stubborn in my will to God, then am I no longer dead to sin? And if I, at that moment, am not dead to sin, is Christ no longer dead to sin because, after all, my death to sin, as we shall presently see, is *with Him*. If I do not reckon it so, then am I alive to sin? If I am alive to sin, then is Christ alive to sin? But we know that is not possible because He died to sin and is now alive to God.

But it gets better! When with honesty I admit that my experience doesn't match this explanation, I am confronted with urgent appeals that make me feel worse!

"The matter of which we are told to take note here is the great federal fact that our old man was crucified with Christ. Perhaps no more difficult task, no task requiring such constant vigilant attention, is assigned by God to the believer. It is a stupendous thing, this matter of taking note of and keeping in mind what goes so completely against consciousness—that our old man was crucified. These words are addressed to faith, to faith only. Emotions, feelings, deny them. To reason, they are foolishness. But ah, what stormy seas has faith walked over! What mountains has faith cast into the sea! How many impossible things has faith done!"[17]

Wow! This is great writing. But it leads me to the conclusion that I, and others who may lapse into sin, are not vigilant enough or that we are lacking in faith. While some Christians have calmed the storm of sin and thrown the mountain of vice into the sea, others are sinking beneath the waves or standing in the shadow of a fearful mountain that will not move in spite of our best faith efforts to relocate it!

Here's one more: "It's tough to act on facts when feelings are screaming something that contradicts the truth. Yet we face that kind of choice many times in our Christian experience. You may be facing that kind of situation right now with this truth about your old nature. If you don't feel as if your sin nature is dead, you may be tempted to reject this truth. But if you don't accept it, what are you going to do with the verses that clearly teach that we died with Christ?"[18]

Once again, I will say that such statements are well-intentioned but misguided, and it is important to expose the fallacy of such statements in order to protect God's people from wrong thinking, unrealistic expectations, and ultimately, from disillusionment with God's Word.

John Stott convincingly shows where this kind of rhetoric can lead. "It is incompatible with Christian experience…scriptural and historical biographies, together with our own experience, combine to deny this. Far from being dead, in the sense of quiescent, our fallen nature is so alive and active that we are urged not to obey its desires, and are given the Holy Spirit to subdue and control them."[19]

"A serious danger of this popular view is that it can easily lead to disillusion or self-deception. If we struggle to 'reckon' ourselves to be 'dead to sin' (i.e. unresponsive to it), when we know full well that we are not, we feel torn between Scripture and experience, and may then be tempted either to doubt God's Word or, in order to maintain our interpretation of it, to resort even to dishonesty about our experience."[20]

Well-stated, and while we once again honor our brothers who have earnestly preached and written about holiness (and do not wish to be argumentative about it), we must be honest in exposing such fallacious thinking that can only lead to inconsistency, heartache, and distrust of Scripture.[21]

If the Eradication and Suppression theories fail us, what, then, shall we do with the verses that clearly teach that we died with Christ? We will search for another interpretation! What does it mean to be dead to sin? Here is what I propose Paul was talking about:

When we died to sin, we died to the penalty of sin, not to the power or influence of sin in our lives, not to an old nature within us, not to the cravings of the flesh, or to any of the descriptions quoted above.[22]

This may elicit an initial disappointment from those looking to gain greater power over sin in their lives. "I don't want another lecture on justification," they may say. "I want something of substance that pertains to my sanctification." I can imagine that my statement will also generate howls of protest, "What? How can you say it's not about the power of sin? Romans 6:1 clearly talks about the problem of *continuing* in sin and 6:2 about *living* in it!"[23]

In due time, I will answer these and other objections, but for now let me say this, especially for those seriously searching for holiness in their lives: When we understand death to sin as death to the penalty of sin, we will discover that perfect, long sought-after puzzle piece that effortlessly locks into place with the other pieces—and it will lead to victory over sin. One leads to the other. Let there be no doubt, Paul wrote Romans 6 through 8 so we can have power over sin, but the phrase "dead to sin" does not mean what so many have said it means—death to the *power* of sin. It is about death to the *penalty* of sin.

I know this statement—Romans 6 is about death to the penalty of sin— cuts across the grain of understanding for many. I made this statement to a friend of mine who is a gifted teacher. She immediately and forcefully said, "No, it means we died to the power of sin," as if her statement would be enough to correct me and settle the matter in my mind once for all.

So many teachers have been saying this for so long that we accept it as "Gospel truth." The reasoning goes, "Romans 1-5 is about the penalty of sin, and 6-8 is about dying to the power of sin in our lives."[24] Like a mantra, Christians repeat this line—or others like it—ad infinitum.

Let me again assure my readers that Romans 6 through 8 is about overcoming the power of sin in our lives. It is about living a holy life. Paul does not want his readers to continue in sin (6:1) or live in it (6:2). He wants them to walk in newness of life (6:4) and does not want sin to reign in their bodies (6:12–13). But in these early verses of Romans 6, all he presents are teasers, hints, and quick referrals to show that his argument has practical, moral value.

In the opening verses of Romans 6, he is not ready for his fully developed exposition of power over sin. But when we try to make it about that, we get into exegetical and practical trouble. In these verses, Paul gives a glimpse of the life of the Spirit and overcoming sin, but he first has to develop his theology about dying to sin and to the Law in the rest of chapter 6, all of 7, and 8:1–12. Paul's primary concern in 6:1 through 8:12 is to develop and conclude themes introduced in the preceding five chapters which, in turn, open the door to his exposition of life in the Spirit in 8:13–39.

We have drawn the organizational divisions of Romans in the wrong place. Most teachers miss it by two chapters and twelve verses! We should draw it in 8:13 where Paul talks about putting to death the deeds of the body by the Holy Spirit and following the Holy Spirit. But even here, we must be careful in the drawing of lines because one topic—our death to sin and to the Law—seamlessly transitions to the topic of concern: how to live a Spirit-empowered life. We are not talking about two unrelated topics—death to the penalty of sin and victory over the power of sin. The subject is one: life in the Spirit made possible by the death of Jesus to sin in which we are included.

Life in the Spirit is what we are after. But, on our journey, we must be patient. I said the trail would be long and sometimes difficult. We are in challenging terrain. But to understand life in the Spirit that overpowers sin, we must first grasp our death to sin and the Law. We can have power over sin through the Spirit because we died to sin. Let's examine what Paul was talking about.

What Does It Mean to Be Dead to Sin?

First, I must recall a humorous scene from a favorite family movie, *The Princess Bride*. In a tragic turn of events, the hero, Wesley, dies in a torturous "scientific experiment." But we learn he may not be dead. His friends take him to an old magician and his wife. At first, the magician is reluctant to have anything to do with the situation. He pronounces Wesley dead and sends away the friends with the "dead" Wesley. But his nagging wife won't tolerate his indifference. "Liar, liar," she shouts at him as he tries to rationalize away his responsibility to help.

Finally, the old magician takes a closer look and says, "Well, he's mostly dead," which means that he was partially alive and could be revived to rescue the damsel in distress.

Whether you liked the movie or not, it is a great illustration of what the verse is *not* saying. Romans 6 does not say we are *mostly* dead, dead only when we consider it to be so, seemingly dead, or dead when we resist the cravings of sin. It says we *died* to sin—zippo, six feet under, out of here, deader than a door nail—whatever phrase you prefer. Paul says we *died*.

It is also important to remember that this is not an obscure, puzzling phrase found only in one place, like "baptism for the dead" in 1 Corinthians 15:29. Paul uses this terminology freely in several places as if his readers would or should know what he is talking about. It seems to be something he taught everywhere. For example, we find it in his letter to the Galatian churches, written about AD 50.[25] We find it in his personal instructions to Timothy about 15 years later.[26] We find it in Romans, 2 Corinthians,[27] and in his letters to the Ephesians and Colossians.[28]

In the course of this book, we will look at them all. But let's start with the key phrases in Romans 6, make two observations, and work from there. Romans 6 contains the greatest cluster of "dead to sin" verses in the entire Pauline corpus.

Romans 6:2 – How shall *we who died to sin* still live in it?

Romans 6:3 – All of us who have been baptized into Christ Jesus have been *baptized into His death*.

Romans 6:4 – We have been *buried with Him* through baptism *into death*.

Romans 6:5 – We have become *united with Him in* the likeness of *His death*.

Romans 6:6 – Our old self was *crucified with Him* in order that our body of sin might be done away with.

Romans 6:8 – We have *died with Christ*.

Romans 6:10 – For the death that He died, *He died to sin*, once for all.

Romans 6:11 – Even so consider yourselves to be *dead to sin*, but alive to God in Christ Jesus.

Two observations are in order here. First, notice that whatever Paul is talking about, it is *all with or in Christ*.[29] It is not independent of Him.[30]

Second, our *death to sin* is only because *He died to sin*. The logic of these verses runs as follows:

"We died to sin" (6:2)
> *with Christ* (6:3, 4, 5, 6, 8)
>> because "He died to sin" (6:10).
>>> Therefore, consider yourselves to be "dead to sin" (6:11).

Paul's logic leads me to the following conclusion: Whatever death to sin *important* means, it can mean nothing more or nothing less than what it meant to Christ. We died to sin only because Christ died to sin.

The key question then becomes: What does Paul mean when he says "Christ died to sin"? What did He die to? And whatever it meant to Jesus when *He died to sin* (6:10), it must mean the same thing for us when *we died to sin* (6:2) because our death to sin was only *with Him* (6:3, 4, 5, 6, 8). Further, we are to consider something (6:11) that already happened, independent of our trying to make it happen.

What did Christ die to when He died to sin? Let's try to answer this question by asking another question: When other New Testament verses speak of Christ's death in reference to sin, what are they talking about? This is not a trick question. It is an easy answer for anyone even vaguely familiar with Paul's writings and the gospel. Other New Testament verses are talking about Christ's atoning sacrifice that removed our guilt before God. Whether it is expiation, propitiation, justification, redemption, or reconciliation, the apostles with one voice speak of Christ's death in reference to sin in a substitutionary way—He died for us.

If that is what His death in reference to sin means throughout the New Testament, why do we think Romans 6, when it speaks of Christ's death to sin, means anything else? On what basis do we inject new meaning into the death of Christ and therefore come up with difficult, not-true-to-life explanations of our co-death with Him?[31] The weight of New Testament verses on the death of Christ is one factor that has led me to this conclusion: When Paul states Christ died to sin he means Christ died to the penalty of sin. When he says we died to sin with Him he means we died to the penalty of sin as well. We did not die to an "old nature" within us, to the cravings of the flesh, or to the power of sin and its enticements. We died to sin's demand that we be executed. We died to sin's penalty.

Some might argue, "Yes, other verses in the New Testament are about Christ's atoning sacrifice, but these verses speak of His dying *to sin*—not *for* sin—and therefore introduce another element of our Savior's work. These verses speak of our co-crucifixion with Him and our death to the power of sin and the old sin nature within us. He not only died for our sins as our sin-bearer; He died to the power of sin so that we could have power over sin and a new life of righteous living."

For example, Watchman Nee in his classic work, *The Normal Christian Life*, distinguishes between the work of the Blood and the work of the Cross (italics are his): "But we must now go a step further in the plan of God to understand how he deals with *the sin principle in us*. The Blood can wash away my sins, but it cannot wash away my 'old man.' It needs the Cross to crucify me. The Blood deals with the *sins*, but the Cross must deal with the *sinner*."[32]

Is this true? Is there such a distinction in Scripture between the Blood and the Cross, between sins and sin, between Christ's Calvary work to forgive and His Calvary work to deliver? Do the "He died to sin" verses speak of another aspect of His work on the cross? Let's place the Romans 6 verses on hold and examine two of Paul's other "death with Christ" passages to see if they point to another aspect of His saving work on the cross or if they point to His substitutionary work for us. They are 2 Corinthians 5:14–15 and Galatians 2:19–20.

THE BELIEVER'S DEATH WITH CHRIST IN 2 CORINTHIANS 5:14-15

"For the love of Christ controls us, having concluded this, that *one died for all, therefore all died*; and He died for all, so that they who live might no longer live for themselves, but for Him who died and rose again on their behalf" (italics mine).

Although this passage does not say we died *with Christ*, it is still a "co-crucifixion" passage because it mentions our "death" in conjunction with His. It is clear that our "death," whatever it is, is only because He died. One died for all; *therefore*, all died. But how does Paul focus on Christ's death in this passage? Does he speak of a secondary aspect that pertains to an old nature or death to the power of sin? Is sanctification in view? These verses and the following verses of 2 Corinthians 5 do not bear this out. They point only to Christ's substitutionary work on the cross to pay the penalty for our sins. Consider these points.

1. Three times Paul says Christ died for all.

    One died *for all* (14).

    He died *for all* (15).

    Him who died and rose again *on their behalf* (15).

    The Greek behind "for all" is *huper panton*. "On their behalf" is simply *huper*. This is the language of substitution[33]—Christ dying *for us* or *in our behalf*. In 14 other verses, Paul uses this language to speak of Christ's atoning death, including these classic verses:[34]

    Romans 5:6 – Christ died *for the ungodly.*

    Romans 5:8 – While we were yet sinners Christ died *for us.*

    1 Corinthians 15:3 – Christ died *for our sins* according to the Scriptures.

    Galatians 1:4 – [Christ] gave Himself *for our sins.*

    Galatians 3:13 – [Christ became] a curse *for us.*

    1 Timothy 2:6 – [Christ] gave Himself a ransom *for all.* This verse uses the identical phrase as 2 Corinthians 5:14–15 – a ransom for all is *huper panton.*

2. The language of Christ's atoning sacrifice continues in the rest of the passage. Second Corinthians 5:19 speaks of God's act of reconciliation and imputation. He was reconciling the world to Himself and not charging the world for its sins or imputing sins to the accounts of people. Verse 21 speaks of Christ becoming a sin offering on our behalf (huper) so that we might become righteous in Him.

3. This act of reconciliation and imputation gave Paul the ministry of reconciliation to the world (5:18, 20) so that others might receive the benefit of Christ's death.

From this evidence, we see that the death of Christ in 2 Corinthians 5 is His atoning sacrifice for our sins and this atoning death affected our death. *One died for all, therefore, all died.* No other aspect of Christ's death is in view here.[35] And it is this death for us that affected our death: One died for all; therefore, all died. Or, to phrase this personally, "Christ died for my sins, therefore I died."

But what did I die to? This is the Romans 6 question! The 2 Corinthians 5 answer is that I died to the penalty of sin. My death to sin made possible by the death of Christ can be nothing other than the purpose of His death. If His death was so that I might not be charged with sin and be reconciled to Him (5:19) because He became sin in my behalf (5:21), then my death in this passage is death to the penalty of sin. God did not charge sin to my account so that I might be reconciled to Him.

This death to the penalty of sin does have a sanctifying effect. Having died to the penalty of my sins, I am now free to live for Him who died and rose again for me rather than live for myself (5:15). Because of His work on the cross and my death with Him, I can now look at people differently (5:16). I am a new creature with new possibilities (5:17), and I have a new focus and purpose in life—the ministry of reconciliation (5:18, 20). His amazing love on the cross compels me (5:14) to a new life, and I can experience it because when Christ died on my behalf to take away the penalty of sins, I died with Him to the same thing.

Sanctification themes are touched upon. They are always there, like an eager actor just offstage who cannot wait to make a grand entrance and recite his lines. But for his lines to have their full effect, he must wait for the other actors to recite their parts and reveal the plot. Otherwise, the lines will have no meaning.

But as inviting as these themes are, we must hold them off for now. Our present purpose is to discover the meaning of Christ's death to sin in Romans 6 so that we might understand our death to sin. And if 2 Corinthians 5 sheds any light on it, it sheds this light: His death to sin is another way of saying He died *for our sins* or *in our behalf*. And if this is what he died to, this is what we died to as well.

THE BELIEVER'S DEATH WITH CHRIST IN GALATIANS 2:19-20

"For through the Law *I died to the Law*, so that I might live to God. *I have been crucified with Christ*; and it is no longer I who live, but Christ lives in me; and the life which I now live in the flesh I live by faith in the Son of God, who loved me and gave Himself up for me" (italics mine).

For these phrases, context is crucial—the context of the book and the context of the immediate paragraph. Concerning the book, Paul was writing this letter to the Galatian churches because they were falling to the error of agitators trying to bring them under the Mosaic regulations as the additional basis by which they could have equal status with Jewish believers. Paul's letter counters this argument by pointing to the work of Christ as the sufficient foundation for our right standing with God and with one another.

The immediate context of Galatians 2:19–20 was Paul recalling his confrontation with Peter in Antioch. The story begins in 2:11: "But when Cephas [Peter] came to Antioch, I opposed him to his face, because he stood condemned." Peter had been enjoying table fellowship with Gentile Christians (2:12a), but when the agitators came to Peter and objected, he lost his courage and withdrew from table fellowship (2:12b). Other Jews who had enjoyed such fellowship also withdrew. Surprisingly, Barnabas was among those who withdrew (2:13b). Paul rebuked Peter for this lapse in the presence of all (2:14). How could he and the others do such a thing?

What was Paul's basis for his stern rebuke of Peter and Barnabas? The next verses explain his reasons and provide the key points so that we can interpret 2:19–20 contextually.

Here is Galatians 2:15–18: "We are Jews by nature and not sinners from among the Gentiles; nevertheless knowing that a man is not justified by the works of the Law but through faith in Christ Jesus, even we have believed in Christ Jesus, so that we may be justified by faith in Christ and not by the works of the Law; since by the works of the Law no flesh will be justified. But if, while seeking to be justified in Christ, we ourselves have also been found sinners, is Christ then a minister of sin? May it never be! For if I rebuild what I have once destroyed, I prove myself to be a transgressor."

Observations on 2:15-18

2:15—Paul begins by speaking of Jewish ethnic identity and the contrast between it and Gentiles who were considered "sinners" or outside the covenant. "We are Jews by nature and not sinners." What does this mean? Weren't Jews sinners too? Of course they were, and God provided the entire sacrificial system for them because of their sin. When Paul speaks in this language, he is using terminology familiar to his Jewish heritage. They were inside the covenant and had the Law of God. Gentiles were outside the covenant, worshipped idols, and were without God.[36] We see in 2:15 that Paul's subject has to do with Jewish-Gentile relations in the church.

2:16—Paul, Peter, and Barnabas, Jews within the long history of covenant relationship with God, still needed justification by faith in Christ Jesus just like the Gentiles. God did not make them right before Him by the works of the Law. If their Jewish Law could not justify them, then God must make them right the same way He made Gentiles right with Him. They, therefore, have no basis for withdrawing table fellowship from the Gentiles. Withdrawing flies in the face of the death of Jesus for all sins— Jew and Gentile—and the proclamation of salvation to all the nations.

2:17—Paul continues with an observation about their justification. If their justification is by faith in Christ rather than by works of the Law, then it proves them to be transgressors[37] of the Law of God. A Jewish opponent, as surely happened many times to Paul, would then point out, "Your Messiah Jesus then is only a minister of sin. All He is doing is showing your sinfulness, and this contradicts the reason why God gave the Law. He gave the Law for us to keep and fulfill." To this Paul replies, "*Me genoito* (God forbid!)."[38]

2:18—Christ is not the minister of sin. We are the ministers of sin! Paul says in this verse, "If I rebuild what I once destroyed, *I prove myself to be a transgressor*" (italics mine). N.T. Wright points out that the rebuilding Paul had in mind would be a rebuilding of the barrier between Jew and Gentile, a rebuilding by reestablishing the Law as the separator between the two groups.[39] But the rebuilding of this wall would sever the oneness God was trying to bring between the two, and it would bring the painful reminder to the Jew that they were incapable of keeping the Law. Thus, withdrawing from table fellowship was a wall rebuilding, but the wall only established the harsh reality that Jews were transgressors and under condemnation just like the Gentiles.

OBSERVATIONS ON 2:19-20

Now we have the context for our death with Christ verses in 2:19–20. The background is about the first-century problem of how Gentiles could be included in the covenant people of God. Did Gentiles have to submit to the Mosaic Law, or could they find full status in God's family with believing Jews without submitting to the Mosaic regulations? As we can see, Paul has nothing in view here related to an internal "old man" or to a death to sinful habits for the Christian life. It is all about status. With this background in mind, we come now to 2:19–20, the verses that speak of the believer being crucified with Christ, and make our key observations.

1. Jew, as well as Gentile, stood condemned before God. This condemnation before the Law of God demanded their death and thus Paul says, "Through the Law I died to the Law." And here we have Paul's first recorded statement of the believer dying to something. But it is not a death to an "old self" but his death to the Law. Once the Law has carried out its sentence, it no longer has any jurisdiction over a person. We can amplify the verse in this way: "Through (the carrying out of the penalty of) the Law I died to (the condemnation of) the Law."

   Once the Law carries out its sentence against a person and that person dies, the Law has fulfilled its purpose and loses its power. The person no longer has to pay for that sentence. It is completed and he is dead to the Law's commands, condemnations, and sentences. And if the Law is finished with that person, then that person is finished with the Law. He is dead to it. Through the Law, he dies to the Law. This is what happened to Paul, Peter, Barnabas, and every Jewish believer in Christ. Through (the carrying out of the penalty of) the Law, *they died* to the Law. Therefore, their withdrawal from table fellowship with Gentiles, who were equally justified in Christ, was an act inconsistent with the gospel they were proclaiming.

2. All this leads to the question: "If they died to the Law, how did that happen?" This question leads to the answer and the famous statement of 2:20, "I have been crucified with Christ." Here, we have one of the most quoted co-crucifixion verses in Paul's writings and one of the most loved verses of the New Testament. Yet, most rarely understand the statement because they do not view it in its context. Paul is not talking about death to an old nature, to temptation, or to sin's influence over us. He is talking about death to the condemning sentence of the Law of God. Why was he, a transgressor of the Law, dead to the Law's demands and condemnation (2:19)? It is because he was crucified with Christ (2:20) for when Christ died, He died *to the Law*.[40]

Our death in this passage, therefore, means that we were crucified to the demands and condemnation of the Law. We died to these because Christ took the curse of the Law in our place and suffered its consequences—death. It is this act of bearing the curse—of Jewish and Gentile sin—that enables Jew and Gentile to have table fellowship. To withdraw from table fellowship because of Mosaic regulations is a failure to be "straightforward about the truth of the gospel" (2:14). But because Christ bore the penalty of the Law on our behalf, we can say that we too have borne the penalty of the Law because we have been crucified with Christ.

3. Paul continues in 2:20 to say that he doesn't live but Christ lives in Him. This is not a mystical statement where Paul is trying to say that the indwelling Christ somehow supersedes his personality or responsibility to obey. Instead, Paul is saying that he does not stand before God or man in his own merits. Christ who sits at the right hand of God has come to live in him through the Spirit and stands as His justification before God. The life that Paul now lives is not by the works of the Law but by faith in the Son of God. This phrase looks back to 2:16 where Paul stated that we are justified by faith and not by the works of the Law.

4. Galatians 2:20 finishes with a strong substitutionary statement: "I live by faith in the Son of God *who loved me and gave Himself up for me*" (italics mine). When Paul speaks of how Christ loved him (past tense) rather than loves him (present tense), he is referring to the love of Christ poured out on the cross in his behalf.[41]

5. The chapter concludes with further substitutionary statements showing that Paul's references to the death of Christ are not about a secondary work of Christ on the cross but about his only work on the cross—His death for our sins. "I do not nullify the grace of God, for if righteousness comes through the Law, then Christ died needlessly" (2:21).

6. The subject of justification continues in chapters 3, 4 and up to 5:12

where Paul presents further reasons why the Galatian churches should not submit to the agitators. Alan Cole provides a succinct explanation for the occasion and purpose of the letter. "Paul wrote the epistle to answer the Judaizers who were troubling the Gentile churches of Galatia with their insistent demands that, to be a good Christian, one had first to become a good Jew. Circumcision and some law-keeping at least were necessary to salvation."[42]

It should also be helpful to summarize these points about Galatians 2 by comparing the themes of Galatians 2 with Romans 6 and the surrounding verses. Notice these striking similarities in Table 1.

TABLE 1	
Galatians 2	**Romans 6**
2:16-17, 21 – Paul precedes his death with Christ statement in 2:20 with the topics of justification and righteousness	5:16, 18, 19 – Paul precedes his crucifixion of the old man statement in 6:6 with the topics of justification and righteousness.
2:17 – Paul interjects an objection to his gospel with the question, "Is Christ the minister of sin?"	6:1 – Paul interjects an objection to his gospel with the question, "Shall we continue in sin?"
2:17 – Paul answers with "May it never be, me genoito!"	6:2 – Paul answers with "May it never be, me genoito!"
2:18 – Paul uses a more specific word for sin, transgressor which translates parabasis.	5:20 – Paul uses a more specific word for sin, transgressor which translates paraptoma.
2:19 – Paul dies to something.	6:2, 11 – The believer dies to something.
2:19 – Paul dies to the Law	6:2, 11; 7:4 – The believer dies to sin and to the Law.
2:20 – Paul says, I have been crucified with Christ, translating sunestauromai.[43]	6:6 – Paul says, the old man was crucified with Him translating the compound sunestaurothe.
2:19 – Paul's death to the Law was so that he might live to God.	6:4, 10-11 – The believer's death to sin is that he might walk in newness of life and just as Christ lives to God the believer can now live to God.

One should be able to see that Paul is talking about the same topic. I ask in conclusion to this examination of Galatians 2: "If Paul is speaking the same language and about the same topic and if the occasion and purpose of the letter and the context is about status in the family of God, then what is Paul referring to when he speaks of our death with Christ to sin?" He is clearly speaking of His—and our death—to the penalty of sin.

But, lest the reader think that this book and its much loved verses have nothing to do with gaining power over sin, let me say that sanctifying power is present in this passage. Like the previously mentioned actor just off the stage who can't wait to recite his lines, it shows up. Paul hints at sanctification when he says, "I [We] died to the Law that I [we] might *live to God* (2:19, italics mine), a phrase found, interestingly, in Romans 6.[44] But it will take Paul a few more chapters in Galatians to get to his full exposition of the Christian life. He must first finish his argument that we died to the Law because we were crucified with Christ and stand by grace alone. He finally gets to the practical sanctifying effects in 5:13ff.

To borrow a question from Romans 6, "What shall we say to these things?" The contexts, language, subjects, and arguments of 2 Corinthians 5:14–21 and Galatians 2:12–21 point in this direction: The death of Christ is a substitutionary death for our sins. This substitutionary death caused our death—"one died for all, therefore, all died" and "I have been crucified with Christ." If this is the meaning of these phrases for the Galatian and Corinthian churches, it seems reasonable that Paul would have the same meaning for the same terminology when writing to the church at Rome. By allowing these passages to guide our understanding of Romans 6 we come to this conclusion: When Paul speaks about Christ and our dying to sin in Romans 6, he is talking about Christ and our dying to the penalty of sin. The logic and flow of Romans 6:1–11, then, runs like this:

> We died to *the penalty of* sin (6:2)
> > with Christ (6:3, 4, 5, 6, 8)
> > > because He died to *the penalty of* sin (6:10).
> > > > Therefore, consider yourselves to be dead to *the penalty of* sin (6:11).

Will these interpretations from 2 Corinthians and Galatians fit into Romans 6? Or, are they like beautiful pieces of art that are exquisite in their own right but out of place in the Romans 6 setting? The following chapters will examine Romans 6 more closely. Is there internal evidence that when Paul speaks about Christ's (and our) death *to sin*, he is speaking about death *to the penalty of sin*? And if he is, how does this help us live a holy life and gain victory over the power of sin?

Chapter Two Endnotes

[1] Origen, second century Christian apologist, quoted by Joseph A. Fitzmeyer, *The Anchor Bible: Romans* (New York: Doubleday, 1992), 433.

[2] Martin Luther, *Commentary to the Epistle of the Romans* (Grand Rapids, Michigan: Kregel, 1976), 100.

[3] Ben Witherington III, *Paul's Letter to the Romans, A Socio-Rhetorical Commentary* (Grand Rapids, Michigan: Eerdmans, 2004), 169.

[4] F. Godet, *Commentary on St. Paul's Epistle to the Romans* (New York: T & T Clark, 1883), 403.

[5] Ibid., 404.

[6] Barclay M. Newman and Eugene A. Nida, *A Translator's Handbook on Paul's Letter to the Romans* (London: United Bible Societies, 1973), 115.

[7] Robert Govett, M.A., *Is Sanctification Perfect Here Below?* (Miami Springs, Florida: Conley & Schoettle Publishing, 1985), 35.

[8] Many commentators will note that the overwhelming majority of verb tenses in Romans 6 and other death to sin verses is aorist, denoting a once-for-all past completed action.

[9] John Stott says, "In every analogy (in which somebody is likened to something), we need to enquire carefully at what point the parallel or similarity is being drawn; we must not press a resemblance at every point." John Stott, *Men Made New*, 42.

[10] H.P. Liddon, D.D., D.C.L., LL.D., *Explanatory Analysis of St. Paul's Epistle to the Romans* (Grand Rapids, Michigan: Zondervan, 1961), 108–109. In a similar vein, Lenski said: "The moment a man is dead he ceases to respond to stimuli. Coax him, command him, threaten him—no response, no reaction. The sphere in which he once moved ("in it") is his sphere no longer. So plain in the physical realm, is it less plain in the spiritual where the genuine realities exist? Once sin was the sphere in which we moved and responded to all this power of sin. Then came grace—oh, that blessed grace so vastly greater than the sin!—and possessed our soul which then and there died to the sin and, being thus dead, ceased living in it, ceased responding to it, the sin reached out to this dead one in vain." R.C.H. Lenski, *The Interpretation of St. Paul's Epistle to the Romans* (Minneapolis, Minnesota: Augsburg Publishing House, 1961), 390.

[11] For example, "Our sin nature died with Jesus Christ on the cross almost 2,000 years ago. If you have trouble accepting that fact, then consider this question:

If it wasn't our sin nature that died, what did die? Paul teaches here that the old self is forever dead. Our sin nature won't be coming back." Steve McVey, *Grace Walk* (Eugene, Oregon: Harvest House, 1995), 60.

[12] Sermons, Vol. 1, p. 124 and Vol. 2, p. 19, respectively; quoted by J. Sidlow Baxter, *A New Call to Holiness* (Grand Rapids, Michigan, Zondervan, 1973), 46.

[13] Ibid., 53.

[14] Ibid., 50. Baxter used material from Ironside's book, *Holiness: the False and the True*.

[15] Ibid., 54.

[16] We will investigate the meaning of 6:11 in Chapters 7 and 8.

[17] William R. Newell, *Romans Verse by Verse* (Chicago Grace Publications 1943), 210.

[18] McVey, *Grace Walk*, 64.

[19] John Stott, *The Message of Romans: God's Good News for the World* (Downers Grove, Illinois: IVP, 1994) 170–171.

[20] Ibid., 171.

[21] Stott says this erroneous teaching of Romans 6 "... cannot stand up to a careful examination but leads people to self-deception, to disillusionment, and even to despair." Stott, *Men Made New*, 37–38.

[22] Stott says, "What is true of Christ is equally true of Christians who are united to Christ. We too have 'died to sin,' in the sense that through union with Christ we may be said to have borne its penalty." Stott, *Romans*, 172.

[23] "The first question in chapter 6, despite popular impressions to the contrary, is about status, not behavior. 'Shall we continue in sin' treats 'sin' as a place where one might go on living, not as an activity one might continue to perform." N.T. Wright, *The New Interpreter's Bible Commentary, Volume X, Romans* (Nashville, Tennessee: Abingdon, 2002), 528.

[24] For example, "We have seen that Romans 1 to 8 falls into two sections, in the first of which we are shown that the Blood deals with what we have done, while in the second we shall see that the Cross deals with what we are. We need the Blood for forgiveness; we need also the Cross for deliverance." Watchman Nee, *The Normal Christian Life* (Wheaton, Illinois: Tyndale House, 1979), 31.

[25] Galatians 2:20; 5:24; 6:14.

[26] 2 Timothy 2:12.

[27] 2 Corinthians 5:14–15.

[28] Ephesians 2:4–6; Colossians 2:11–15, 20; 3:3.

[29] Paul uses three compound verbs in the space of a few sentences to drive this point home. He says we have been "buried with Him" (*sunetaphemen* – 6:4), "united with Him in His death" (*sumphutoi* – 6:5), and "crucified with Him" (*sunestaurothe* – 6:6). Moo investigates Paul's "with Christ" terminology throughout his epistles and concludes, "In the case of both Adam and Christ, the union between them and those whom they represent is primarily—and in Christ's case perhaps exclusively—forensic. Because he is our representative, the judgment or decision that has fallen on Christ falls also on those who come to belong to him." Douglas Moo, *The Epistle to the Romans* (Grand Rapids, Michigan: Eerdmans, 1996), 395.

[30] "We must therefore find an explanation of this death to sin which is true both of Christ and of Christians. We are told that 'he died to sin,' and that 'we died to sin.' So, whatever this death to sin is, it has to be true of the Lord Jesus and of us." Stott, *Men Made New*, 39.

[31] "If we answer these questions from Scripture rather than from analogy, from biblical teaching about death rather than from the properties of dead people, we shall find immediate help. Death is represented in Scripture more in legal than in physical terms; not so much as a state of lying motionless but as the grim though just penalty for sin. Whenever sin and death are coupled in the Bible, from its second chapter...to its last two chapters...the essential nexus between them is that death is sin's penalty. This is plain also in Romans, in which we read that those who sin 'deserve death' (1:32), that death entered the world through sin (5:12), and that 'the wages of sin is death' (6:23)." Stott, *Romans*, 171–172.

[32] Nee, *The Normal Christian Life*, 34. The Keswick Conferences popularized this idea and spread it across the globe. For example, "Calvary...is God's answer to the problem of man's *sin* as well as his *sins*." By faith, we must lay hold of this experience of the cross in order to gain victory over the power of the old man and sin inside us. See Steven Barabas, *So Great Salvation*, (Eugene, Oregon: Wipf and Stock Publishers, 2005), 88–90.

[33] "In the papyri *huper* is the ordinary preposition for the notion of substitution where benefit is involved as in this passage." A.T. Robertson, *Word Pictures in the New Testament, Volume IV, Epistles of Paul* (Nashville, Tennessee: Broadman, 1931), 568.

[34] The other apostles also use this language to speak of Christ's atoning death. See Hebrews 2:9; 10:12; 1 Peter 2:21; 3:18; 1 John 3:16.

[35] "In what sense did they all die? The answer lies in *huper*, in Christ's substitution. It is indicated in Matt. 20:28 and Mark 10:45: he gave his life as a ransom in the stead of many. He laid down the price, and that price was reckoned as though we had laid it down. Each of us might die a thousand times, and this would amount to nothing even for those who did this: we are sinners who are damned to die. The death of the sinless Son, the Lamb without spot or blemish, this and this death alone, equals the death of all for whom he died." R.C.H. Lenski, *The Interpretation of St. Paul's First and Second Epistles to the Corinthians* (Minneapolis, Minnesota: Augsburg Publishing House, 1961), 1031.

[36] Paul puts it this way in Ephesians 2:12: "[Gentiles were] excluded from the commonwealth of Israel, and strangers to the covenants of promise, having no hope and without God in the world." In Romans 2:17–20 he lists the reasons why Israel was superior to the Gentile world.

[37] In this passage, Paul does what he did in Romans 5:20. Paul is not just a generic "sinner." Paul is a transgressor (of Law), a covenant-breaker. The Greek is *parabasis*, a synonym for *paraptoma* used in Romans. Paul is a transgressor of a known command, just like Adam.

[38] In this exchange, we see the same verbal sparring as in Romans 5:20—6:2. There, the Law came in that transgression might increase and God met this increased transgression with abundant grace. The Jews answered, "Then let's sin more and get more grace," to which Paul answered, "*Me genoito* (God forbid!)." Here Paul has them identifying Christ as one who incites sin, a minister of sin. In Romans 5:20—6:2, God's increased grace is the cause of greater sinning in the mind of Jewish opponents.

[39] N.T. Wright, *Justification* (Downers Grove, Illinois: IVP Academic, 2009), 119.

[40] I believe one should be able to see by now that the distinction between dying "for" something and dying "to" something, a distinction important in the arguments I am seeking to refute, becomes irrelevant. Christ died to the Law and to sin; i.e., He died to put away the condemning Law brought about by our sin. When we died *to sin* it means we died to the condemning effect of the Law because of our sin. All this is another way of saying that Christ died for our sins.

[41] Romans 8:37: "But in all these things we overwhelmingly conquer through

Him who *loved us*" (italics mine). Ephesians 5:2: "And walk in love, just as *Christ also loved you and gave Himself up for us, an offering* and sacrifice to God as a fragrant aroma" (italics mine).

[42] Alan Cole, *The Epistle of Paul to the Galatians* (Grand Rapids, Michigan: IVP, 1972), 23.

[43] The Greek word is the same as in Romans 6:6: *sunestauromai* in Galatians and *sunestaurothe* in Romans. These are the only places this compound shows up in the New Testament.

[44] Romans 6:10: "He died to sin once for all; but the life that He lives, He lives to God."

DEAD TO SIN IN ROMANS 6

What shall we say then? Are we to continue in sin so that grace may increase? May it never be! How shall we who died to sin still live in it? Or do you not know that all of us who have been baptized into Christ Jesus have been baptized into His death?

Therefore we have been buried with Him through baptism into death, so that as Christ was raised from the dead through the glory of the Father, so we too might walk in newness of life. For if we have become united with Him in the likeness of His death, certainly we shall also be in the likeness of His resurrection, knowing this, that our old self was crucified with Him, in order that our body of sin might be done away with, so that we would no longer be slaves to sin; for he who has died is freed from sin.

Now if we have died with Christ, we believe that we shall also live with Him, knowing that Christ, having been raised from the dead, is never to die again; death no longer is master over Him. For the death that He died, He died to sin once for all; but the life that He lives, He lives to God.

ROMANS 6:1–10

HOW DOES PAUL SPEAK OF THE DEATH of Christ in Romans 6? If the Galatians and Corinthian passages are great pieces of art, can we display them in the Romans 6 wing of Paul's gallery? Will they fit there and enhance the beauty of that room? Or, is Romans 6 different, a contrasting shade of color or a different technique that clashes with the Galatians and Corinthian pieces?

I suppose that even though 2 Corinthians 5 and Galatians 2—passages with strikingly similar terminology to Romans 6—speak of Christ's death in substitutionary ways, Romans 6 still could have a different shade of meaning. Paul could be introducing a new topic or revealing a new application to Christ's death that he doesn't mention in other places. The question is, does he?

We will attempt to answer this question by looking at four points in the opening verses of Romans 6—the death of Christ language, baptism, the phrase "once for all," and the idea of death as master.

THE DEATH OF CHRIST LANGUAGE IN ROMANS 6

What strikes me first in Romans 6 is that Paul speaks of Christ's death to sin with little or no explanatory notes. Having spoken of Christ's death as a substitutionary death in his other writings, it would seem that if he is going to give it a new meaning, he would preface his "death to sin" statements with such an explanatory note.[1] But he doesn't; instead, he employs already used language in Romans and takes for granted that his readers know he is talking about familiar themes. Previously, Paul made these statements about the death of Christ:

- We have been justified by grace through His redemption (3:24).
- God displayed Him publicly as a propitiation in His blood (3:25).
- He was delivered over because of our transgressions and raised because of our justification (4:25).
- Christ died for the ungodly and for sinners (5:6, 8).
- We have been justified by His blood (5:9).
- We have been reconciled through the death of His Son (5:10).

Redemption, propitiation, justification, and reconciliation—major biblical themes describing Christ's accomplishment on the cross—are Paul's words of choice in the early chapters of Romans. When he speaks of Christ's death in 6, should we not assume he is talking in the same realm of substitution unless otherwise noted? No transition to another kind of death shows up. Paul speaks simply of His death (6:3, 5) and the death that He died (6:10).

In the immediately preceding context of 5:12–21, Paul contrasts Christ with Adam. Adam disobeyed and brought condemnation. Christ obeyed and brought justification. Adam brought the reign of death; Jesus brought the reign of grace to eternal life. In short, Christ reversed the devastation of Adam's disobedience. But how did He do it?

Paul explains it in 5:18–19[2]: "So then as through one transgression there resulted condemnation to all men, even so through one act of righteousness there resulted justification of life to all men. For as through the one man's disobedience the many were made sinners, even so through the obedience of the One the many will be made righteous."

In order to grasp the significance of these verses that help form the background to the death of Christ references in chapter 6, let's take a closer look at the contrast between Adam and Christ in 5:15–21. First, I will set the key phrases next to each other in Table 2. Then, I will make several observations pertaining to the question before us about Romans 6.

TABLE 2			
Adam			**Christ**
The transgression –	15		The free gift –
by the transgression of the one	15		by the grace of the One Man
the many died.	15		the grace of God and the gift by the grace abounded to the many.
The judgment arose	16		The free gift arose
from one transgression	16		from many transgressions
resulting in condemnation.	16		resulting in justification.
By the transgression of the one	17		Through the one Jesus Christ
death reigned through the one.	17		those who receive ... the abundance of grace and the gift of righteousness will reign
Through one transgression	18		Through one act of righteousness
there resulted condemnation to all.	18		there resulted justification of life to all.
Through one man's disobedience	19		Through the obedience of the One
the many were made sinners.	19		the many will be made righteous.
Transgression increased.	20		Grace abounded.
Sin reigned in death.	21		Grace reigns through righteousness to life.

In 5:15, Paul emphasizes *the nature of Adam's and Christ's actions*. The nature of Adam's action was transgression—the breaking of a known command or the crossing of a boundary. The essence of Christ's action was grace. Adam broke God's command, but Christ—the free gift mentioned in the opening phrase—offered Himself. Stott eloquently speaks of "this enormous disparity" between Adam's "self assertion" and Christ's "self sacrifice."[3] Many commentators also point out the abundance of "gift" words in this verse[4]—free gift (*charisma*), grace (*charis*), and the gift (*dorea*) by that grace.

- "Free gift" (*charisma*) refers to Christ offering Himself in submission to the Father on the cross.
- The "grace" of God (*charis*) refers to the gracious disposition of God towards sinners.
- The "gift" (*dorea*) by the "grace" (*charis*) of the One Man refers to the status of righteousness conferred upon those who believe.[5]

In 5:16, Paul emphasizes *the immediate effects of Adam's and Christ's actions.* Adam's transgression caused a judgment (judicial decree) to arise. The judicial decree was condemnation. Paul contrasts the judgment arising with the free gift (of Christ offering Himself) arising, which led to a different judicial decree— justification.

Paul makes one other contrast in 5:16: One transgression/many transgressions. Adam's one transgression led to condemnation for all. But the many transgressions of the world, including the ones that put Christ on the cross, led to justification! Stott points out, "The secular mind would have expected *many sins* to attract more judgment than one sin. But grace operates a different arithmetic."[6]

Stott then goes on to offer a famous quote from Charles Cranfield: "That one single misdeed should be answered by judgment. This is perfectly understandable. That the accumulated sins and guilt of all the ages should be answered by God's free gift, this [is] the miracle of miracles, utterly beyond human comprehension!"[7]

In 5:17, Paul emphasizes *the ultimate effects of Adam's and Christ's actions.* Adam's transgression brought the reign of death. But Christ's abundant grace brought the gift of righteousness (the verdict of justification), which means those who receive this abundant grace will reign. But Paul does not just make a one-to-one contrast. He uses the phrase "much more" and the word "abundance" to show how Christ's work overwhelms the effects of Adam's sin.[8]

In 5:18–21, Paul uses the "just as…even so" contrast to finish the thought he began in 5:12 where he spoke of Adam's sin bringing death to the whole world: Just as Adam…even so Christ…. In 5:18 he re-emphasizes the immediate results of Adam's and Christ's actions, in 5:19 he re-emphasizes the nature of their acts, and in 5:20–21 he re-emphasizes the ultimate effects of their courses of action.[9] When we look at Christ's actions, we find these immediate and long-term effects:

- 5:18 – Justification of life
- 5:19 – The many are made (constituted, given the status of[10]) righteous
- 5:20 – Grace abounded
- 5:21 – Grace reigns through righteousness to eternal life

What is the purpose of this examination of Romans 5:12–21? Commentators and pastors, when trying to explain the meaning of Romans 6, frequently overlook these verses that provide insight for the interpretation of Romans 6. But these verses are the background to his thinking! What do these verses emphasize?

This immediate context to Paul's thoughts in Romans 6 and his 14 contrasts between Adam and Christ in Table 2 speak at every point of Christ's work on the cross to rescue us from condemnation and to bring us into a justified position before God. If this is the background to Paul's thinking, why should we think Romans 6 is about anything else?

When we add this to the several statements of His death in chapters 3:24—5:11, why would that death suddenly mean something other than His substitutionary death, especially if Paul does not explain it in any other terms or say He is introducing a new subject? Thus, when we find statements by Christian authors distinguishing the work of the Blood vs. the work of the Cross or statements that *His death to sin* is somehow different than *His death for our sins,* do we have any textual ground upon which to stand?

When we hear that we have to find an extra meaning to the Cross, experience some kind of inner death to a sinful nature within to get the upper hand over sin, or seek a "second blessing" to eradicate sin within, and when we hear that all of this comes from Romans 6, are we hearing from the Word of God or listening to the words of man?

Paul says in 6:3 and 6:5 that we are baptized into *His death* and united in the likeness of *His death*. No other aspect of *His death* comes into view, and Paul does not introduce any new meaning. The only new factor Paul introduces is to teach the Romans that *their* baptism into Christ was also a baptism into *His* death. This leads to our second point.

OUR BAPTISM

Three times Paul mentions baptism, twice in 6:3 and once in 6:4: "Or do you not know that all of us who have been *baptized* into Christ Jesus have been *baptized* into His death? Therefore we have been buried with Him through *baptism* into death, so that as Christ was raised from the dead through the glory of the Father, so we too might walk in newness of life" (italics mine).

I remember my pastor teaching through Romans 6 years ago when I was in high school. In his efforts to remain faithful to evangelical theology that one finds salvation by grace alone through faith alone with no works attached, and because he feared that some might construe baptism as a "work," he valiantly proclaimed that Romans 6 did not contain one drop of water! He was fearful that by speaking of Christian baptism, he would be walking perilously close to the treacherous waters of baptismal regeneration apart from personal faith. He therefore proclaimed that Paul had Spirit-baptism in mind in this section.

This effort to remain true to justification by faith alone does not require one to force such a strained reading upon Paul's text. John Stott points out that whenever a writer mentions baptism without any other modifier such as the Spirit or fire, water baptism is what the writer, or speaker, has in mind.[11]

Paul, therefore, was clearly speaking of Christian baptism—the climax of a conversion process that began by responding with faith to the preaching of the Gospel and culminated in their public confession of Christ as Lord at their baptism. Lest any reader be confused at this point, Douglas Moo has offered the following helpful comment:

> "How, then, can we preserve the cruciality of faith at the same time as we do justice to the mediatorial role of baptism in this text?" Here the suggestion of J. Dunn is helpful. He points out that the early church conceived of faith, the gift of the Spirit, and water baptism as components of one unified experience, which he calls 'conversion-initiation.' Just as faith is always assumed to lead to baptism, so baptism always assumes faith for its validity. In vv. 3–4, then, we can assume that baptism stands for the whole conversion-initiation experience, presupposing faith and the gift of the Spirit. What, we might ask, of the Christian who has not been baptized? While Paul never dealt with this ques-

tion—and his first reaction would undoubtedly have been 'Why hasn't he been baptized?'—we must assume from the fact that faith is emblazoned in every chapter of Romans while baptism is mentioned in only two verses that genuine faith, even if it has not been 'sealed' in baptism, is sufficient for salvation."[12]

I agree completely and affirm that the passage is about Christian water baptism. At the climactic moment of the conversion process, when men and women confessed Jesus as Lord, they passed out of death into life, from the realm of the first man, Adam, with its sentence of condemnation to the realm of the Second Man, Jesus, with its sentence of justification.

Sin used to reign in their lives. Now, grace reigns over them (5:21). If you look back at Table 2 contrasting Adam and Christ, you could say that one passes from the left column to the right column. Thankfully, a lot more than moving from one slot on a table to another is involved. Our status before God, conditioned at one time by our solidarity with Adam, has now changed. Now we find our status before God conditioned by our solidarity with Jesus Christ!

With this contrast fresh in his mind, Paul asks in 6:3, "Don't you know this? Don't you remember and know that when you confessed Christ as Lord and were baptized into Him, you were also baptized into His death? You were not only baptized into His death, you were also buried into that death which transferred you from the realm of Adam with its consequences to the realm of Christ with its benefits."

Why does Paul ask this question: "Don't you know?" He seems to think that because they recall one thing—their baptism into Christ—they should therefore know another thing—their baptism into Christ was a baptism into His death.

Perhaps Paul assumed that at (or prior to) their baptism, they were instructed in this association. Or perhaps Paul assumed they would naturally make the connection that if you come into union with Christ, this means that you come into union with all that He did for you—His death, burial, and resurrection.

It's easy for us to make this association, having heard it times without number in sermons and in baptism services, but for some the association may not have been quite as easy. Young believers (not to mention us older ones!) often need reminding and reassurance. In addition, Dunn points out that in the ancient world the linking of baptism with death was not a natural one[13] and was most likely a Christian innovation going back to Jesus' own association of His death with baptism.[14]

Dunn also points out that baptism would not necessarily be identified with burial as burials were not necessarily underground but above ground in tombs or caves. Thus, baptism by immersion would not provide a self-evident link with death unless they had been taught this.[15]

But Paul wants to make sure they know this or call it to mind and asks, "Do you not know?" Dunn then shows that Paul wants to make sure they associate their union with Christ with His death. He states: "The new step Paul takes here is that of combining two strands of his own teaching which he had not hitherto linked—baptized into (union with) Christ (as in Gal 3:27 and 1 Cor 12:13), and dying with Christ (as in Gal 2:20 and 2 Cor 4:10–11). Whatever knowledge of these traditions Paul could assume on the part of his readers, he certainly points back to the Adam/Christ contrast of 5:12–21; they have died to sin (v2) because they have died with Christ and because Christ now lives beyond sin and death, a life which they can share."[16]

What does all of this mean in relation to our topic? By referring to the believers' baptism whereby they escaped condemnation and entered into justification and by linking it with the death of Christ, Paul cannot be talking about anything other than His substitutionary work and their identification with Christ who died for their sins. Paul, then, in this chapter is not referring to a secondary work of Christ in His death (in which we mystically share) to overcome sinful impulses.[17] When he speaks of our union with Christ in that death, he identifies it as our baptism/conversion. This is an event of justification, not sanctification.

But as with the other passages, it *leads to* sanctification. Paul gives a glimpse of this when he talks about our walking in newness of life in 6:4. It is a subject he will address in 6:11–14 when he draws out the implications of our death and resurrection with Christ. He addresses it in 6:15–23 when he looks at it from the master/slave analogy, in 7:1–6 when he uses the husband/wife metaphor, and finally in 8:13ff in his full-blown exposition of life in the Spirit.

But for now, we are answering the question about the meaning of Christ's death in the opening verses of Romans 6. We have looked at the wider context of Romans 6, which points to it being a justification event, and we have looked at the baptism by which we participate in His death. Let's move to the third topic, the "once for all" language found in 6:10.

ONCE FOR ALL

If any verse could serve as a perfect lead-in to an additional meaning for Christ's death to sin, it is verse 10. Paul begins by saying, "For the death that He died…" If he had wanted to give a meaning other than the substitutionary meaning to Christ's death, this would have been an ideal place to give such an additional meaning. For example, Paul could have said, "For the death that He died…was a death that slew the old man within you in order to give you victory over those sinful desires." But he didn't say this or anything like it. Instead, he states, "For the death that He died, He died to sin once for all."

Inside this concluding statement[18] is a remarkable and enlightening phrase: "once for all." If you're an above average Bible student, or one who has heard sound biblical teaching, this phrase will be familiar to you. We find it in several other New Testament passages, primarily in the book of Hebrews (italics mine):

"[Christ] does not need daily, like those high priests, to offer up sacrifices, first for His own sins and then for the sins of the people, because this He did *once for all* when He offered up Himself" (7:27).

"And not through the blood of goats and calves, but through His own blood, He entered the holy place *once for all*, having obtained eternal redemption" (9:12).

"By this will we have been sanctified through the offering of the body of Jesus Christ *once for all*" (10:10).

In the first passage (7:27), the author of Hebrews is contrasting the sacrificial ministry of Christ with that of the high priests under the Mosaic Law. They offered sacrifices for their own sins and for the sins of the people every day. But Christ did not have to offer a sacrifice for Himself because He was sinless. However, He did offer Himself for the people, and when He did it was *once for all*. Christ does not have to die every day or every year. His *once for all* death on the cross was enough to cover the sins of His people.

In the second passage (9:12), Christ entered *once for all* into the heavenly holy place. He entered through His blood and obtained eternal redemption.

Unlike the high priest, He doesn't have to enter the Holy of Holies every year on the Day of Atonement and sprinkle blood on the mercy seat. His blood was better than that of calves and goats. His blood was sufficient for our eternal redemption. He entered the heavenly holy place *once for all*.

In the third passage (10:10), the writer says Jesus offered His body *once for all* in order to sanctify[19] His people. He follows up this statement in 10:11–14 where he emphasizes His one sacrifice for sins for all time: "Every priest stands daily ministering and offering time after time the same sacrifices, which can never take away sins; but He, *having offered one sacrifice for sins for all time*, sat down at the right hand of God, waiting from that time onward until his enemies be made a footstool for His feet. For *by one offering He has perfected for all time* those who are sanctified" (italics mine).[20]

It is clear what the writer of Hebrews is talking about: the substitutionary work of Christ. His sacrifice is better than that of calves and goats. He obtained eternal redemption for us. He entered the heavenly holy place for us and set us apart to God. Nothing else has to be done. What Jesus did was sufficient to make us right with God.

This understanding of the work of Christ—made emphatic by the writer's use of the "once for all" vocabulary—must guide our understanding of the death of Christ to sin *once for all* in Romans 6.[21] If it means one thing in Hebrews, why would it mean something else in Romans 6, especially when these are the only uses of the phrase in the New Testament?

And we must not forget how Paul uses the once for all statement in Romans 6. He does not simply say that Christ died *for our sins* once for all, but that He died *to sin* once for all. This is our key phrase that many have so often misunderstood. But its use with the "once for all" terminology sheds light on its meaning. Christ dying to sin means He put away our sins by His substitutionary death on the cross. And if that is what it meant for Him, then that is what our death to sin must mean.

Finally, when Paul says that Christ is dead to sin, he does not mean that Christ is dead to sinful impulses within Him. After all, He had none.[22] Paul means that Christ no longer has to face its consequence—death—on our behalf. Or, another way of putting it: Because of His *once for all* sacrifice, death is no longer master over Him.

DEATH IS NO LONGER MASTER OVER HIM

Romans 6:9 contains the final phrase that will help us determine what Paul is talking about in Romans 6 when he speaks of the death of Christ and our death with Him: "Knowing that Christ, having been raised from the dead, is never to die again; death no longer is master over Him."

Christ has been raised! Christ never has to die again! What great news! But because Paul presents it as an accomplished fact, years after death lost its grip when He died and rose, we overlook an unsettling truth: At one point death was master over Him. Compounding the oversight of this unsettling truth is the fact that we live centuries after the great event and perhaps years after we have received Him and lived in fellowship with Him. We have come to know Him as Sovereign Lord and a gracious Savior. To think that at one time something was master over Him is strange to our ears. Yet, this is what the text clearly implies. If death is *no longer* master over Him, then at one time, death was master over Him.

It's strange to think of anything having mastery over Jesus. Sinful habits certainly did not. He lived a perfect life. Disease and demons did not. He healed the sick and cast out evil spirits with a word. The difficulties of life did not. He calmed the storms on the Sea of Galilee, raised people from the grave, and in His darkest moments in the Garden of Gethsemane and on the Cross, He still displayed control, placed all His faith in His Father, laid down His life on His own authority, and forgave His executioners. Nothing had mastery over Him, except, according to Paul's statement, death. How do we explain this?

Death was Jesus' master because Jesus voluntarily took the role of the substitute for our sins. Once Jesus took this role, He could take no other path than the one that led to death, if He was to come out on the other side of death with our justification.

Jesus entered into this role at His birth. Paul tells us in Galatians 4:4 that Christ was "born of a woman," emphasizing His full entrance into and participation in our humanity. Though He did not partake of our sinful nature, He did partake of human nature and voluntarily entered into the realm of Adam conditioned by his sin. But the realm of Adam has no way out of its predicament except through death. As Paul said in 5:12, "death spread to all men" and in 5:14, "death reigned."

Death became the master of every man, including the Perfect Man, because He willingly accepted the role of the One who would bear death on behalf of all and reverse the effect of Adam's sin. Once He entered into this realm where death reigned, no way out existed except to let death have its way with Him, to let death be His master.

Paul says more in Galatians 4:4. He says that He was also born "under the Law." To be born under the Law means one is born under the obligation to keep the Law and therefore under the curse of the Law if one does not keep it. And even though Christ never broke the Law, He came to bear the curse of the Law on our behalf.[23] Therefore, from His earthly beginning, even though He was no law-breaker, the curse of the Law—death—hung over Him and would not depart from Him until He satisfied its demands.

Theologians have sometimes called this Recapitulation Theology where Jesus voluntarily reenacted the life of the man Adam and of the nation, Israel. Jesus walked the steps they walked. But whereas they failed, He succeeded. Adam was tempted at the beginning of his commission to rule creation and failed. Jesus was tempted at the beginning of His commission to inaugurate the kingdom and obeyed.[24] Israel was tested in the wilderness shortly after their passing through the waters of the Red Sea and failed. Jesus was tested in the wilderness after passing through the waters of baptism and succeeded.[25]

Thus, Jesus entered this world with the full recognition of what His ministry would entail—reversing the judgment Adam brought into the world and the covenant curses on Israel. Where mankind disobeyed, He had to obey. Where Israel strayed, He had to stay faithful, and in doing so, He put Himself in a position to bear the judgment of Adam's sin and the curses of the covenants His people violated. All 14 contrasts between Adam and Christ laid out in Table 2 should now take on a richer significance. And the phrases in 5:18–19— "through one act of righteousness" and "through the obedience of the One"— should become much more pointed.

Is this not why, when John tried to refuse Jesus from entering baptism, Jesus replied, "Permit it at this time [John]; for in this way, [we will] fulfill all righteousness" (Matthew 3:15)? Baptism was a symbol of cleansing for sin and something Jesus did not need. Yet Jesus voluntarily submitted to this rite, identifying as the sinless One with those who were repenting of their sins.

He began His ministry with the end in mind: total identification with sinners. What He began in the waters of baptism ended on the cross where He bore the curses of the covenant.[26] "Permit it at this time, John, for *in this way* we will fulfill all righteousness," or, to put it in covenant language: "In this way we will fulfill the demands of the covenant and bring the covenant promises to our people." In what way? In the way of voluntarily identifying with sinners, picking up a cross, denying self, obeying all the way to the cross, and letting death do its worst to Him.

There was no easy way out. Death, the consequence of sin, could rightfully demand that He give Himself up to death if He was going to take upon Himself the sins of the world. Death, therefore, can be said to have been His master for it would not allow any other way to redeem mankind.[27]

Again, its mastery over Jesus was not due to His sins or weaknesses. He had none. But because He willingly took our sins upon Himself, He therefore had to suffer their consequence—death. There was no escaping it. He had to take in hand the cup He so earnestly prayed would pass away. He had to drink, in full, the cup of the wrath of God. Death rightly demanded that the Sin-Bearer give up His life. Jesus could take no other route. He had to submit to the demands of death because of our sin.

Romans 6:9 is another way of drawing out the implications of Romans 5:12: "Through one man sin entered into the world, and death through sin." Death was the unwelcome intruder upon God's creation, the uninvited partner that accompanied sin when Adam fell. It spread to all men (5:12), even over those who were unwittingly sinning and not rebelling against known commands (5:14). Twice in chapter 5 (verses 14 and 17), Paul stated that death "reigned." Death was master over all. It touched and ended every life. Because Jesus entered this world of humanity where death was king, and because He chose to bear the sins of humanity, He therefore subjected Himself to sin's consequence—death. When Jesus chose this route, and held fast to it, He allowed death to become His master and overpower Him on the cross.[28]

But by His death, He satisfied death's demands. He suffered the consequence of man's sin, and in paying for sin, death lost all rights to exercise mastery over Him. With sin paid for, Jesus could rise from the grave to an immortal life. By stating that He died to sin once for all in 6:10, Paul affirms that His death was a sufficient payment for the sins of Adam's race. He never has to die again

(6:9) and death can no longer make any claims upon Him since the penalty for sin, now satisfied, can be laid to rest once for all and destroyed. If the penalty for sin no longer exists, death, therefore, can no longer exert its mastery over Him.

DEATH TO SIN IN ROMANS 6

It's time to bring all of this together. We have viewed four points in this chapter to determine the meaning of the death of Christ in Romans 6.

- The death of Christ terminology in the verses leading up to Romans 6, especially in 5:15–21
- Baptism/conversion as the key moment of identification with His death
- The "once for all" terminology of Hebrews and Romans 6
- The one-time mastery of death over Jesus which has now been broken

When we understand these four points as major markers in the path Paul walks in Romans 6, can there be any remaining doubt what "death to sin" in Romans 6:2 and 6:10 is about? Paul is not talking about a secondary aspect to the work of Christ that dealt with a supposed old sin nature. Instead, He is talking about the substitutionary work of Christ on the cross. His death to sin was to the penalty of sin as our sin-bearer—the same as in 2 Corinthians 5 and Galatians 2. And if His death to sin was to the penalty of sin, then our death to sin must be the same. This takes us back to a key premise in chapter 2: *Whatever "death to sin" means, it can mean nothing more or nothing less than what it meant to Christ. We died to sin only because Christ died to sin.*

Now, we can confidently answer the question of 6:1: "Are we to continue in sin so that grace may increase?" Paul's answer in 6:2 with our interpretation answers: "May it never be! How shall we who died to [the penalty of] sin still live in it?" In other words, with condemnation removed, it is foolish, illogical, and inconsistent to live a sinful life.

To continue living in sin in order to get more grace would show a complete misunderstanding of why Christ died and what He accomplished on the cross to remove the judgment and the curses from us. It would show a complete failure to grasp the mastery of death and how that mastery has been broken and the reason for which we submitted to baptism—to be united with Him in His death so that we could be united with Him in His resurrection to walk in new-ness of life.[29]

"But wait!" some will say. "You have overlooked the key verse in Romans 6. What you have said is well and good, but you have failed to talk about 6:6, which speaks about our sin nature being crucified with Christ. Here, Paul speaks explicitly in co-crucifixion terms and says that our old self was crucified with Him with the result that the body of sin might be done away with, leading to a further result: that we should be freed from sin's slavery. This is where we learn that Christ's death to sin has freed us from the power of sin's impulses."

Here are verses 6 and 7: "Knowing this, that our old self was crucified with Him, in order that our body of sin might be done away with, so that we would no longer be slaves to sin; for he who has died is freed from sin".

Yes, these are the verses! But they are verses over which many scholars, stu-dents, and saints have puzzled—and, as I will show, upon which they have stumbled.

Let's continue our journey in the rough terrain of Romans 6, but rather than stumbling in our understanding or taking a path that leads to a dead end (no pun intended), we will discover that 6:6 and 6:7, when properly understood, are talking about something very different from what most popular speakers say. When they are properly understood, it leads to the freedom in Christ we are searching for. In our next chapter, we will examine this question: "What is the 'old man' who was crucified?"

CHAPTER THREE ENDNOTES

[1] Such as, "Now let me tell you what else He did on the cross."

[2] Almost all commentators point out that Paul did not finish his thought in 5:12 but broke it off in 5:13–14 to handle a couple of side issues relating to sin and death before the Mosaic Law. Then in 5:15, he starts the Adam/Christ contrast and in 18–19 completes the thought he introduced in 5:12. Wright calls it "the key sentence…in which Paul at last says what he has been waiting to say for five verses." N.T. Wright, *The New Interpreter's Bible Commentary*, Volume X, *Romans*, (Nashville, Tennessee: Abingdon, 2002), 528.

[3] "Paul has called Adam the type or prototype of Christ (14). But he has no sooner made this statement that he feels embarrassed by the anomaly, the impropriety, of what he has said. To be sure, there is a superficial similarity between them in

that each is one man through whose one deed enormous numbers of people have been affected. But there indubitably the likeness between them ends. How can the Lord of glory be likened to the man of shame, the Savior to the sinner, the giver of life to the broker of death?" John Stott, *The Message of Romans: God's Good News for the World* (Downers Grove, Illinois: IVP, 1994), 154–155.

[4] "This reiteration of emphasis upon grace is not redundancy but, in a manner characteristic of the apostle, an eloquent fullness and variety of expression to advertise the freeness from every angle of thought." John Murray, *The Epistle to the Romans* (Grand Rapids, Michigan: Eerdmans, 1965), 193–194.

[5] See Douglas Moo, *Epistle to the Romans* (Grand Rapids, Michigan: Eerdmans, 1996), 334–337 for a full explanation of the nuances of each Greek word in Paul's sentence.

[6] Stott, *Romans*, 155.

[7] Ibid.

[8] Ibid., 156. "The words *how much more*, together with the reference to God's abundant provision of grace and of the gift of righteousness, alert us to expect a greater blessing. Even so, we are not prepared for what follows, namely that the recipients of God's abundant grace will themselves reign in life. Formerly death was our king, and we were slaves under its totalitarian tyranny. What Christ has done for us is not just to exchange death's kingdom for the much more gentle kingdom of life, while leaving us in the position of subjects. Instead, he delivers us from the rule of death so radically as to enable us to change places with it and rule over it, or reign in life."

[9] I am indebted to John Stott's work, *The Message of Romans,* 155–156, where he identifies the three contrasts—the nature of their acts, the immediate results, and the ultimate results. Here is how they line up with one another:

5:15 speaks about	the nature of Adam's and Christ's	and is re-emphasized in 5:19.
5:16 speaks about	the immediate consequences of Adam's and Christ's actions	and is re-emphasized in 5:18.
5:17 speaks about	the ultimate effects of Adam's and Christ's actions	and is re-emphasized in 5:20–21.

[10] "This making righteous however must be interpreted in the light of Paul's typical forensic categories. To be 'righteous' does not mean to be morally upright, but to be judged acquitted, cleared of all charges, in the heavenly judgment. Through Christ's obedient act, people become *really* righteous; but 'righteous' itself is a

legal, not a moral, term in this context." Moo, *The Epistle to the Romans*, 345.

[11] Stott, *Romans*, 173.

[12] Moo, *The Epistle to the Romans*, 366.

[13] Baptism, instead, was more naturally related to cleansing, which Christians also used as Ananias said to Paul, "Get up and be baptized and wash away your sins, calling on His name" (Acts 22:16).

[14] "Jesus himself was remembered as having made the link (Mark 10:38–39; Luke 12:50), that is, explicitly using baptism as a metaphor for his own death, the imagery of death as an overwhelming torrent of destruction (Ps 69:2 [Aq 68:3]; Josephus, *War* 4.137). The *hagnoeite* therefore may refer implicitly to this tradition as something the Roman believers should know: Paul speaks of their being baptized to share Jesus' death because Jesus before him had spoken of his own death as a 'baptism' (cf. Cullmann, Baptism, 19–20; Robinson, Wrestling, 69; other bibliography in Halter, 530 n.25). If the Baptist had spoken of a baptism which all must undergo, and Jesus was remembered as having focused that baptism on himself then Paul here combines the two: all must be baptized with his baptism (see further Dunn, 'Birth of a Metaphor')." James D.G. Dunn, *Word Biblical Commentary, Vol. 38A, Romans 1–8*, (Nashville, Tennessee: Thomas Nelson Publishers), 312.

[15] "This is the new or further teaching which Paul presumably wants to draw to their attention.... Despite frequent assertions to the contrary...baptism was not an obvious symbol for death.... The symbolism of cleansing was much more obvious; and since death did not necessarily mean burial under the surface of the earth (but typically in tombs and caves) the symbolism of immersion provided no self-evident link. The association of baptism and death is probably distinctively Christian." Dunn, 312.

[16] Ibid., 312–313.

[17] The Greek text is explicit: "We have been buried with Him through *the* baptism (*tou baptismatos*) into *the* death (*ton thanaton*)."

[18] This verse and 6:2 are like bookends. 6:2 says *we* died to sin. 6:10 says *He* died to sin and in between (6:3, 4, 5, 6, 8) Paul explains what His death to sin was about and therefore what our death to sin is about. Then 6:11 begins the application of this theology.

[19] In this book I have been contrasting justification (our once-for-all right standing with God) and sanctification (the process by which we become holy in our

character and behavior). The New Testament writers, however, often use sanctification in a positional sense—we are "set apart" for God. This is one of those cases. Other verses that use sanctification in a positional sense are 1 Corinthians 1:2; 6:11 and Hebrews 2:11.

[20] This terminology is also affirmed in Hebrews 9:26, "*Once* at the consummation of the ages He has been manifested to put away sin"; in 9:28, "Christ... having been offered *once* to bear the sins of many"; and in 1 Peter 3:18, "For Christ also died for sins *once for all*, the just for the unjust."

[21] Dodd, in his article, "The Old Testament in the New," makes the following observation: "If it can be shown that one particular sentence has been quoted in two or more writings of the New Testament, where we have no reason to suspect literary dependence of one writer on another, there is surely a fair presumption that the sentence had been recognized as having special significance for Christians at a date earlier than the first such quotation." G.K. Beale, editor, *The Right Doctrine from the Wrong Texts?* C.H. Dodd, "The Old Testament in the New" (Grand Rapids, Michigan: Baker Academic, 1994), 170. Although Dodd is talking about Old Testament quotations in the New Testament, the principle would hold true for phrases found in the New Testament. Romans and Hebrews were written by two authors at two times to two groups. Their use of the same phrase—*once for all*—could indicate a pervasive use of the phrase in first-century churches, or, it could mean that Paul's use became so widespread that the writer of Hebrews picked up on it and used it to refer to the substitutionary death of Christ.

[22] To this idea Stott remarks, "What does verse 10 mean by saying 'he died to sin, once for all'? It cannot mean He became unresponsive to it, because this would imply that He was formerly responsive to it. Was our Lord Jesus Christ at one time so alive to sin that He needed subsequently to die to it? And indeed was He so continuously alive to sin that He had to die to it decisively once and for all? Of course not. That would be intolerable." John Stott, *Men Made New* (Grand Rapids, Michigan: Baker Book House, 1988), 39.

[23] "Christ redeemed us from the curse of the Law, having become a curse for us—for it is written, 'Cursed is everyone who hangs on a tree'" (Galatians 3:13).

[24] Thus, Paul contrasts Adam and Christ in Romans 5 and in 1 Corinthians 15. Christ becomes the last Adam (15:45) and the Second Man (15:47).

[25] Many commentators have noted that Jesus defeated Satan by quoting Scrip-

ture from Deuteronomy where Israel was in the wilderness. See Deuteronomy 8:3; 6:13; 6:16.

[26] Jesus referred to His death as a baptism, thus linking the two. See Luke 12:50.

[27] In personifying death and sin in this way, I hope no reader will make the mistake of thinking that death was a power working independently of God, sort of as a rival god. Man's choice brought sin and death into the world and they remain as powers subject to the sovereignty of God. He allows them to run their course and do their worst, but He ultimately overrules and reverses their destruction through Christ.

[28] In his comments on 5:12, N.T. Wright says, "Sin and death, here personified, continue as 'characters' in Paul's narrative through to chap. 8. In terms of his overall argument for assurance, they are the forces that must be defeated if the Christian is to be sure of eternal life...Paul imagines them as alien powers, given access to God's world through the action of Adam. Once in, they had come to stay; staying, they seized royal power. Linked together as cause and effect, they now stride through their usurped domain, wreaking misery, decay, and corruption wherever they go. No one is exempt from their commanding authority." N.T. Wright, *The New Interpreter's Bible Commentary*, Volume X, Romans, (Nashville, Tennessee: Abingdon, 2002), 525.

[29] Stott summarizes it well: "We died to sin [in the past]; how then shall we live in it [in the future]? It is not the literal impossibility of sin in the believers which Paul is declaring, but the moral incongruity of it. J.B. Phillips catches the point in his rendering: 'We, who have died to sin—how could we live in sin any longer?' Paul is drawing attention to the essential anomaly of living in sin when we have died to sin." Stott, *The Message of Romans*, 169.

THAT OLD MAN

Knowing this, that our old self was crucified with Him, in order that our body of sin might be done away with, so that we would no longer be slaves to sin.

ROMANS 6:6

WE HAVE CALLED HIM A VARIETY OF NAMES; the old man, the old self, the sin nature, the old nature, and sometimes, the flesh. Different translations and paraphrases get in on the name-calling:

- Old self – NIV, NASB, ESV, HCSB
- Old man – KJV, NKJV, ASV
- Old way of life – Message
- Old unrenewed self – Amplified
- Old sinful selves – NLT
- The persons we used to be – CEV

What is the old man?[1] A common opinion is that the old man is something within us, something that is part of our human nature inherited from Adam and corrupted by his sin, and further corrupted by our own sin. We hear that the old man is another name for our sinful human nature that causes our sin problems. Sinning is not just something we do. It is something we are, something that stems from our sinful nature—the old man—and something Christ dealt with decisively on the cross. He not only died for our sins, He also crucified our sin nature to get at the root of the sinful impulses within so that we can live free from sin. Consider these statements:

Charles Hodge– "Our old man, that is, our corrupt nature as opposed to the new man, or holy nature, which is the product of regeneration, and the effect of our union with Christ …. The old man, the nature which is prior in the order of time, as well as corrupt, is crucified, and a nature new and holy is induced."[2]

H.P. Liddon– He speaks of "the crucifixion of the old sinful nature with Christ."[3]

Godet– "Our old man, denotes human nature such as it has been made by the sin of him in whom originally it was wholly concentrated, fallen Adam reappearing in every human ego that comes into the world."[4]

Dr. J. Sidlow Baxter– He quotes those before his time and from his time (early to mid-20th century) who taught the same.

"It is called, in the New Testament, 'the flesh,' 'the body of sin,' our 'old man,' 'sin that dwelleth in me,' and the simple term 'sin' in the singular number…. Now all Christian denominations are agreed as to the real existence of this inbred sin….

"Instead of leaving me to struggle with my sinful nature and its promptings, Christ took that nature with Him to be crucified….

"Some declare that sin must remain in the heart of the believer until death, but in Romans, chapter 6, verse 6, we read that our corrupt sinful nature can be destroyed, that henceforth we should not serve sin."[5]

In our day, the voices continue:

Steve McVey– "Paul says that the old has 'passed away.' You know what it means when someone has 'passed away.' To put it plain, they're dead. That's what happened to our old sin nature. It passed away and is never coming back. Maybe you haven't believed that your old sin nature is dead. But just for a moment, ask yourself this question: Wouldn't it be wonderful if my sin nature was honestly dead? This is where things get exciting because the Bible shows that our sin nature is dead!"[6]

McVey quotes Charles Stanley in support of this view: [7]"What he is saying is that God cut away—He took away that old sinful nature we received from our parents. That nature that has been poisoned by the Adamic nature. That old sin nature is that within us which causes us to disobey and rebel. God deals with that in salvation. God has taken away from us that which was given at birth—that old sinful nature. Some will say, 'Do you mean to tell me that my old sinful nature with which I was born has been taken away?' It has been taken away. That is what he is referring to when he speaks of circumcision, that cutting away."

If you have followed me this far in our journey, you might suspect that I have trouble with this common interpretation. I do—big time! But first, I want to re-emphasize that I have no quarrel with the noble intentions of my brothers to help the family of God. I admire their work and rejoice in their efforts to give help and guidance to Christians who struggle with sin. I only believe they have misinterpreted key verses that have unfortunately created greater confusion about the Christian life.

Some questions I have asked upon hearing or reading such statements are: "If my old man, something inside me, my corrupted nature that causes me to sin, was crucified with Christ, why am I still having trouble with sinful thoughts, desires, tendencies, and habits? What is it inside me that keeps screaming for attention and says, 'feed me'?"

In a recent email exchange, a pastor friend of mine asked, "Why do some of the same selfish desires keep reoccurring, even though I've been convinced very clearly that they're wrong and destructive?" Like a veteran of guerilla warfare, the old (crucified) man attacks, does his damage, and disappears into darkness, making him hard to find and deal with. Like that character from horror movies, he keeps showing up long after we thought he was dead.

What is it inside us that keeps resurfacing and enticing us to sin? We can't blame the devil for everything, and we can't place all the blame on the world, even though it sets a beautiful table and invites us to indulge. Ultimately, it's down to you and me—we are responsible. We can be on a Christian retreat, surrounded by godly people, in a picture postcard environment with praise to God surrounding us and the name of Jesus everywhere exalted. It's about as close to heaven as one can get on earth, yet evil thoughts can still arise from within!

On more than one occasion, I have been at my desk reading or studying, deeply moved by the Spirit of God, only to find my mind wandering to unwholesome topics just a few short minutes later! We can run from the world, but ultimately we have to face the evil within. More than one mystic and monk who sought to run from evil discovered that wherever he went, evil went with him—because it was on the inside.

And so I ask again, if my sin nature inherited from Adam was crucified with Christ, where does all this junk inside me come from?

Some commentators, recognizing the problem, have resorted to a clever distinction between crucifixion and death. Godet states, "This old man has been crucified so far as the believer is concerned in the very person of Christ crucified. The apostle does not say that he has been killed. He may exist still, but like one crucified, whose activity is paralyzed…not an immediate death certainly, but the reduction of it to powerlessness."[8]

Govett picks up this distinction. "The man nailed to the cross, unable to stir hand or foot, could serve no one. Such should be, in God's scheme, the position of the justified in Christ toward sin. His old nature is not dead, while he is yet alive in the body. But it is to be on the tree of the curse, powerless, declining in force day by day, till actually dead. See then, in Jesus crucified, the present place of enforced inactivity, and the future doom of 'the old man' of the justified."[9]

But is this what Scripture says—that the "old man" was crucified, but not dead and still lingering on the cross? Or to use the words in the previous quote: "*declining in force day by day, till actually dead* and in a place of *enforced inactivity*"?[10] That would make the destruction of the old man still to come, as Govett says, "the future doom of the 'old man.'" Yet all the verb tenses in Romans 6 signify a past, completed action![11]

And if we are crucified but not dead, did Christ not die completely? But Romans 6:3 says we were baptized into *His death*, and 6:4 says we were *buried with Him*. In the 18th and 19th centuries, European theologians and philosophers, captured by anti-supernatural biases, concluded that the resurrection of Christ could not have happened. Some proposed that Christ did not die on the cross but only swooned or went into unconsciousness and was resuscitated by the coolness of the tomb and therefore did not rise from the dead.

We know this as the Swoon Theory, and we know that no thinking person who studies the evidence could hold to such a position. But aren't the above quotes a variation on the swoon theory—not the swoon theory about Christ, but about us! Our old man hasn't yet died, but has only lost consciousness. He has swooned and from time to time reemerges from the tomb to cause horror and panic!

It is clear that such statements, although an ingenious way to deal with the ever-emerging sinful impulses within, are not consistent with Scripture. When Paul states we were crucified with Christ in 6:6, he means that we died with Christ. We cannot accept such a view that our corrupt sinful nature is still lingering on the cross, paralyzed, weakening, and made ineffective by the nails of Calvary.

In addition to it being inconsistent with Scripture, it is also a poor way of describing our sinful tendencies that at times seem anything but paralyzed and weakening. It is also a dismal metaphor for the kind of life Paul expects us to experience—a Spirit-empowered life where we overwhelmingly conquer!

Some have offered another solution. We are "to reckon" that our old nature is dead. We hear that the devout believer must learn to pair Romans 6:6 with 6:11 where Paul states, "therefore consider yourselves dead to sin." We are told something like this: "The reason many have trouble with their old sinful nature is that they don't know that it has been crucified. They need to learn this truth: Their old nature was crucified with Christ, which is why Paul begins 6:6 with 'knowing'—and then "consider" it, "reckon" it, and "act upon" it by faith according-ing to 6:11. Only when we acknowledge that our sin nature was crucified does the power of the cross take effect upon our old sinful nature and quell the sinful desires within. We are to accept this by faith and not trust our feelings." If any-one thinks my sample statement doesn't reflect popular teaching, consider these words from Mike Quarles and Steve McVey:

Mike Quarles– "It was at that moment that the lights came on and in that moment I knew the truth. I knew I had died with Christ and the old sin loving sinner had died and was no more. Oh I had believed the lie and acted like it for all these years, but that was not who I was. I now knew the truth was that I was dead to sin whether I acted like it, felt like it, looked like it or anyone else believed it—because God said I was."[12]

Steve McVey– "When God began to teach me about my identity in Christ, the truth about the death of my old nature was the most difficult thing for me to accept. Even when confronted with Scripture that clearly shows that the old nature was crucified with Christ, I thought that my old nature felt very much alive. But the truth is that the old Steve—the person I was before I was saved—is dead. I really wrestled with this fact. And even when God revealed the truth to me, I couldn't understand how it could be true."[13]

I cannot state the dilemma we face any better than McVey: "I thought that my old nature felt very much alive!" That is the problem! It feels very much alive. Yet we continually hear that it is dead and we have to accept faith over feelings. I guess I haven't had enough faith or I have failed in my responsibility to keep constant vigilant attention and keep my old man crucified.

Newell exhorts: "We must not confound our relationship to sin with its presence! Distinguish this revealed fact that we died, from our experience of deliverance. For we do not die to sin by our experiences: we did die to sin in Christ's death. For the fact that we died to sin is a Divinely revealed word concerning us, and we cannot deny it! The presence of sin 'in our members' will make this fact that we died to it hard to grasp and hold: but God says it. And He will duly explain all to our faith."[14]

Does anyone else see the inconsistencies and fallacies in this statement? 1) It is a divinely revealed fact that we died to sin, but we must not confuse it with the experience of deliverance; 2) Yet sin is still present in our members making the fact hard to grasp; and 3) God will duly explain all to faith.

Why does God have to explain it *to faith* at some later point? What happened to the facts? If we died to sin within us, why is sin still present in our members?[15] Why does it have to be a divinely revealed word—a second blessing or a mystical union with Christ in His death achieved by reckoning it so?—when the paragraph trumpets the supremacy of fact over feeling? This is the typical problem when people approach Romans 6 with the wrong questions and try to make it talk about something far from Paul's mind.

In addition to the obvious inconsistencies, I cannot accept such exhortations, pleas, interpretations, and self-blaming. I know I have believed and reckoned with great earnestness only to find that my sinful nature isn't dead or even in some stage of crucifixion nailed helplessly to a cross. The reason it has felt very much alive is that it is very much alive! Listen to these words from the great Bible expositor, John Stott: "Scriptural and historical biographies, and our own experience, combine to deny these ideas. Far from being dead in the sense of being quiescent, our fallen and corrupt nature is alive and kicking. So much so that we are exhorted not to obey its lusts; and so much so that we are given the Holy Spirit for the precise purpose of subduing and controlling it. And what would be the purpose of that if it were already dead?"[16]

Whether it has been lust, anger, impatience, indifference to the things of God, worry, self-loathing, unbelief, or any other number of sins, I have found them rising up within me. Maybe the devil can plant thoughts in our minds, but I can't blame him or the world all the time. I thank the well-intentioned teachers who have had nothing but blessing in mind for us all. But I, and countless others who care to admit the truth, have found their solutions wanting.

What do we do, then, with Romans 6:6? How do we understand and interpret Paul's statement that our old self was crucified with Him? What is the old self, the old man? To understand Paul's thought, we must return to Romans 5:12–21 and let those verses set the interpretive framework for his statement in 6:6 that our old man was crucified.

THE OLD MAN OF ROMANS 5

Romans 5:12–21 is one of the greatest of Paul's passages. Moo says it rivals 3:21–26 "for theological importance."[17] The density of its Greek has often challenged translators to smooth it into readable English faithful to the Greek text. Wright says its paragraph is "as terse and cryptic as the previous one was flowing and lucid."[18] Yet, as we discovered in the preceding chapter, with painstaking effort, we can discover rich resources that will help us on our journey in understanding Paul's better known statements in Romans 6.

Wright makes the insightful comment that in 5:12–21, Paul is "setting up the grid on which all that follows will be plotted."[19] Another way of saying this is that he is setting up the theological framework by which we can interpret chapters 6 through 8, and for our present purposes, the old man of 6:6. What is this grid, or theological framework, that is determinative for understanding Romans 6? I cannot improve on the overview given by Douglas Moo: "All people, Paul teaches, stand in relationship to one of two men, whose actions determine the eternal destiny of all who belong to them. Either one 'belongs to' Adam and is under sentence of death because of his sin, or disobedience, or one belongs to Christ and is assured of eternal life because of his 'righteous' act, or obedience. The actions of Adam and Christ, then, are similar in having 'epochal' significance.[20]

Moo says Paul's perspective in this section is "corporate rather than individual,"[21] and in this statement we find our first clue. The interpretive framework for 6:6 is a corporate framework. Paul is talking about all of humanity in solidarity with one of two men—either solidarity with Adam in his sin or with Christ in His righteousness.

He introduces this truth in 5:12: "Therefore, just as through one man sin entered into the world, and death through sin, and so death spread to all men, because all sinned." Sin found its entrance into the world through one man, and death came along with sin. And in this way, death spread to every person because all sinned. All sinned? We know everyone is a sinner, but Paul seems to be saying something else in this verse: When Adam sinned, everyone sinned with him. Such words singe the ears and offend the sensitivities of modern hearts. How can everyone be said to have sinned in Adam? Surely, I am not accountable for what Adam did, am I?

Christians have long debated the precise interpretation of that last phrase—"all sinned"—in 5:12. Some have said it simply refers to everyone's sinning. Others have said that it is our sin "in Adam." When he sinned we were "in him" and we therefore sinned with him. We could create a spectrum of opinion and plot various shades of interpretations where one slightly differs from another.[22]

I have read brilliant expositions from the brightest minds setting forth convincing opinions on the various sides of the debate but still have not found that one convincing argument that silences all others (except for the silencing of the Pelagian view). Paul Enns, in *The Moody Handbook of Theology* has provided a helpful overview of the main viewpoints as seen in Table 3.[23]

TABLE 3			
Pelagian	**Arminian**	**Federal**	**Augustinian**
Adam's sin has no effect experientially or judicially upon us.	Adam's sin affects us experientially in that we are born with a sin nature, but we are not guilty before God because of Adam's sin.	Adam's sin affects us experientially in that we are born with a sin nature, and we are guilty before God because of Adam's sin.	Adam's sin affects us experientially in that we are born with a sin nature, we are guilty before God because of Adam's sin, and we sinned in Adam.

Whichever viewpoint you take, Arminian, Federal, or Augustinian, one thing we can all be sure of is that Adam's sin was—at the very least—determinative in guaranteeing that we would become sinners.

In 5:15–19, Paul even goes beyond this when he speaks of the consequences of sin. Once in each verse Paul states that the actions of one man, Adam, brought condemnation and death to everyone.

- 5:15 – by the transgression of the one, the many died.[24]
- 5:16 – the judgment arose from one transgression resulting in condemnation.[25]
- 5:17 – by the transgression of the one, death reigned through the one.[26]

- 5:18 – through one transgression there resulted condemnation to all men.
- 5:19 – through one man's disobedience the many were made sinners.[27]

It's hard to escape Paul's logic and, for many, harder to accept this truth: Adam's sin brought a guilty verdict to everyone before God. Yet, before we brush off such thoughts, we should remind ourselves that if we had been in Adam's place, we would have done the same thing, and we have plenty of our own sin, whether the ignorant type or the defiant type for which we are accountable.[28]

No room exists for self-righteousness or crying out against God, "Foul!" When God opens the books on the Day of Judgment and recounts *our* deeds, every mouth will close (Romans 3:19), every head will hang in shame, and no excuse will sway the verdict brought to us by Adam and reinforced by our own sin in our favor, unless—

Yes, unless! Unless we can somehow break that solidarity with the sin of Adam that led inevitably to our own sin and the added weight of our guilt on top of the guilt Adam brought. This is the other side of Paul's solidarity argument in 5:12–21. Another Man once lived. This man never sinned. Everywhere Adam failed, He lived for God. Everywhere we fail, He succeeded. And, as we saw in the preceding chapter, this Man voluntarily entered into solidarity with Adam's race and offered Himself as a sin offering on behalf of the human race. He is Jesus of Nazareth, the Messiah of Israel, and the Savior of the world. Here's how Paul contrasts His work with the work of Adam.

- 5:15 – Did the many die by the transgression of the one? "The gift by the grace of the one Man, Jesus Christ, abounded to the many."
- 5:16 – Did the judgment of condemnation arise from one transgression? "The free gift arose...resulting in justification."
- 5:17 – Did death reign through the transgression of the one? "Those who receive the abundance of grace and of the gift of righteousness will reign in life through the One, Jesus Christ."
- 5:18 – Did one transgression bring condemnation to all? "Through one act of righteousness there resulted justification of life to all men."
- 5:19 – Did one man's disobedience constitute many as sinners? "Through the obedience of the One the many will be made righteous."

These verses provide an overwhelming corporate framework. In Adam all sinned. Because of Adam, the verdict of judgment came to all. Because of Adam, death reigned over all. Yet, whereas Adam's action brought disaster to the world, Christ's action brought salvation! Christ's action had worldwide, epochal significance affecting every person apart from anything we did (just as Adam's did), yet more so because of the abundance of grace that far surpassed the sin of one man and all mankind.

Paul, then, utilized an idea (and biblical truth) that people in ancient times readily understood and accepted (and still do in many parts of the world)[29]: We are not lone, isolated individuals free to do anything we want without consideration of others. We are part of a race and what we do affects the human community. We stand in solidarity with the entire human race before God—either in Adam or in Christ.

Several years ago, a movie told the story about a small town in California infected with a deadly disease that threatened the nation and world. One man was responsible for the infection. This one man's action led to everyone in that town becoming sick. The government quarantined the entire city, and worse, could not come up with a cure quickly enough to avert worldwide disaster. In an effort to save the world from dying, the government set up barriers around the town so that no one could go in or out. Yet knowing that airborne particles could spread above and outside the roadblocks, the president learned the awful truth: The entire town had to die. The Air Force would explode a device above the city that would suck all the oxygen out of it, effectively destroying the disease. One man's infection brought death to many.

The theology of Romans 5, the anthropological insight of solidarity, and even the Hollywood story should help us understand Romans 6:6. But our problem has been that when we approach Scripture, we approach it with an individualistic frame of mind. Of course, our intentions are good. I read Scripture and seek to apply it to *my life*. You read it and do the same. We come across the verse that says our old man was crucified with Christ and in our hunger for holiness we think, "*my* old man, *my* sinful human nature, something inside *me* was crucified."

But why do we assume Paul is addressing each of us individually? Upon close inspection we discover that Paul combines the plural "our" with the singular "old self."[30] Could he be speaking of humanity in a corporate sense?

When he says "old" man in 6:6, could he be thinking of "old" in the sense of the old epoch or old standing in Adam in contrast to the "new" standing in Christ?

And when he says old "man," could he be thinking of the man, Adam, and our solidarity with him that he just talked about in 5:12–21? Could it be that Paul was not talking about human nature at all? Could it be that he was not talking about something inside us when he talked about our old man being crucified? That's a lot of questions! Let me give my answer. Paul was not talking about something inside us but was talking from the grid of Romans 5:12–21. In light of this Romans 5 background, I would like to propose an alternate meaning for the old man: *The old man is the legal standing humanity inherited from Adam and that each of us shares with all others before God as a condemned sinner.*

Rather than it being something *inside us*, the old man is something *about us*. It is a description of the inherited status we received from the first man, Adam. In the phrases of 5:15–19, the old man is humanity constituted as sinners (5:19), under condemnation (5:16, 18), and legally dead (5:15, 17) because of Adam's sin (5:12). It is a disturbing truth about our shared humanity and about each of us individually. We stand before God as a condemned sinner. Whether I am thinking about myself or about humanity, the result is the same. Apart from Christ, my status before God is "guilty as charged." Apart from Christ, the whole world stands as one old man, guilty before God.

When we think, therefore, of the "old man," we must not think of something inside us like a weakened, wrinkled, graying, grizzled, toothless, ornery old codger who will not give up his ways, and who, somehow, while hanging helplessly on a cross overpowers us or comes creeping out of a burial vault. That's not Paul's intention for the use of "old." Instead, he used "old" to contrast the newness found in Christ—the new standing/status, the new possibilities for life, and the new world that is to come.

Paul uses this language in 1 Corinthians 15:45–49 when he contrasts the first man, Adam, with the second man, Jesus. Obviously, billions of men have walked this earth. But for Paul only two men have influenced every man— Adam and Jesus, the old man and the new man, the first man and the second man. Every person will ultimately take his identity and his destiny from one of these men and his actions.

Dunn points out how Paul used "old" and "new" to distinguish the different epochs of history and the two men who stand at the head of their epochs—Adam and Christ. "Old," *palaios,* is used consistently by Paul to refer to life prior to conversion (1 Cor. 5:7–8; Col. 3:9; Eph. 4:22) and life under the age prior to Christ, the old covenant (2 Cor. 3:14; Rom. 7:6). He says, "So here, *ho palaios anthropos* [the old man] is man belonging to the age of Adam, dominated by sin and death (5:12–21)…the new man is Christ and those in him."[31]

All of humanity stands in one of these epochs and all of humanity stands in solidarity with one of these men. At one point, all people stood in solidarity with Adam. But Christ breaks this solidarity and enables a new solidarity to emerge—a solidarity with His righteousness and immortality.

A question now begs to be asked: "How do we step out of one solidarity into the other? How do we step from an old epoch where we stand as condemned criminals into a new epoch where we are justified?" We do this by exercising faith in the New Man. And Paul's argument in 6:3–4 is that when we express our faith through baptism, we experience union with Him. We become united with Him in the likeness of His death so that we might be united with Him in the likeness of His resurrection. This is the message of 6:5: "For if we have become united with Him in the likeness of His death, certainly we shall also be in the likeness of His resurrection."

The word "united" comes from the Greek word *sumphuo,* which means to cause to grow together like "the edges of a wound or fusing of the broken ends of a bone."[32] Paul uses it only here in his letters[33] to provide a vivid picture of our fusion or merging into the effect of Christ's death. He continues with the logic: If we have been so fused with Christ through baptism into His death, then certainly, we shall experience the same union with His resurrection.

How can we *know* this? How can we know that we have changed sides, that we have a new solidarity with the New Man? This is where 6:6 fits and why Paul begins this sentence with the word, "knowing." We know we have changed sides because our (humanity's) old man (standing in Adam) was crucified with Christ! When Christ died, our legal standing with Adam was crucified upon the cross, the solidarity with the old man broken.

Do you see it? Paul isn't talking about something *inside us* that was somehow crucified. He was speaking of something *about us* that was crucified—our old identity and standing with the old man, Adam, the old humanity that stood condemned before God. Christ took the sins of the old man upon Himself when He was crucified. Through faith/baptism, we now stand in solidarity with Christ and what He has done for us.

This is why we can have the certainty of 6:5. If we have become united in His death, *certainly* we shall have union with the resurrection. Why such certainty? Because of something we know: Our old man, our old status in the "old man Adam," was crucified with Him! If my old status was crucified with Him, then I have no fear of judgment and have certainty of eternal life.

This interpretation may not coincide with the well-intentioned and oft-repeated commentators of the past and present who are trying to find power over the problem of sin within us,[34] but it does line up with Paul's entire thought in Romans 6:1–11, Galatians 2:14–21, 2 Corinthians 5:14–21, and Romans 5:12–21. Dunn points out that Paul's co-crucifixion verb in 6:6 is located in only one other place (Galatians 2:20: "I have been crucified with Christ"). We have already observed that in Galatians 2 Paul is speaking of our justification by faith in the Messiah because He died to the demands of the Law for us. We can safely assume he is speaking in the same categories here.

Dunn also points out that the phrase "crucified with Him" is the third of three compounds in Romans 6:4-6: *sunetaphemen* in 6:4 ("buried with Him"), *sumphutos* in 6:5 ("fused with Him in His death"), and *sunestaurothe* in 6:6 ("crucified with Him"). It seems unlikely that Paul would use this series of compounds to refer to different functions of the death of Christ—one dealing with sins, another with sin, one dealing with the penalty of sin, another with the power of sin. It is much more likely that he would use them to refer to the same effect of His death: He took away our guilt.

It is also unlikely that Paul would use this series of compounds to refer to a part of our humanity—an old nature, or a corrupt part of us that can never change and is therefore crucified and disposed. We should note the holistic and corporate way Paul speaks of us. In 6:4, *we* were buried with the One. In 6:5, *we* were fused with the One. In 6:6, *our* old man was crucified with the One—the same concept he introduced in 5:12–21. Paul has *the whole person* in legal union with Adam in view. The whole person in Adam was crucified, buried, and yet resurrected in Christ!

Let's go back now to the premise of chapter two where I said that our death to sin could only be what His death to sin was because we died with Him. In the same way, I propose that the crucifixion of our "old man" could only be what it was for Christ. The "old man" Christ died to was not something in Him, but the legal standing of Adam's race that He bore when He voluntarily entered into solidarity with Adam's race when He was born of a woman and born under the Law (Galatians 4:4). He died as the substitute "old man" to sin so that He could forever bury the old man, thus paving the way for a "new man" to arise.

Paul says exactly this in Ephesians 2:14–16: "For He Himself is our peace, who made both groups into one and broke down the barrier of the dividing wall, by abolishing in His flesh the enmity, which is the Law of command-ments contained in ordinances, so that in Himself He might make the two into *one new man*, thus establishing peace, and might reconcile them both in one body to God through the cross, by it having put to death the enmity" (italics mine).

Who is the "new man" of this passage? Paul is speaking of all believers—Gentile on equal footing with Jew—as the new man. He uses another corporate term—one body—to describe this new reality. How did Christ create this? By abolishing the enmity (the curse—see Galatians 3:13) of the Law through the Cross on which He crucified the old man. This enabled Him to create a new man, a new body, a new corporate solidarity that stands justified before a holy God.

We might even say that Adam and Jesus Christ are the old man and the new man. All of humanity stands with one or the other of these two key men of history—the old man, Adam, disobedient and guilty before God or the new man, Jesus Christ, obedient and righteous before God.[35] To personalize this, my individual "old man" was my status I inherited from Adam with all others. It was never something *within me*. It was always something *about me*. My indi-vidual "new man" is my status I gained by virtue of my union with Christ's death and resurrection by baptism/faith. It is not something *within me*. It is something *about me*.

Here is the glorious good news: Where Adam disobeyed, Christ obeyed—all the way to the cross where God imputed the sins of the world to Him. Here is where the climax of the death-with-Christ passage in 2 Corinthians 5 sheds light. In 5:21 Paul says, "He made Him who knew no sin to be sin on our behalf, so that we might become the righteousness of God in Him." When Christ suf-fered for our sins, our condemned standing before God in the old man, Adam, was crucified with Him. Because One died for all (by His becoming sin for us), all died (5:14).

In conclusion, we must humbly but forcefully reject the emphasis many of our brothers have promoted through the years. Our old man is not something inside us. It does not refer to our old sinful nature somehow nailed to the cross. We can stop puzzling over how something that supposedly died can still cause problems. We no longer have to chide ourselves for a lack of faith to reckon the old man dead. We no longer have to pit feelings versus the supposed facts of Scripture. We therefore can stop looking within with despair, wondering how something dead seems to be very much alive. And we don't have to keep trying to convince ourselves, by faith, of something we know perfectly well is not true. But something did die—the judgment that arose against us, the verdict of condemnation from Adam's sin, and the eternal death that awaited us. The old man's dreadful and hopeless status before God was crucified with Christ.

Paul is far from done. He provides a reason why our "old man" was crucified with Christ. It was crucified with Him "in order that our body of sin might be done away with." We turn now to the next key phrase in this epochal verse— another phrase long puzzled over and misunderstood. We turn to an examination of "the body of sin."

CHAPTER FOUR ENDNOTES

[1] Paul uses "old man" and "new man" in Ephesians 4:22–24 and Colossians 3:9–10. See Appendix A, "The Old Man and New Man in Ephesians and Colossians" for Paul's meaning in these passages.

[2] Charles Hodge, *Commentary on the Epistle to the Romans* (Grand Rapids, Michigan: Eerdmans, 1976), 197.

[3] H.P. Liddon, D.D., D.C.L., LL.D., *Explanatory Analysis of St. Paul's Epistle to the Romans* (Grand Rapids, Michigan: Zondervan, 1961), 111.

[4] F. Godet, *Commentary on St. Paul's Epistle to the Romans* (New York: T & T Clark, 1883), 415.

[5] J. Sidlow Baxter, *A New Call to Holiness* (Grand Rapids, Michigan: Zondervan, 1973), 48–49.

[6] Steve McVey, *Grace Walk* (Eugene, Oregon: Harvest House, 1995), 59.

[7] McVey quoted this in *Grace Walk*, 62, and said it was a statement he heard in a sermon by Charles Stanley on "The Sufficiency of Christ" at First Baptist

Church in Atlanta. Stanley is speaking about Colossians 2, which parallels Romans 6 about dying and rising with Christ.

[8] Godet, *Commentary on St. Paul's Epistle to the Romans*, 415.

[9] Robert Govett, M.A., *Is Sanctification Perfect Here Below?* (Miami Springs, Florida: Conley & Schoettle Publishing, 1985), 35.

[10] Surprisingly, even Dunn, who—as much as any other author—gives outstanding insight on Romans 6, falls into this trap of distinguishing between crucifixion and death! "Does Paul then turn his back on the idea of the believer's identification with Christ in his death as a lifelong process? Does he mean his readers to understand that their attachment to the present world was already completely ended?—that they have been crucified, destroyed, and have died? And does he therefore mean that the believer as such is in fact free from sin and so sinless? One answer might be that he did not intend the two verses to be read quite so abruptly. To nail someone to the cross was not to kill him there and then but to subject him to a suffering which inevitably resulted in death after some hours or even days; the verb translated 'might be done away with' could be rendered 'might be made ineffective, powerless,' or be taken to describe the end result of the crucifixion, in the believer's case at the end of this early life." James D.G. Dunn, *Word Biblical Commentary, Vol. 38A, Romans 1–8*, (Nashville, Tennessee: Thomas Nelson Publishers), 332. In an effort to make the passage say what it was not intended to say in order to try to make it practical for Christian living, Dunn forgets that we were not only crucified, but we died and were buried!

[11] Eight phrases in 6:1–10 speak of death or death with Christ. Seven of the eight are in the aorist tense, signifying past completed action. The other (6:5) is a perfect tense, signifying past completed action with a continuing result.

6:2 – We *died* to sin

6:3 – We *were baptized* into His death

6:4 – We *were buried* with Him

6:5 – We *have been united* in the likeness of His death

6:6 – Our old man *was crucified*

6:8 – We *died* with Christ

6:10 – The death He *died*

[12] Mike Quarles, *The Strange Odyssey Of a Legalistic Preacher Who Became a Drunk, Discovered Grace And Was Set Free*, http://www.ficm.org.uk/deeperissues/miketestimony.html.

[13] McVey, *Grace Walk*, 56.

[14] Quoted in Mike Quarles testimony, http://www.ficm.org.uk/deeper-issues/miketestimony.html.

[15] I believe it is futile to talk about members as only "the flesh," i.e., sins of the body, when Paul identifies and labels several *internal* sins in Galatians 5:17–19 as "the flesh." Paul also tells us to cleanse ourselves from all defilement of the flesh *and spirit* in 2 Corinthians 7:1. We, therefore, cannot resort to a distinction between "sins in our members," as an "out" to explain away the reality that we who are dead to sin still have trouble with sin.

[16] Stott, *Men Made New*, 41.

[17] Moo, *The Epistle to the Romans*, 314.

[18] Wright, *Romans*, 523.

[19] Ibid.

[20] Moo, *The Epistle to the Romans*, 315. Dunn notes that in 5:1–11 Paul used "personal and individual language," but in 5:12–21 he changes to the third person "in which the whole sweep of human history is embraced by the two epochs instituted by Adam and Christ." See Dunn, 271.

[21] Ibid.

[22] Wright, *Romans*, 526: "Faced with this dilemma, some scholars emphasize the responsibility of each individual, while others, not least those anxious to maintain Paul's parallel between Adam and Christ, emphasize the primal sin as somehow involving all subsequent humanity …. Others, maintaining a delicate balance between these alternatives (the former unlikely, the latter unwelcome), suggest that this is a shorthand way of saying that when humans actually sin, as they all do, they are not merely imitating the primal sin but acting from within a human nature, and indeed within a world, radically conditioned by that prior disobedience."

[23] I adapted this chart from Enns' thoughts on pp. 311–313 of *The Moody Handbook of Theology*.

[24] "Death to the many—aorist tense—it need not, of course, mean that Paul views the infliction of death as a "one-time" event; he simply portrays the condemnation of all people as a comprehensive whole…Paul in this passage always presents the effects of Adam's act as a completed fact, while the effects of Christ's act are always viewed as continuing or future. The aorist tense…may, then, suggest that the sentence of death imposed on all people took place immediately

in conjunction with the trespass of Adam." Moo, *The Epistle to the Romans*, 336, footnote 98.

[25] In this verse, judgment stands for a verdict.

[26] "This emphasis on the one man Adam and his sin as the instrument by which death exercises its rule reveals again the concern of Paul to tie the fate of all people in some direct way with the sin of Adam." Moo, *The Epistle to the Romans*, 339.

[27] To be made a sinner or to be made righteous must be interpreted legally rather than morally in this verse. Moo says that people are "inaugurated into the state of sin/righteousness," 345. In footnote 144 he shows how the Greek word *kathistemi* can be translated "to constitute" with legal connotations. Ibid., 345.

[28] "No one sins entirely alone and no one sins without adding to the collective burden of mankind." Dunn, *Romans*, 274.

[29] "The concept of our having sinned in Adam is certainly foreign to the mindset of western individualism. But are we to subordinate Scripture to our own cultural perspective? Africans and Asians, who take for granted the collective solidarity of the extended family, tribe, nation and race, do not have the difficulty which western people experience." Stott, *Romans* 153.

[30] "The singular…is normal style, but does help emphasize the idea of a common humanness worn out by its bondage to sin and death (8:10). The societal and salvation-history dimension here should not be reduced to the pietistic experience of the individual; but the reference is to Christians ('our old man') for whom the domination of sin has been broken by their identification with Christ's death. Nor should 'the old man' be taken as a dispensable part of the Christian…." Dunn, *Romans*, 318–319.

[31] Ibid.

[32] Ibid., 316.

[33] A cognate form is in Luke 8:7 where Jesus speaks of thorns growing up with the plant.

[34] I find it strange that commentators can take note of the many corporate ideas and judicial aspects of Romans 6, yet still lapse into an assumption that Paul is talking about overcoming the power of sin. Murray, for example, can speak of the strong justification background to the passage (212), speak of the old man in a corporate way (219–220), recognize the finality of the crucifixion of the "old man" (220), and link our death to sin with Christ's death to sin, and then,

almost in the next breath say, "As applied to believers in verses 2 and 11 the thought is that they died to the power of sin" (225). I can only attribute this to a mind-set or way of thinking so ingrained in us that it is hard to expel. John Murray, *The Epistle to the Romans* (Grand Rapids, Michigan: Eerdmans, 1965).

[35] "The baptized are no longer 'Adam-people' but, by a divine transference, 'Christ-people,' members of the new humanity, whose terms of existence are defined, not by Adam's disobedience, but by the obedience and righteousness of Christ." Stephen Westerholm, *Understanding Paul* (Grand Rapids, Michigan: Baker Academic, 2004), 108.

YOUR BODY OF SIN WAS DESTROYED

Knowing this, that our old self was crucified with Him, in order that our body of sin might be done away with, so that we would no longer be slaves to sin.

ROMANS 6:6

OUR OLD MAN—OUR OLD STANDING with Adam as a condemned sinner—was crucified with Christ so that something very important might happen. The crucifixion of the old man occurred so that our body of sin could be done away with. While "our body of sin" or "the body of sin" is the standard translation of the first part of Romans 6:6, translators have employed various phrases in the latter half of 6:6 to translate *katargethe* to describe what happens to it. The NIV and the NKJV, along with the NASB, say that the body of sin is "done away with." The original KJV uses the strong word "destroy," and the ESV renders it "brought to nothing." Table 4 on page 106 shows the cause and effect sequence of Romans 6:6 in various translations.

As you can see, the NLT and HCSB strongly inject standard Christian interpretation into the phrase by saying "so that sin might lose its power in our lives" or "in order that sin's dominion over the body may be abolished." These translators must see the entire verse in an internal way, starting with a crucifixion of a supposed old sin nature. This crucifixion with Christ is so that sinful habits might be abolished, or lose their power over us. They give the second part of 6:6 a freer translation to ensure that the reader will pick up this idea.

We would probably be right in assuming that they would view 6:11 as key to understanding 6:6. In order to make 6:6 work, we must reckon the old man dead and as we do so, "the body of sin" will lose its power/dominion over our lives with the ultimate result of it one day being completely abolished. This theology does not come out as explicitly in the other translations, but most commentators, as we will presently see, take it this way.

Romans	6:6a Cause	6:6b Effect (1st part)	6:6b Effect (2nd part)
NASB	Our old self was crucified with Him	in order that our body of sin	might be done away with.
NIV	Our old self was crucified with Him	so that the body of sin	might be done away with.
NKJV	Our old man was crucified with Him	that the body of sin	might be done away with.
KJV	Our old man is crucified with Him	that the body of sin	might be destroyed.
ESV	Our old self was crucified with Him	in order that the body of sin	might be brought to nothing.
NLT	Our old sinful selves were crucified with Christ	so that sin	might lose its power in our lives.
HCSB	Our old self was crucified with Him	in order that sin's dominion over the body	may be abolished.

TABLE 4

We all look forward to the day when sinful tendencies and practices will lose their grip on us completely. And we rejoice in greater victories as we become more like Christ in this life. But the purpose of this book is to explain how this happens—and how it doesn't happen. Unfortunately, in order to explain what Paul meant in Romans 6, we must first clear up many misconceptions. We have already looked at the misconception of what Paul meant when he said we died to sin and the identity of the old man. We have to take this route again in Romans 6:6. What is the body of sin, and what happened to it?

One fact should be clear to everyone—no matter what one believes about "the old man" and "the body of sin": They are not the same thing. Paul says our old man was crucified with Him *in order that* the body of sin might be done away with. The death of the old man leads to the destruction of the body of sin. As noted in Table 4 at the beginning of this chapter, one is the cause and the other the effect. They cannot be the same thing.[1]

But believing the "old man" to be something within us, most commentators continue on this internal path and speak of the body of sin as sin's desires or active powers *within us*. As we noted, some modern translations have attempted to bring out this internalization of sin more strongly than warranted in the Greek text when they speak of sin losing its power in our lives or the abolishing of sin's dominion over our body.[2]

Here are some examples of the common "internal interpretation" of the body of sin:

Hodge– "The design of our crucifixion with Christ is the destruction of the old man, or the body of sin; and the design of the destruction of the inward power or principle of evil, is our spiritual freedom."[3]

Fitzmeyer– "The 'body of sin' is not merely the material part of a mortal human being, as opposed to the soul, but the whole person considered as earth-oriented, not open to God or his Spirit, and prone to sin."[4]

Newman & Nida– "The TEV takes the phrase 'the body of sin' with the extended meaning of the power of the sinful self; this assumes that Paul is speaking of the power that the sinful self holds over one's person rather than of the sinful self itself."[5]

Fraser– "The body of sin...doth not mean the human body, but that whole system of corrupt principles, propensities, lusts, and passions, which have, since the fall, possessed man's nature and is co-extended and commensurate to all the human powers and faculties."[6]

We are grateful for such men who want to guide us into a godly life. But if these commentators wrongly interpreted "dead to sin" as being dead to the power of sin, and if they wrongly interpreted "old man" as an old sinful nature somehow mystically crucified with Christ, the chances are good their understanding of the body of sin and its demise is wrong also. If this is the case, they have become ineffective guides attempting to lead people out of a dangerous wilderness area. Their intentions are good, but if they keep interpreting the map incorrectly and taking wrong paths, they will lead everyone farther into the wilderness.

Those who have misinterpreted "dead to sin" and "old man" have taken the wrong path, and as they venture deeper into Romans 6:6–7, they find themselves in more trouble. It is clear in the examples I quoted above that the writers interpret "body of sin" along the lines of sinful desires. Hodge called it "the inward power and principle of evil"; Fitzmeyer spoke of our being "prone to sin"; Newman and Nida, "the power that the sinful self holds"; and Fraser "the whole system of corrupt principles, propensities, lusts, and passions."

All of these phrases present us with a new dilemma. These and other writers are hard-pressed to define in what way the body of sin is done away with, destroyed, or brought to nothing when they and other Christians still deal with sinful tendencies! Usually they resort to interpreting the Greek for "done away with" (*katargethe*) as some kind of quasi, conditional nullification of sin's power in our lives accomplished by the co-crucifixion of the old man with Christ, yet somehow not complete and a process in which we still play a pivotal role. For example:

Brauch– "What we have here is the presence of a real tension between the affirmation that we died to sin and are therefore free from its bondage, and the assertion that such freedom is always and only present as a possibility which must be actualized."[7]

Morris– "As a result of crucifixion with Christ this sinful body is rendered powerless, completely nullified."[8]

Luther– [The destruction of the body of sin] "...is done through the continuous progress of the new (spiritual) life. This destruction must therefore be understood in a spiritual sense."[9]

Bruce– "For the destruction of the sinful self (NEB), i.e., that the 'flesh,' the unregenerate nature with its downward tendency, the 'old Adam' in which sin found a ready accomplice, might be rendered inoperative."[10]

Pick your word! Pick your phrase! Pick something hard and definitive like "destroyed." Pick a softer translation such as "nullified" or "done away with." It doesn't matter what you pick because the body of sin *as currently defined* isn't destroyed, done away with, rendered inoperative, or nullified. We have fallen into the accepted trap of temporarily pacifying our understanding with a new translation for *katargethe*; yet, deep in our heart we wonder how something that is destroyed can still live, or, something that is done away can still hang around!

Look at these words again and think about them. For example, does it really solve the dilemma to say that the old man's crucifixion with Christ led to our sinful desires becoming *inoperative* instead of *destroyed*? Recently, my wife and I popped in a DVD, but we couldn't watch it because the remote was *inoperative*. I pushed the power button. I pushed it hard. I pushed lots of buttons, very hard, but it remained inoperative. If only my sinful desires were inoperative in this way! But, alas, I have to admit that temptation has, at times, "pushed my buttons" and received a quick power surge. The translation "inoperative" isn't helpful because sinful desires still *operate* inside us.

Pick the word "nullified"—another attempt at softening the intent of Romans 6:6b. The online Merriam-Webster dictionary defines it as "counteracting completely the force, effectiveness, or value of something." The sentence example they provide is "the penalty nullified the touchdown."[11]

How I have wished the offensive force of sin to be "counteracted completely"! But it is not. Sin has scored on me many times, and when I have looked for a flag on the field to nullify the score, I have found none. The translation "nullify" doesn't help because the death of the old man with Christ did not nullify sinful desires. They still emerge.

No, sinful impulses working through "the body of sin" as currently defined remain, at times, quite active with ungodly desires that dishonor Christ. We are back to the same problem when discussing our "old man." If the old man refers to something within us, our sinful human nature, why does this human nature continue to sin if it has been crucified and buried with Christ?

In the same way, how can we say that the body of sin—if defined as "the principle of evil," "being prone to sin," or "the sinful self" (pick your favorite phrase) working in and through our body and soul—is inoperative or powerless when it is obviously operational and assertive?

Just a few verses after making this statement, Paul warns believers not to let sin *reign* in their bodies (6:12). He's not warning about an occasional slip up from which we automatically and quickly recover. Instead he holds out the possibility of sin continuing *to reign* (to have *dominion* over) the person whose "body of sin" was supposedly done away with by co-crucifixion with Christ!

Why warn them of this danger if our co-crucifixion with Christ has made "the body of sin" inoperative or has nullified it? It really doesn't matter which word one picks to translate *katargethe*. None of them makes this interpretation work because, as Paul says, our old man was crucified and buried so that the body of sin might be *destroyed* or *done away with.*[12] What happens to someone who dies by crucifixion and is buried? What is the purpose of crucifixion and burial? Why did the Romans crucify Jesus, oversee His burial, put a seal on the tomb, and post a guard? They didn't banish Jesus to an island in the Mediterranean or put Him under house arrest in order to minimize His influence. They carried out the full extent of their horrifying procedure.[13]

The goal of the crucifixion was to obliterate Jesus in order that they might have no further trouble. Our old man was crucified with Christ so that "the body of sin" might cause no further trouble. I, therefore, believe Paul intended *katargethe* to convey a definitive, line-in-the-sand meaning. On one side of the line, the body of sin is active and powerful. On the other side of the line, it is completely destroyed—like a man crucified and buried.

The venerable expositor, Dr. J. Sidlow Baxter, whom I had the privilege of meeting and learning from when I was a young man, brings out this point clearly. The capitalized words are his emphasis: "Romans 6:6 does not teach counteraction; it teaches destruction through crucifixion as anyone can see. One after another counteractionist preachers will 'explain' to us that the word 'destroyed' in Romans 6:6 does not really mean destroyed, but only 'rendered inoperative' or (according to viewpoint) 'done away.' Those among them who say that 'the body of sin' means our 'sinful old nature' insist on 'rendered inoperative.' Those among them who say that 'the body of sin' means our 'unregenerate former self' prefer to read it 'done away.' But these superfine distinctions are mere hair-splitting; for in Romans 6:6, as any straight-thinking mind must see, the word, 'destroyed,' is the completive counterpart of the verb, 'was crucified'—'Our old man was CRUCIFIED with Him, that the body of sin might be DESTROYED.' Therefore, 'destroyed' here cannot mean anything less than what crucifixion brings about. Or, more pointedly, Romans 6:6 teaches DESTRUCTION BY CRUCIFIXION."[14]

Good point! The old man was crucified with Christ (6:6), united in death with Christ (6:5) and buried with Christ (6:4). If something is nailed to a cross, dies, and is buried, it is dead and gone! Just as the scourging of Christ, the crown of thorns, the nails in His hands and feet, and the spear in His side brought about the death of His body, in the same way, the crucifixion of the old man brought about the literal destruction of the body of sin.

By this time, if you are following the logic and plain sense of how these phrases work, you must be wondering what the body of sin is. In keeping with the context of Romans 6, I would like to propose the following definition:

> *The body of sin is the list of our sins and faults held against us that rendered us guilty before a holy God. The body of sin is a legal term referring to the "body of sinful evidence" held against us that required us to die.*

Just like the old man, the body of sin does not refer to something *within us*. Rather, it refers to something *about us* or as we shall see something *against us*. It refers to the fact that in Adam we stood guilty before God because our sins created insurmountable evidence against us. Our sins created a body of sin, a body of evidence, a legal case against us that rendered us guilty before a holy God. When our "old standing in the old man Adam" was crucified for those sins with Christ, the body of sin, the body of evidence, the legal case that took Christ to the cross completely lost its power. It no longer had any effect because the blood of Christ sufficiently paid for those crimes, rendering the body of sin null and void. Now, we can pick any word to translate *katargethe* and it will work!

Our old standing in Adam as a guilty sinner was crucified with Christ in order that the body of sinful evidence might be:

- rendered powerless
- made null and void
- made ineffective
- done away with
- abolished
- destroyed [15]

When a sentence against a crime is finished, the sins that brought the punishment (or, as Paul says, "the body of sin") no longer have any control over the person.

The question before us now is: Is this the correct interpretation? Is there evidence in and outside the New Testament that would confirm this interpretation? That is the subject of the next section of this chapter.

IS THE BODY OF SIN A LEGAL TERM REFERRING TO OUR ACCUMULATED GUILT BEFORE GOD?

If we are to interpret the body of sin in this way, the first point we must establish is if the word "body" is a versatile word that can refer to more than our physical bodies. This is an easy point to make and not one that has ever been contentious. Many commentators, even if they do interpret "the body of sin" as our sinful impulses, nevertheless already see *the body* of sin as a metaphor and not as a reference to our physical body. Of course, sin exercises and expresses itself through our physical bodies, but when Paul says our body of sin is done away with, he is not talking about our mortal body[16] but using the word in another way.

Fitzmeyer refers to it as "the whole person considered as earth-oriented."[17] Newman and Nida closely follow by referring to it as "one's total being."[18] Calvin says it does not refer to our flesh and bones but the "corrupted mass."[19] Murray follows Calvin in this view.[20] Even though these commentators are incorrect in viewing the body of sin as something internal and part of our sinful nature, they are correct in understanding it metaphorically as a totality or a mass.

This concurs with one of the many ways we use the word "body" today. The word "body" has more than 20 definitions, and many of these point to its metaphorical use as a mass, group, or collective. Here are a few:

> *The Oxford Encyclopedic English Dictionary* – A group of persons regarded collectively, especially as having a corporate function (*governing body*). (usually followed by *of*) a collection (*body of facts*).[21]
> *The American Heritage Dictionary* – A mass or collection of material that is distinct from other masses: *a body of water*.[22]
> *Webster's New World College Dictionary* – A group of people or things regarded or functioning as a unit (a body of soldiers, an advisory body).[23]

I trust that everyone can see these metaphorical uses. With so many definitions, one can see that the word is versatile and most of the definitions do not refer to our physical body. In the *Webster's New World College Dictionary*, one should also see how my interpretation of "body of sin" fits this usage. The body of sin would be the grouping of our sins into a unit with the function of condemning us.

One other definition caught my eye. It comes from a 1949 *Webster's*

Unabridged Dictionary. Definition 22 defines body as *the statement of the complainant's case in a suit in equity*.[24] You can see why this caught my attention. It catches the full forensic flavor of 6:6, of Paul's argument in the opening verses of chapter 6, and of 5:12–21, which forms the interpretive framework for chapter 6. Utilizing this definition, the body of sin would refer to the statement against us in a legal suit. The statement against us would consist of the grouping of our sins into a collective whole in order to bring a charge against us.

With these definitions, we can see that the word body has *metaphorical, collective,* and *legal* usages. With such versatility, I propose that we interpret "body of sin" in this manner in order to provide the correct interpretation of Romans 6:6. When we do so, it locks into place with the other pieces of the Romans 6 puzzle. Paul, therefore, is not talking about the physical body, nor is he talking about something sinful in us that was somehow rendered ineffective through the cross, yet still somehow mysteriously and frustratingly effective. Rather, he is talking about the totality of humanity's sin and guilt before God that led to God's "statement of complaint" in His suit against us.[25]

But I do not believe these definitions conclusively prove my interpretation of the body of sin in Romans 6:6. After all, these are modern definitions of the word "body." Did the ancient world use the word "body" in these ways? And the answer is a resounding, "Yes!"

THE USE OF "BODY" IN THE ANCIENT WORLD

In classical Greek leading up to Plato, from Plato to Aristotle, in the fourth through third centuries BC, and in the period 100 BC to AD 100[26], "body" was a versatile word used in a variety of ways including the following:

- "Body" could represent the five elements[27] and the entire cosmos.[28]
- "Body" had the idea of totality.[29]
- "Body" referred to the state[30] and an assembly (*ecclesia* from which we get "church").[31]
- "Body" referred to the totality of music heard in the body of music.[32]

What about Jewish writings? The Old Testament, extra-canonical Jewish texts, and the first-century Alexandrian Jewish scholar Philo used "body" metaphorically and to refer to a totality arising from many parts.[33] But the most striking example is from Josephus, a contemporary of Paul's, who spoke of *the body of history* and wrote it this way: το σωμα της ιστοριασ (*to soma tes historias*).[34] This is the way Paul writes "the body of sin" in Romans 6:6, exchanging, of course, the word "sin" for "history": το σωμα της αμαρτιασ ("the body of sin"). Let's chart this to see the striking similarity of the words they employed.

TABLE 5		
Josephus	το σωμα της ιστοριασ to soma tes historias	the body of the history
Paul	το σωμα της αμαρτιασ to soma tes hamartias	the body of the sin

Again, we can see that the word "body" was as versatile in the ancient world as it is in the modern world. We can also see that the versatility of the word provides new possibilities for interpreting Romans 6:6 the way I have proposed. But I do not believe these arguments yet prove the point for my interpretation of Romans 6:6. Although this usage of "body" in Romans 6:6 would be acceptable both to the Hellenic and Hebrew worlds, does Paul use the word "body" in a metaphorical way to refer to a mass, a collectivity, or a group of things? Yes, he does so in a number of places.

PAUL'S USE OF "BODY"

One of Paul's favorite applications of the word "body" is the aggregate usage where many parts comprise a whole. This is when he speaks of believers as the *body* of Christ. He does this in about a dozen places in familiar verses.[35] The church, the *ecclesia*, a concept the Greeks also used, is the body of Christ comprising many individuals.

Second, in Colossians 2:17 he uses *body* as the sum total of all that Christ is and all that He has done. Having talked about food and drink regulations, festivals, new moon celebrations, and Sabbath days, he refers to them as "things which are a mere shadow of what is to come; but *the substance* belongs to Christ" (italics mine). "The substance" ("reality" in NIV) is, in the Greek, *to soma tou Christou*, "the body of the Christ." Paul is referring to all that Christ is and all that He has done as the "mass, the totality, the object, or the body" that casts the shadows that people looked at and followed before He came. Here again, "body" is a totality or a whole consisting of many parts.

By this time, any reader should be able to see that Paul, like his contemporaries in the surrounding Jewish and Greek cultures, was comfortable with using the word *body* in a metaphorical way and as a totality or aggregate that arose from many parts. But the real question is: Does he use "body" in any other place in a way similar to Romans 6:6 that would confirm the interpretation I am proposing? The answer is another resounding, "Yes!"

Once again, we must turn to another of Paul's letters, the book of Colossians. Just as we looked at 2 Corinthians 5:14–15 and Galatians 2:14–21 to give us background for understanding "dead to sin" in Romans 6, we will find in Colossians 2 a wealth of information that will give us understanding about the body of sin in Romans 6:6.

Colossians 2:11-15 and the Body of the Flesh

Whereas Galatians 2 and 2 Corinthians 5 contain *phrases* that parallel Romans 6, Colossians 2 contains a *paragraph* that mirrors the death, burial, and resurrection terminology of Romans 6.

[11]"And in Him you were also circumcised with a circumcision made without hands, in the removal of the body of the flesh by the circumcision of Christ; [12]having been buried with Him in baptism, in which you were also raised up with Him through faith in the working of God, who raised Him from the dead. [13]When you were dead in your transgressions and the uncircumcision of your flesh, He made you alive together with Him, having forgiven us all our transgressions, [14]having canceled out the certificate of debt consisting of decrees against us, which was hostile to us; and He has taken it out of the way, having nailed it to the cross. [15]When He had disarmed the rulers and authorities, He made a public display of them, having triumphed over them through Him."

Let's make four initial observations:

1. We quickly and easily find two Romans 6 themes in this passage—our burial and resurrection with Christ. Both are in verse 12: "Having been buried with Him in baptism" and "you were also raised up with Him." The resurrection theme repeats in 13: "He made you alive together with Him."
2. We notice both the burial and resurrection events are the experience of

the believer by virtue of their union with Christ, just as in Romans 6. We were buried *with Him* (12), raised up *with Him* (12), and made alive together *with Him* (13). These phrases confirm the earlier argument of chapter 2: Whatever dying and rising with Christ means, it can mean nothing more or nothing less than what it meant to Christ because the burial and resurrection were only *with Him*.

3. The "together with Him" stated in verse 13 strengthens the corporate emphasis Paul wishes to convey. All of the verbs and pronouns are plural as Paul is speaking to the corporate church and telling what Christ did for the new humanity. Of course, it all applies individually, but Paul is speaking of what Christ did for all.

4. We see in this passage a stronger description of the expression of faith than in the Romans passage. Earlier, I referenced the concern some might register at the strong emphasis of water baptism in Romans 6 as part of the conversion experience of believers. Here, Paul also speaks of baptism in verse 12—"buried with Him in baptism"—but he also states that we were raised up with Him through "faith in the working of God," that work of God being that "He raised Him from the dead." This is another way of making the confession of Romans 10:9: "If you confess with your mouth Jesus as Lord, and believe in your heart that God raised Him from the dead, you will be saved." Baptism may have been part of the conversion process in the first century, but it always presupposed faith in the person and work of Christ, which Paul makes abundantly clear in 2:12.

Having listed these similarities, let me now point out a major difference—a difference, not in theology or meaning, but only in expression. Paul does not use the terminology of "dying with Christ." Instead, in verse 11, he speaks of our being circumcised in Him: "In Him you were also circumcised with a circumcision made without hands, in the removal of the body of the flesh by the circumcision of Christ."[36] But as I will show, the circumcision of Christ is a synonymous phrase for the death of Christ.

Our first impulse is to interpret the last four words, "the circumcision of Christ," as His act of circumcising us. In other words, we were circumcised because Christ circumcised us. But upon closer inspection we find this not to be the case. The circumcision of Christ refers to *His* being circumcised, not His physical circumcision when He was eight days old, but a spiritual circumcision that occurred when He was on the cross. Something was "cut off" of Christ when He died. I come to this conclusion for these reasons:

1. In the flow of the passage, it stands in the location where the death of Christ should stand. Right after this phrase, we have the burial and resurrection statements. Instead of the death, burial, and resurrection of Christ we have the circumcision, burial, and resurrection of Christ. This is our first clue that circumcision stands for His death, and if so, then it refers to Christ being "circumcised" on the cross.

2. Our experience of circumcision is "in Him":"in Him you were circumcised." To stay consistent with Paul's "union theology," our burial into death and resurrection to a new life is only because He was buried and resurrected. Our circumcision, therefore, is ours only by virtue of our union with His circumcision.

3. Some might point out that the last five words of verse 11 say "*by* the circumcision of Christ." This appears to show the means by which we were circumcised, i.e., He circumcised us. But the Greek at this point says "in the circumcision of Christ." The Greek word *en* can sometimes have the meaning of "by," but Paul had other prepositions available to express method. Instead, he chose *en* that He uses emphatically in this verse and in the preceding verses to show that spiritual realities are true for us because they are first true *in Him*. In 2:9, all the fullness of deity dwells in bodily form *in Him*. In 2:10, God makes us complete *in Him*—in the One who is the head over all rule and authority. These verses immediately precede 2:11–15 to show who Christ is so that we might know we are in union with the One who has supremacy over all things and we therefore do not have to resort to other so-called spiritual realities. Having established this amazing fact, Paul is now ready to tell us what this Supreme Person did for us and in which we participate by faith/baptism.

4. In 2:11–12, we find that we were circumcised, buried, and raised *with* or *in* Him. Our circumcision is only *in Him*. Therefore, when Paul speaks of the removal of the body of the flesh, He cannot be speaking of something that He did internally to us in some mystical way. This was the mistake Charles Stanley and countless others have made in their inter-

pretation of this passage.[37] Instead, the removal of the body of the flesh is something we experience only in Him. God removed the body of the flesh from Christ. Because we are in Him, the body of the flesh was removed from us also. Another way of saying this is that when Christ was circumcised on the cross, we were circumcised, too.

Peter O'Brien, in the *Word Biblical Commentary* states: "...The New Testament meaning is that the body of flesh was stripped off when Christ was circumcised, that is, when he died ..."[38] and "It is better to regard the statement as denoting the circumcision that Christ underwent, that is, his crucifixion, of which his literal circumcision was at best a token by way of anticipation."[39]

We now see that Paul was teaching the Colossian Christians the same truth as the Roman Christians and that circumcision is another way of referring to Christ's death and our death with Him. The parallel, then, remains intact. We have been circumcised (crucified), buried, and resurrected in or with Christ. But I'm sure you noticed that Paul added an important detail about what happened when Christ was circumcised and we were circumcised in Him. He says that when our circumcision took place in Him it resulted "in the removal of the body of the flesh."

Here then is the answer to the question I asked earlier in this chapter. Let's review the question first: "Does Paul use "body" in any other place in a way similar to Romans 6:6 that would confirm the interpretation I am proposing for Romans 6:6?" My answer then was a resounding "Yes," and I hope you can see why. In Colossians 2 we have a passage that parallels the thought of Romans 6 and a phrase that matches *the body of sin*! Look at the following comparison of Romans 6 and Colossians 2 in Table 6 below—first the entire verse then the key components.

TABLE 6	
Romans 6:6	**Colossians 2:11**
Our old self was crucified with Him, in order that our body of sin might be done away with	*In Him you were also circumcised with a circumcision made without hands, in the removal of the body of the flesh by the circumcision of Christ*
our old self	you
was crucified	(were) circumcised
with Him	in Him
our body of sin	the body of the flesh
done away with	removal

The Greek text brings out the parallel between the key phrases with even greater clarity, as seen in Table 7 below.

TABLE 7	
Romans 6:6	Colossians 2:11
The body of the sin	The body of the flesh
το σωμα της αμαρτιασ	του σωματοσ της σαρκοσ
to soma tes hamartias	tou somatos tes sarkos

But exactly what does Paul mean when he speaks of "the removal" of the body of the flesh? The Greek word for removal is *apekdusis* and refers to the stripping of garments[40], a fitting picture of the removal of our guilt before God! One wonders if Paul had the story of Joshua, the high priest, standing before God in filthy garments and the angel removing them and replacing them with clean garments to indicate his right standing with God.[41]

When we look deeper into the Colossians passage, we will see that everything about it points to the removal of a *guilty standing* before God and that it has nothing to do with the removal of an internal fleshly entity residing within us or a weakening of sinful desires.

WHAT IS THE EMPHASIS IN COLOSSIANS 2:11–15?

Let's take a closer look, then, at Colossians 2. Having stated in verses 11–12 that we have been circumcised, buried, and raised with Christ, Paul circles back in verses 13–15 to show our condition before God. Instead of speaking of an inner sinful nature mystically crucified (or circumcised), he speaks of our guilty status before a holy God and that guilt being removed—all *with* or *in* Him!

1. You were dead in your transgressions (13), making you legally guilty before God.
2. Your flesh was uncircumcised (13). Paul uses the words circumcised and uncircumcised in his letters to refer to three things:

   - physical circumcision or uncircumcision.[42]

   - a synonym for Jew/Gentile.[43]

   - one's *status* before God either inside or outside a covenant relationship with Him.[44]

According to these definitions, to be spiritually circumcised/uncircumcised has nothing to do with our inner self or human nature.[45] Uncircumcised means to be outside the covenant and guilty before God. Spiritual circumcision removes this guilt and places us in a covenant relationship by justification. When he speaks of *your flesh* being uncircumcised, he is using flesh in a forensic way as in Romans 7:5[46] and 8:9,[47] the whole man outside the covenant and in a guilty status before God.

In 2:13, "the uncircumcision of your flesh" is a synonymous phrase to "being dead in your transgressions," and we can diagram it this way:

You were dead   *in your transgressions*
       and   [in] *the uncircumcision of your flesh*

3. He made you alive together with Him (13). When you were in this condition of guilt ("dead in your transgressions") and outside the covenant ("the uncircumcision of your flesh"), He made you alive with Christ. How did He do this? By crucifying some sin nature within us? No, this would introduce a thought foreign to the argument Paul has been building. Instead, Paul says He made us alive together *with Him*. Paul continues the union with Christ theology he has carefully been developing. This line of thinking parallels Romans 6: We were crucified and buried *with Him*, and we were raised *with Him*. Why could this happen? He could raise us with Him because of His *having forgiven us all our transgressions*. Verse 13 begins with our deadness in transgression and ends with our resurrection in Him because those transgressions were forgiven, or, to put it another way, the uncircumcision of the flesh was cut away or removed by virtue of Christ's circumcision on the cross. As you can see, the judicial themes of forgiveness and justification keep coming. But Paul, typically, is just warming up!

4. Having canceled out the certificate of debt (14), Paul uses another phrase to amplify why God could make us alive with Christ. The first is "having forgiven us all our transgressions" (13). Now we have a further reason. He "canceled out the certificate of debt" (14). Certificate of debt is a translation of the Greek word, *cheirographon*. O'Brien comments on its meaning: "*Cheirographon* denotes a document, especially

a 'note of indebtedness' written in one's own hand as a proof of obligation.... This meaning is well-attested in both the Jewish and Greco-Roman world.... A common thought in Judaism was that of God keeping accounts of man's debt, calling in the debt through angels and imposing a just judgment based on the records kept in the ledger.... Our preference is to understand *cheirographon* as the signed acknowledgment of our indebtedness before God. Like an IOU it contained penalty clauses.[48]

Are you seeing how Colossians 2 is lining up with Romans 6 and how it supports my interpretation of the body of sin? If our death, burial, and resurrection canceled a legal IOU before God in Colossians 2, then our death, burial, and resurrection canceled the "body of sin" or "body of debt" in Romans 6. But let's keep probing.

5. What was the content of that certificate of death? Paul says it consisted of "decrees against us" that were "hostile to us" (14). In this phrase, we hear many echoes of our earlier discussion. We first hear the echoes of Galatians 2:19: "Through the Law I [we] died to the Law." We died through the Law because *the decrees* that we broke brought the hostility of the Law upon us, the hostility that Christ bore (Galatians 3:13). But having died through the Law's condemning function, we are now dead to the Law's demands. We next hear echoes of Romans 5:12–21 where in Adam we found a sentence of condemnation to death rising against us because of our *transgressions*. We finally hear the echoes of Ephesians 2:15 where Paul says that in His flesh He abolished *the enmity*, the Law of commandments contained in ordinances. All of these sound like the *decrees against us* that were *hostile to us* and the content within a legal document composed to condemn us. As you can see, multiple scriptural passages are fitting, adhering to one another, complementing one another, and pointing to a legal framework of condemnation and release from condemnation.

6. What did Christ do with the certificate of debt? He "[took] it out of the way" and "nailed it to the cross." God did not crucify an old sin nature with Christ. He took away our guilty legal standing that consisted of a document outlining the charges against us for our transgressions. That

document was "taken out of the way," a concept that parallels the "removal" of the body of the flesh in verse 11.

7. Verse 15 tells us that something else did happen on the cross. There was another dimension to the work of Christ. But it was not a dimension internal to our dealing with a supposed old sinful nature. It was a dimension that had to do with the cosmic powers arrayed against the people of God and the plan of God. Paul says, "When He had disarmed the rulers and authorities, He made a public display of them, having triumphed over them through Him."

The other dimension of Christ's sacrificial death was to disarm Satan and the powers of their weapon. What was that weapon? It was the fact that mankind, the apple of God's eye, stood guilty before Him. Humanity, created for an eternity of joy and pleasure with God, forfeited that pleasure by sin and stood condemned in Adam. The powers knew that God would not and could not compromise His justice and holy character. The fear of impending judgment and death gave the devil his greatest weapon against God by holding God to His character. The fear of impending judgment and death also gave him his greatest weapon against mankind by preying on the fears of condemnation and death, deceiving them into erroneous methods of dealing with those fears through false religion.

But when Christ died for our sins, He paid the price of guilt in full and therefore could cancel our debt. The Greek word for "cancel" in 2:14 is εχαλειπσασ (exaleipsas) and refers to the blotting out of a written record[49], a fitting image for the nullifying of the body of sinful evidence in Romans 6:6. Christ took that document and nailed it to the cross. Christ suffered the curse of the decrees against us, the decrees that were hostile to our well-being, and forgave us all our transgressions. In doing so, he disarmed Satan and the powers of their primary weapon. And we remind ourselves that the Greek word for "disarmed" in 2:15 is the same word for "removal" in 2:11. They were one and the same event—the removal of our guilty verdict (the body of flesh) disarmed Satan of his greatest weapon.

8. Finally, we should note that the circumcision solution in verse 11 must match the circumcision solution in verses 13–14. If in 13–14 the solution was to forgive us and cancel the certificate of debt by nailing it to the cross of Christ, then, in verse 11, the solution—the removal of the body of the flesh—must carry the same meaning. Once again, it does not refer to the removal of a sin nature but the removal of the certificate of debt. By this close examination, we can see that the idea of the removal of some type of sin nature, or its nullification, or its being rendered powerless is completely out of place with Paul's subject matter.

Paul uses many images to drive home a single point. Let's list these images in summary.

- the removal or stripping off garments (11)
- cutting off skin/circumcision (11, 13)
- burial (12) and resurrection (12, 13)
- dead (13)
- forgiving (13)
- cancelling a debt (14)
- wiping a record clean (14)
- disarming (15)

Paul uses all these images to drive home this single point: When Christ died, we died with Him. Because He died to remove our guilt before God, therefore our death with Him means our guilt has been removed, stripped off, cut off, buried, forgiven, cancelled, and wiped clean. This great act disarmed the powers that used our guilty status against God and us. The body of fleshly deeds that rendered us guilty before God and were contained in a certificate of debt hostile to our eternal well-being was removed in Christ. We have now been raised with Christ to a new life.

To put all of this in Romans 6 language: Our old man, our old legal standing, was crucified with Christ in order to destroy the body of sin. The body of sin—the cumulative evidence against us—was destroyed, nullified, rendered ineffective, made inoperative, and is null and void! God did not destroy something *in us*, but destroyed something *against us*! Our old guilty status was crucified that the document of guilt might be completely removed. With these multiple and varied images, we can see that Paul was speaking of Christ's propitiatory and justifying work on the cross, not death to an old sin nature!

BACK TO ROMANS 6

It's time to return to Romans 6. We have explored the Greek use of the word "body" extensively. We have discovered its flexible and metaphorical usages in modern English, ancient Greek, and in the writings of Paul. We have examined Colossians 2 with its parallel theology of death, burial, and resurrection in or with Christ. We have discovered the meaning of the phrase "the body of the flesh" and how it parallels and explains "the body of sin." We have discovered that Colossians 2:11–15 is not about victory over an old sin nature, but its multiple images all point to forgiveness of sins, justification before God, and victory over the powers that used our guilt to enslave us.

If these interpretations are accurate, what grounds do we have to give the body of sin in Romans 6:6 any other meaning such as sinful desires? We have no scriptural grounds. Instead, we find every reason to conclude that Romans 6:6 is judicial through and through.[50]

Now we can see what Romans 6:6 is about. The old man and the body of sin do not denote something within us. Instead, they refer to something about us. The "old man" is our status in the old man (Adam) as a condemned sinner because of his sin and ours. Our old standing is one of condemnation because of the compelling body of evidence accumulated against us, the body of flesh in Colossians 2 and the body of sin in Romans 6. But that old standing in Adam was crucified with Christ. And it was crucified so that the body of sin, the body of evidence against us, could be destroyed.

With no charges against us, we can be set free from the prison house of sin and condemnation. A man is held under lock and key if charges against him remain, but when the charges have been satisfied or dismissed, he is free to go.

This is Paul's last point in Romans 6:6: "Knowing this, that our self was crucified with Him, in order that our body of sin might be done away with, *so that we would no longer be slaves to sin*" (italics mine). This is the subject of our next chapter.

Chapter Five Endnotes

[1] Some commentators have missed this point.
William S. Plumer, *Commentary on Romans* (Grand Rapids, Michigan: Kregel, 1971), 277: "The body of sin may mean the mass of corruption in us, substantially the same as the old man."
F.F. Bruce, *The Epistle of Paul to the Romans* (Grand Rapids, Michigan: Eerdmans, 1963), 138: "For the destruction of the sinful self (NEB), i.e., that the 'flesh,' the unregenerate nature with its downward tendency, the 'old Adam' in which sin found a ready accomplice, might be rendered inoperative."
Charles Hodge, *Commentary on the Epistle to the Romans* (Grand Rapids, Michigan, Eerdmans, 1976), 197: "The body of sin is only another name for 'the old man' or rather for its concrete form."

[2] This is an example of the blurring of the line separating translation and interpretation.

[3] Hodge, *Commentary on the Epistle to the Romans*, 197.

[4] Joseph A. Fitzmeyer, *The Anchor Bible: Romans* (New York: Doubleday, 1992), 436.

[5] Barclay M. Newman and Eugene A. Nida, *A Translator's Handbook on Paul's Letter to the Romans*, (London: United Bible Societies, 1973), 115.

[6] James Fraser, *A Treatise on Sanctification*, 61, quoted by John Murray, *The Epistle to the Romans* (Grand Rapids, Michigan: Eerdmans, 1965), 220.

[7] Manfred T. Brauch, *Hard Sayings of Paul* (Downers Grove, Illinois: IVP, 1989), 39.

[8] Leon Morris, *The Epistle to the Romans* (Grand Rapids, Michigan: Eerdmans, 1988), 252.

[9] Martin Luther, *Commentary to the Epistle of the Romans* (Grand Rapids, Michigan: Kregel, 1976), 102.

[10] F.F. Bruce, *The Epistle of Paul to the Romans* (Grand Rapids, Michigan: Eerdmans), 138.

[11] http://www.merriam-webster.com/dictionary/nullify

[12] And when he says that it *might* be destroyed, Paul is not introducing uncer-

tainty as if maybe it will be destroyed or maybe it won't be. When he says that it *might* be destroyed, he means that the one act (the crucifixion of the old man) has inevitably led to the second act—the destruction of the body of sin. It is like saying, "I received Christ so that I might be saved." Such statements do not intend uncertainty.

[13] Sorin Sabou explains that crucifixion was not just one method among many to kill people, but it was designed to advance horror among people in order to subjugate them. Sorin Sabou, *Between Horror and Hope* (Waynesboro, Georgia: Paternoster Biblical Monographs, 2005), 79–89.

[14] J. Sidlow Baxter, *A New Call to Holiness* (Grand Rapids, Michigan: Zondervan, 1973), 66.

[15] Please see Appendix B, "The Uses of *Katargeo* in Romans 6 and Beyond," for a fuller discussion of how and why Paul uses this word in his letter to the Romans.

[16] I find it interesting that just a few sentences away, Paul must distinguish between the body of sin and our physical body by referring to the latter as our *mortal* body. He obviously had something other than the physical body in mind in 6:6.

[17] Joseph A. Fitzmeyer, *The Anchor Bible: Romans* (New York: Doubleday, 1992), 436.

[18] Barclay M. Newman and Eugene A. Nida, *A Translator's Handbook on Paul's Letter to the Romans* (London: United Bible Societies, 1973), 115.

[19] John Calvin, *Commentaries on the Epistle of St. Paul to the Romans* (Grand Rapids, Michigan: Eerdmans, 1947), 225.

[20] Murray, *The Epistle to the Romans*, 220: "'The body of sin' has been interpreted figuratively by many commentators and sin is viewed as an organism with many members. Substantially the same view is represented by those who take body in the sense of 'mass' and interpret Paul as referring to the mass of sin and corruption." Murray then quotes from Fraser, Calvin, Hodge, and Philippi.

[21] These are definitions 4a and 4b from *The Oxford Encyclopedic English Dictionary* (New York: Oxford University Press), 158–159.

[22] *The American Heritage Dictionary of the English Language*, 3rd Edition (Boston: Houghton Mifflin Company, 1992), 211.

[23] Definition 6 from *Webster's New World College Dictionary* (New York: Macmillan, 1996), 155.

[24] *Webster's New International Dictionary of the English Language*, Second Edition Unabridged, (Springfield, Massachusetts: Merriam Company, 1949), 301.

[25] Courtroom and lawsuit imagery would be familiar from the Old Testament: Isaiah 41:1 – "Coastlands, listen to Me in silence, and let the peoples gain new strength; let them come forward, then let them speak; let us come together for judgment."

Isaiah 43:26 – "Put Me in remembrance, let us argue our case together; state your cause, that you may be proved right."

Hosea 4:1 – "Listen to the word of the LORD, O sons of Israel, for the LORD has a case against the inhabitants of the land, because there is no faithfulness or kindness or knowledge of God in the land."

Hosea 12:2 – "The LORD also has a dispute with Judah, and will punish Jacob according to his ways; He will repay him according to his deeds."

Micah 6:2 – "Listen, you mountains, to the indictment of the LORD, and you enduring foundations of the earth, because the LORD has a case against His people; even with Israel He will dispute."

[26] These eras are from *Kittle's Theological Dictionary of the New Testament* to organize the article on body.

[27] Gerhard Friedrich, editor, *Kittle's Theological Dictionary of the New Testament* (Grand Rapids, Michigan: Eerdmans, 1971), Gerhard Delling, Volume VII, "Body-Soma," 1026.

[28] Ibid.: "…The cosmos is understood as an ensouled and rationally controlled being…so that there is reference to the σωμα του παντοσ or σωμα κοσμου," *soma tou pantos* ("the body of everything") or *soma kosmou* ("the body of the world"), 1028.

[29] Ibid., 1031.

[30] Ibid.: "Finally, it is of interest that he also transfers the image of the body to the state, which proves that as a totality this is more original than the individual, just as the totality of man is more original than the individual member, which being dead bears only the name of hand or foot," 1032. Here we see the same usage of body that Paul employed for the body of Christ.

[31] Ibid.: "Often a single body consists of many separate bodies like an assembly and an army and a chorus from which, however, life and thought and instruction comes to each individual," 1035.

[32] Ibid., 1041.

[33] Ibid., 1045–1055.

[34] Ibid., 1056.

[35] See Romans 12:5; 1 Corinthians 10:17; 11:29; 12:13, 18, 27; Ephesians 1:23; 2:16; 4:4, 12, 16; 5:30; and Colossians 1:18.

[36] But why use "circumcised"? Why not use "crucified"? The answer is that Paul is killing two birds with one stone. He has been addressing the problem of Judaistic syncretizers who were leading the Colossians astray. Their desire was for Gentile believers to submit to circumcision as a requirement for full incorporation into the new people of God. But Paul's argument in the book and this section is that this is unnecessary. The circumcision that really counted was the one that took place on the cross and in which believers partook by faith.

[37] See Chapter 4 where Steve McVey quotes Stanley's comment of Colossians 2.

[38] Peter T. O'Brien, *Word Biblical Commentary, Volume 44, Colossians and Philemon* (Waco, Texas: Word Books, 1982), 117.

[39] Ibid.

[40] Its noun form is used only here in the New Testament, and Paul may be the first to use it in this way. But he also uses the verb form in 2:15 to refer to the stripping or disarming of the powers and in 3:9 where he says the old man was laid aside. See, William F. Arndt & F. Wilbur Gingrich, *A Greek English Lexicon of the New Testament* (Chicago: University of Chicago Press, 1963), 82–83.

[41] See Zechariah 3.

[42] See Romans 4:10 as an example. By my count, he uses it this way 30 times.

[43] See Galatians 2:7–9 for an example. By my count he uses the word 14 times this way.

[44] See Romans 2:25–29 and Ephesians 2:11ff for examples. By my count Paul uses the word 9 times this way.

[45] I realize that in Romans 2:29, Paul speaks of circumcision of the heart, but even there, the topic is one of status before God and not some inner working to bring about sanctification.

[46] "For while we were in the flesh…" the implication being that we are no longer in the flesh because we have been released from the Law.

[47] "However, you are not in the flesh but in the Spirit…" speaks of a transfer from one realm to another.

[48] O'Brien, *Word Biblical Commentary, Volume 44, Colossians and Philemon*, 125.

[49] Arndt & Gingrich, *A Greek English Lexicon of the New Testament*, 272.

[50] For a continued discussion of the options for interpreting body of sin, see Appendix C, "Options for the Body of Sin in Romans 6:6."

CHAPTER SIX

No Longer Slaves

Knowing this that our old self was crucified with Him, in order that
our body of sin might be done away with, so that we would no longer
be slaves to sin; for he who has died is freed from sin.
ROMANS 6:6–7

WHEN MY WIFE AND I VACATIONED in British Columbia one year, we asked a local
if he knew a great place to hike—some place off the beaten path where we might
see beautiful parts of God's creation.

Without hesitation, he said, "Jaffrey Lakes." Jaffrey Lakes is a series of three
alpine lakes at ascending levels that were not that well-known or visited.

We took his advice and drove to the site. The first lake was at ground level
and beautiful, but we were eager to see the other two and so we set off. For the
next three hours, we trudged up a path, beautiful in its own right, but up, up,
and up. It seemed like we climbed a stairway for three hours. And then we came
to the second lake, surrounded by pine trees with snow-capped mountains in
the background. It was one of the most beautiful places we had ever been. We
took our share of pictures and had others get one of us as we stood in front of
the lake with the mountains behind it.

But we were not quite finished. The third lake was still another 45 minutes
ahead on a winding, upward trail, and we were not about to turn around without finishing our journey.

✳ ✳ ✳

That's where we are in our journey through Romans 6. We have climbed some
steep, rugged trails of word studies, text comparisons, and historical consider-
ations in our efforts to find the meaning of key phrases in Romans 6. The added
difficulty of the journey is that we have had to pause and examine some familiar
side trails. Many have taken these side trails only to find themselves surrounded

by ideas not true to Scripture or human experience. We have explained why these trails are wrong in a dogged effort to stay consistent with God's Word, believing that, in the end, we will find ourselves in the place we all want to be—a place of beauty and joy where we experience His grace and find power to live in victory over sin.

If you're ready, let's get back on the trail one last time for the final upward ascent as we probe the last part of Romans 6:6 and Romans 6:7. Here is the text again: "Knowing this, that our old self was crucified with Him, in order that our body of sin might be done away with, so that we would no longer be slaves to sin; for he who has died is freed from sin."

We have learned that our old man—our guilty status in Adam—was crucified with Christ that the body of sinful evidence held against us might be done away with. But the doing away with the body of sin occurred so that something additional might take place. Paul puts it this way: "So that we would no longer be slaves to sin [because] he who has died is freed from sin." This is the subject of this chapter. What did Paul mean when he said we are no longer slaves to sin? What did he mean when he said we are freed from sin?

NO LONGER SLAVES

The words "no longer" should jump out at us. They have a sense of finality to them. They also have a sense of "now-ness" to them. Paul did not say the body of sin was destroyed so that *in the future* we would not be slaves to sin. He said the body of sin was destroyed so that we would no longer, no more, not ever again be enslaved to sin. This is one of three places in the immediate context where Paul says "no longer." The other two places are in 6:9 and do not point to an indefinite future but to the current reality that Jesus experiences. The first reality is that He *no longer* has to die—"Christ no longer dies"—or, as the NASB translates it: "Christ is never to die again." The second reality explains the first. He no longer has to die because death *no longer* is master over Him.[1]

Here in 6:6c we find that we are *no longer* slaves. It seems clear that in this first of the three "no longer" phrases, Paul is wishing to communicate that what once was—enslavement to sin—*no longer* is a fitting description of the person who has died and risen with Christ. Just as Christ experiences the current reality that He no longer has to die because death no longer can claim any mastery over Him, so also, we are now no longer slaves of sin.

Translations are somewhat consistent with their rendering of this passage as you can see in Table 8.

TABLE 8		
Romans	6:6a – The Cause 6:6b – The 1st Effect	6:6c – The 2nd Effect
NASB	Our old self was crucified with Him in order that our body of sin might be done away with	so that we would no longer be slaves to sin;
NIV	Our old self was crucified with Him so that the body of sin might be done away with	that we should no longer be slaves to sin—
NKJV	Our old man was crucified with Him that the body of sin might be done away with	that we should no longer be slaves of sin.
KJV	Our old man is crucified with Him that the body of sin might be destroyed	that henceforth we should not serve sin.
ESV	Our old self was crucified with Him in order that the body of sin might be brought to nothing	so that we would no longer be enslaved to sin.
NLT	Our old sinful selves were crucified with Christ so that sin might lose its power in our lives.	We are no longer slaves to sin.
HCSB	Our old self was crucified with Him in order that sin's dominion over the body may be abolished	so that we may no longer be enslaved to sin,

But what does Paul mean when he says we are no longer slaves to sin? Normally, we read the 6:6c phrase as enslavement to sinful tendencies or habits. We do this because of our usual (and inaccurate) reading of the first part of the verse. I present it to you again:

6:6a – Our old sinful nature was crucified with Christ

6:6b – So that our sinful impulses rising from within might be counteracted

6:6c – With the result that we no longer are enslaved to those sinful tendencies or habits.

But if we read and interpret it this way, we encounter our old problem in a new guise. If we are no longer slaves to sin, why are some Christians still addicted to certain types of sin? Please don't tell me they are not Christians!

While that may be true with some—they have not really met Christ and been born again—it is not true of all. Some people meet Christ, are born again, and still struggle with sinful addictions in their lives. It could be alcohol, illegal drugs, sexual sin, or anger. It could be less noticeable sins such as bitterness, gluttony, or divisiveness. They are still enslaved to harmful habits, character deficiencies, and attitude problems.

Commentators, having taken the dangerous side trails of interpreting the first parts of verse 6 internally have wandered into another dangerous side trail in 6:6c. They have not been able to reconcile Paul's finality of the severing of our servitude to sin with reality—we unfortunately still serve sin in our lives! Here are some examples of our brothers who have tried to cope with this problem, but unsuccessfully.

Liddon– "There can be no more service of the sinful principle. The instrument of such service will have disappeared."[2]

Calvin– Paul "points out the end for which this destruction [of the body of sin] is effected, when he says, so that we may no longer serve sin. It hence follows, that as long as we are children of Adam, and nothing more than men, we are so in bondage to sin, that we can do nothing else but sin; but that being grafted in Christ, we are delivered from this miserable thralldom; not that we immediately cease entirely to sin, but that we become at last victorious in the contest."[3]

In his full quote, Liddon, when speaking of the disappearance of the instrument of sin, is referring to the "disappearance" of the body of sin in 6:6b, the instrument through which the sinful principle expresses itself. But he would have a hard time convincing me of this "invisible man" act because my body of sin—if defined as sinful tendencies—has not disappeared at all! His "no more service of the sinful principle," i.e., sinful tendencies within us, is wishful thinking and no help in explaining the true condition of many of God's people and the meaning of Paul's statement.

Calvin's statement fares only a little better. He indeed says Christ delivered us from "this miserable thralldom," yet, in the next breath he has to concede that we still sin in this life although we will one day be "at last victorious." At last? One day? Someday? Evidently, *no longer* doesn't mean *no longer*.

Even the clear thinking and erudite contemporary scholar Dunn slides far down the slippery slope of this side trail! Listen to his surprising words: "The very formulation…implies that the possibility of the believer's continuing to serve sin is very real." And he speaks of the believer "succumbing once again to sin at any particular point," in spite of the fact that Paul said we are no longer enslaved to sin![4] How can he, or anyone for that matter, say that we continue to serve sin when Paul clearly says *we died* with Christ *to destroy* the body of sin so that we would *no longer* be sin's slave?

This is the continuing dilemma of commentators, preachers, and Christians. We faced this dilemma when we encountered the common thinking of dead to sin, old man, and body of sin. And we are facing it again with Romans 6:6c. But when we adjust the reading of the first part of this verse, as I have proposed in the preceding chapters, we discover fresh possibilities for 6:6c that harmonize with Paul's thoughts here and in his other letters, and we avoid making statements not true to life.

First, look at the logic of the verse. I will emphasize the connecting phrases to show the logic:

> 6:6a – our old man was crucified with Christ　　*in order that*
> 6:6b – the body sin might be destroyed　　　　*so that*
> 6:6c – we would no longer be slaves to sin.

Now, look at the logic and the meaning using the legal interpretation:

> 6:6a – our old status in Adam as a guilty sinner was crucified with Christ
> 　　　　　　　　　　　　　　　　　　　　　*in order that*
> 6:6b – the body of sinful evidence might be destroyed
> 　　　　　　　　　　　　　　　*so that*
> 6:6c – we are no longer enslaved to (the penalty of) sin.

Everything falls into place when we view all parts of the verse from the legal standpoint. We don't have to explain how a person is no longer a servant to sin, yet still fights sin in his life because Paul is not talking about behavior in this phrase, but status.[5] But is this the meaning of Romans 6:6c? I believe it is for two reasons. First, consider these illustrations.

How many times have we heard stories of people convicted of crimes and held in jail, yet who are released because the evidence used against them was found to be inadmissible in court? Many times. How many times have we heard stories of people convicted of crimes and held in jail, only to be released when the evidence against them was found false? Or, new evidence came up pointing to the true perpetrator of the crime? Again, many times. One day they are enslaved to a crime. On the next, they are free.

Here's another scenario: A man, justly convicted of a crime, is sentenced to prison for 1,000 days. He is led away and begins serving his time. He is "enslaved" to his crime for 1,000 days. Every day, for two years and nine months, he must remain confined to his quarters. He is not allowed out of jail. He does not have freedom to participate in the normal activities of society.

But on day 1,001, the prison officials come to his cell, unlock the door, tell him to gather his possessions, escort him to the prison gate, and tell him, "You are free to go. You have served your time. We can no longer justly keep you 'enslaved' here. You are a free man." Why would the prison officials say this to him? They would say this because the sentence against him has been satisfied, and the list of charges against him—the body of sin—no longer has any force or effect over him.

This is Paul's thought in Romans 6:6. Our old standing with Adam was crucified with Christ in order to make the body of sinful evidence against us null and void so that we would no longer be slaves to the sentence that our sinful behavior brought. Our sinful behavior put us in a guilty standing before God. But because Christ satisfied the demands of the accusing Law against us, the evidence no longer has any binding force, and we can walk free.

To put this in the language of Colossians 2, Christ cancelled the certificate of debt against us and raised us up with Christ. To put this in the language of Romans 6: We died to sin with Christ so that we might walk in newness of life. We no longer have to sleep in our prison cell. We no longer have to exercise only in the prison yard. We no longer have to follow the strict regimen imposed upon us within the prison walls. Our sentence has been paid for and the evidence against us nullified. We have been set free from our sin.

I hope you can see this. Paul, though very much concerned about the conduct and behavior of the members of the churches he founded, is not talking about freedom from sinful habits *in this verse*. Instead, he is talking about legal freedom from the consequences of our sinful behavior, the same topic of 5:12–21 and of every major concept in 6:1–11.

Some could read these words and say, "You're reading a lot into Romans

6:6c!" But I would counter that I am not reading into this phrase a greater amount of theology than other commentators read into it. They have read their theological perspective into it, and I am reading mine. This is interpretation. I believe the difference is that they have read a faulty theological interpretation into 6:6c based upon a faulty interpretation of dead to sin, old man, and body of sin in 6:2 and the first parts of verse 6.

I am reading a consistent interpretation of all these concepts. Many commentators have noticed the legal aspects of some of these phrases, but no one has connected them all together with a coherent interpretation.

I said I had two reasons why I believed we should interpret 6:6c legally. Here is the second reason, which I believe is the clinching argument. The clinching argument is in Romans 6:7, which says, "For he who has died is freed from sin."

You Have Been Freed from Sin

Romans 6:7 completes the thought and the logic Paul introduced in verse 6. If 6:6a is the cause, 6:6b the first effect, and 6:6c the second effect, how does 6:7 function in the sentence? In Chart 1, I illustrate 6:6–7 with its key connecting words.

As you can see, Romans 6:7 circles back to the cause by stating a generally held principle: When a person dies, he is freed from sin's penalty. And in stating this principle, Paul reaffirms his underlying theology of death and resurrection with Christ. We can say that we are no longer slaves to sin (6:6c) because when a person has died, he is freed from the sin that locked him up in prison (6:7).

Earlier in this chapter, I presented several scenarios of how a man in prison can walk out of prison with no continuing legal consequences because of inadmissible evidence or the completion of a sentence. I failed to mention one other scenario: A person no longer stays in prison if he dies!

Imagine yourself on death row. You are there because of heinous crimes against humanity. You deserve your penalty. The day of execution comes and the authorities strap you to a bed and inject deadly fluid into your bloodstream. In a matter of minutes, you stop breathing, all organs in your body, deprived of oxygen, cease functioning, your heart stops beating, and you die. Your lifeless body lies on that table. The doctor examines you—there is no heartbeat. There are no brain waves. He examines every vital part of you and declares no life present. One hour passes, two hours pass, three hours pass and the authorities send

Chart 1

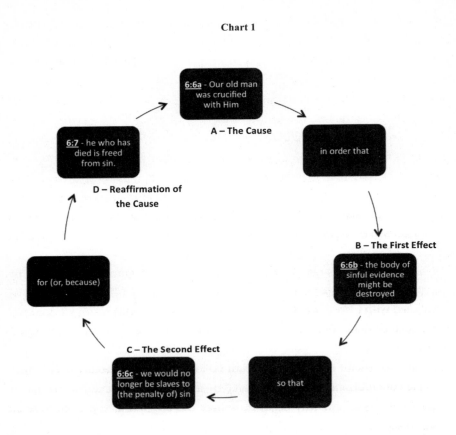

your body to the mortuary for burial preparation. But, while your body is there something amazing happens: Your heart starts beating, blood flows through your veins, your organs start functioning. Warm and vibrant skin replaces the cold, white pallor of death. You open your eyes. You sit up. You are alive!

What will the state do? The state can do nothing against you. The state executed you for your crime. You paid the penalty. You are now free to walk from that mortuary and no longer have to return to prison. You experience a new life free from the condemnation you lived under for your crimes. This is Paul's thought in 6:6c, which he substantiates in 6:7.

Because of our death with Christ and the destruction of the body of sin that held us captive, we are no longer prisoners or slaves to the sin we committed. We know this because of the universally understood truth that when a man dies he is freed from sin. Paul is not talking about freedom from sinful habits (although that is desirable). He is talking about freedom from condemnation.

In this little verse consisting of only nine words, Paul gives the big reason and the final argument why we can have certainty of eternal life. Remember the thought of 6:5? If we have been united with His death, then *certainly*, we shall be united with His resurrection. The point of all this "death talk" is so that we can get through it and get to the other side, which is resurrection. In 6:5 Paul expresses certainty about this: We shall be united with His resurrection—*certainly*!

Why can we have such assurance? It is because of what we know in 6:6— "knowing this"—our old status was crucified so that the body of evidence against us could be destroyed with the result that we are no longer on death row, no longer slaves to our spiritual crimes. But how do we know that we are no longer slaves to sin? Verse 7 gives the final answer: Everyone knows that "he who has died is freed from sin."

After Paul makes his freedom statement in 6:7, he starts recapitulating his entire death-and-resurrection-with-Christ theology. In 6:8 he says, "Now, if we have died with Christ, we believe that we shall also live with Him." How can we have such certainty of resurrection? It is because of something we know. In 6:9, he says we know this because Christ no longer dies (for our sin). His death was sufficient to pay for our sins, and death no longer has any mastery over Him.

He concludes his argument in 6:10 by telling us why we know that He no longer has to die and why death no longer has any mastery. It is because He died to sin *once for all*![6]

DEDIKAIOTAI – A Surprising Word!

But 6:7 has more to say to us. When Paul says he who has died is "freed" from sin, he uses an unusual word. It was not unusual for Paul, but the translation "freed" is unusual and unwarranted. The word is *dedikaiotai* ("has been justified"). He who has died has been justified from sin!

Notice what the following commentators say about this. The bold type in the quotes are mine for emphasis.

Fitzmeyer– Has been freed from sin – "Understood in a **forensic sense**, *dikaioun* would mean that from the standpoint of Jewish law a dead person is absolved or 'freed,' for **sin no longer has a legal claim or a case** against such a person. It is said to have the meaning of *dikaioun* that is often given to it (rightly?) in Acts 13:38. Possibly, too, Paul is echoing **a Jewish universal legal**

principle, formulated thus in the late Babylonian Talmud: "When one died, one is **freed of the obligation of the law and its precepts**."[7]

Sanday and Headlam– "The sense of *dedikaiwtai* is still **forensic**: 'is declared righteous, **acquitted from guilt**.' The idea is that of a master claiming **legal possession** of a slave: proof being put in that the slave is dead, **the verdict** must needs be that **the claims of law are satisfied** and that he is no longer answerable. **Sin loses its suit**."[8]

The translator into English of Calvin's commentary contributes a revealing footnote about this. The italics are mine for emphasis. "The verb…"is" or "has been justified" has been considered by the early and most of the later commentators in the sense of being freed or delivered. This is the view, among others, of Chrysostom, Basil, Oecumenius, Beza, Pareus, Hammond, Grotius, Doddridge, and Macknight. *But it must be added that it is a meaning of which there is no other clear instance in the New Testament, though the verb occurs often*."[9]

No other clear instance in the New Testament? If no other clear instance of translating *dedikaiotai* with the English word "freed" exists, why do commentators and translators render it this way here? It is because they stumble over the same stumbling stone we have found in many other places. They have misunderstood dead to sin, old man, body of sin and slavery to sin, and they have injected meaning into Romans 6:2 and 6:6 that is not there!

They have followed the initial trajectory of their interpretation to its logical destination and have found themselves in a different orbit from Paul's thought. Every other use of the verb in every other place in the New Testament has one meaning, but in Romans 6, it means something else! What is the basis for translating it "freed" (from sinful habits)? None exists![10] But because of our faulty interpretation of 6:6, commentators and translators have followed this faulty trail of thinking for centuries on 6:7.[11] Listen further to Leon Morris and John Stott on this point as they have sought to point the way out.

Morris– "Anyone who has died in this way has been 'justified (NIV, freed) from sin.' Robin Scroggs stresses the importance of seeing Jesus' atoning death behind the passage …. The person who has died with Christ enters into Christ's atonement and is justified from his sin.

"It is also possible that the imagery is pointing to a master claiming a slave who proves to be dead. The legal verdict is that the slave is no longer answerable.... But Paul is not speaking only of a cancelling of evil; he refers to a positive act of justification. He has just said that the believer is not enslaved to sin. Why not? Because he has died with Christ and has thus been justified."[12]

John Stott– "The only way to be justified from sin is that the wages of sin be paid, either by the sinner or by the God-appointed substitute. There is no way of escape but that the penalty be borne. How can a man be justified who has been convicted of a crime and sentenced to a term of imprisonment? Only by going to prison and paying the penalty of his crime. Once he has served his term, he can leave prison justified. He need have no more fear of police or magistrates, for the demands of the law have been satisfied. He has been justified from his sin."[13]

These helpful comments reinforce the main point of this chapter: Paul is not talking about freedom from the slavery of sinful habits at this point in his long argument, but freedom from the imprisonment of sin's guilt for when a guilty man dies he is acquitted or justified from all crimes committed.[14]

Of course, this is hardly a comfort to a criminal on death row. It is no comfort to say to a man on the day of his execution, "Don't worry, tomorrow you will be free from this miserable place." No comfort, that is, unless someone pays the penalty for him. That is what has happened for those who are in Christ Jesus and why we are no longer enslaved to sin. We have died to sin's demands for death, have been acquitted of all charges, and are justified before God because our old status in Adam was crucified with Christ!

As we think on Romans 6:6, we find another kind of freedom, freedom from the slavery of contradictions, puzzles, inconsistencies in interpretation, and fallacious interpretations that try to explain that we are dead to an old sinful nature, yet somehow that old nature keeps rising up and causing problems. No longer do we have to wrestle with the question of how our "body of sinful desires" can be rendered inoperative, yet still have it be operational. No longer do we have to make excuses for Christians who still struggle with sinful habits even though Paul says Christ freed them from sin's slavery. Let us step away from these fallacious interpretations and contradictory explanations of the Word and of our human experience once for all and rediscover Paul's great truths of our death and resurrection with Christ.

Here, then, is a summary paraphrase of Romans 6:1–10 based on the legal interpretive framework I have provided in this and in the preceding chapters.

6:1 – What shall we say, then, in light of this great fact that God met the increased sin of our people with super abounding grace? Shall we, as some argue, continue in sin like our forefathers so that we may receive super-abounding grace?

6:2 – May it never be! If this is what some think, they have completely missed my point! How shall we who died to the penalty of sin still live in it?

6:3 – Don't you know that when you confessed Christ as Lord in baptism, you were baptized into Him and what He did for you? Don't you realize you were baptized into His death to sin?

6:4 – Therefore, if you were baptized into His death to sin, you were also buried with Him into His death with the goal that just as Christ was raised by the Father's glorious power you might have a new life!

6:5 – If we have been fused with Him into His death to sin, certainly we shall also be fused with Him in His resurrection.

6:6 – We know this: We have such certainty of this resurrection because our old condemned standing we shared in Adam because of his sin and ours was crucified with Him so that the body of sinful evidence against us could be completely wiped clean so that we would no longer be enslaved to the penalty of sin.

6:7 – For everyone knows this general principle: When a guilty man dies he is justified from his sin.

6:8 – So, let me repeat, if we have died with Christ, we believe we shall one day live with Him.

6:9 – We know that we shall live with Him because we know that Christ has been raised from the dead and never has to die again! Death no longer has any mastery over Him!

6:10 – Death no longer has any mastery over Him because the death that He died was a death to the penalty of sin once for all. But the life that He lives, He lives continually to God!

Glorious, life-changing truth! Jesus Christ receives all the glory! Our focus is completely on Him and His great accomplishment for us! His work on the cross takes center stage! To Him be all the praise!

✳ ✳ ✳

After my wife and I rested for a bit and enjoyed the glories of God's creation at the second of the three lakes, we set off on our journey again. We were not disappointed. Another 45 minutes on the trail and we arrived at the third lake with rushing streams from melting glaciers cooling our tired feet. At one spot, I called to my wife and encouraged her to jump onto a boulder on the side of the trail. From this boulder, we could see lake two below us and lake three ahead of us— a scene I will never forget. When we returned to our accommodations that night, we were exhausted, and the hot tub was a welcome amenity for our sore muscles. But we never regretted and the effort we put into our journey that day.

I hope you have not regretted the effort of walking with me on the difficult terrain of Romans 6. But now that we have mastered it and have arrived at our destination, we are ready to walk in the clear fresh air of His grace that he talks about in 6:11–14. We are ready to explore its glories fully and find the power to overcome the sinful tendencies that trouble us all from time to time.

After all, we began this journey with the hope that we might find power over sin. In the next chapters, we examine how our union with Christ's death and resurrection leads to a life of victorious living, a life where we find ourselves changing miraculously into the ways of the New Man to the glory of God!

Chapter Six Endnotes

[1] We examined this phrase in chapter three and discovered its important place in Paul's overall argument in Romans 6.

[2] H.P. Liddon, D.D., D.C.L., LL.D., *Explanatory Analysis of St. Paul's Epistle to the Romans* (Grand Rapids, Michigan: Zondervan, 1961), 111.

[3] John Calvin, *Commentaries on the Epistle of St. Paul to the Romans* (Grand Rapids, Michigan: Eerdmans, 1947), 225.

[4] James D.G. Dunn, *Word Biblical Commentary, Vol. 38A, Romans 1–8* (Nashville, Tennessee: Thomas Nelson Publishers, 1988), 320.

[5] Moo adds this helpful comment on these verses: "Paul's point, then, is that the real, though forensic, inclusion of the believer with Christ in his crucifixion means that our solidarity with, and dominance by, Adam, through whom we are bound to the nexus of sin and death, has ended." Douglas Moo, *The Epistle to the Romans* (Grand Rapids, Michigan: Eerdmans, 1996), 376.

[6] See chapter three for the significance of the "once for all" statement in understanding Paul's meaning of dead to sin.

[7] Joseph A. Fitzmeyer, *The Anchor Bible: Romans* (New York: Doubleday, 1992), 436.

[8] William Sanday and Arthur Headlam, *The Epistle to the Romans* (New York: Scribners, 1906), 159.

[9] Calvin, *Commentaries on the Epistle of St. Paul to the Romans,* 226.

[10] "True, there is some slight evidence from early Jewish literature that *dikaioo* could mean to 'make free or pure' (BAGD). But there is a perfectly good word in Greek for to 'set free,' namely *eleutheroo*, which in fact Paul uses in verses 18 and 22, whereas *dikaioo* comes fifteen times in Romans, and twenty-five times in the New Testament, in all of which occurrences the natural meaning is to 'justify.' So surely the verse should be translated 'he who has died has been justified from his sin.'" Stott, *Romans,* 177.

[11] Two translations have it right, the ASV ("for he that hath died is justified from sin") and the HCSB ("since a person who has died is freed from sin's claims").

[12] Leon Morris, *The Epistle to the Romans* (Grand Rapids, Michigan: Eerdmans, 1988), 253.

[13] Stott, *Romans,* 177.

[14] Hodge says that Paul refers to the Jewish idea of death being the expiation for sin. "Others say he is to be understood as speaking only of sin or guilt in relation to human law: 'He who had died for his crime is freed from guilt or further liability.' Either way, the only relation which this verse, when understood of physical death, can have to the apostle's argument, is that of an illustration: 'As the man who has suffered for his crime is freed from it, so he who is crucified with Christ is free from sin.'" Charles Hodge, *Commentary on the Epistle to the Romans* (Grand Rapids, Michigan: Eerdmans, 1976), 198.

PART 2

DEAD MEN RISING

CONSIDER YOURSELVES DEAD TO SIN

> Even so conisder yourselves to be dead to sin, but alive to God in Christ
> Jesus.
>
> ROMANS 6:11

I BEGAN THIS BOOK BY TALKING about a contradictory reality. The reality is that all
of God's people sin from time to time. No one is perfect. The contradiction is
that our sin is the opposite of the way we should live. We were baptized into
Christ's death so that just as He was raised, we might live a new life. Jesus Christ
is Lord of all and we are born again with an eternal destiny of purpose and
delight. Yet, in spite of these and countless other truths, we fail Him and live in
ways that contradict this joyful reality.

This is more than a *contradictory* reality. We are not just dealing with an
intellectual anomaly or theological puzzle. We are dealing with a *painful* reality.
Sin causes pain and grief—internally and relationally. We who follow Christ
have to deal with the sorrow and disappointment that comes when we sin—
sorrow for ourselves and for others. Just when we thought we were shifting into
a higher gear, or turning our walk with Christ into a run, we trip, stumble, and
find ourselves sprawled on the pathway. It can be discouraging, and we sometimes wonder if we will ever sustain a consistent walk with Christ or overcome
that weak area.

For good reason, the writer of Hebrews urged believers to lay aside weights
and sins that so easily entangle our feet (Hebrews 12:1). Paul urged the Romans,
several chapters after his famous statements in chapter 6, to lay aside deeds of
darkness, behave properly, and give no opportunity for fleshly lusts (Romans
13:11–14). James asked, "What is the source of quarrels and conflicts among
you? Is not the source your pleasures that wage war in your members?" (James
4:1) We could find admonitions on almost every page of the apostolic letters to
turn away from the sin that fights against us and within us and pursue a life of

righteousness. While the world around us and the devil have a role in our sin, the primary war is within ourselves.

But how do we obey these verses consistently? And how do we win the long war? If no once-for-all Holy Spirit experience eradicates every sinful impulse of an old nature within us, to whom or to what can we turn?[1]

If my interpretation is correct—that the Romans 6 phrases "dead to sin," "old man," "body of sin," "slaves to sin" and "freed from sin" pertain to the destruction of our guilt and not to the destruction of something within us—then the common teaching that Romans 6:11 directs us to reckon an old sinful nature as dead, is wrong too. Let me recap this way of thinking: "Your old sinful nature was crucified with Christ, but the death to that old nature is effective only when you reckon it so. You, by faith, must claim that your old nature died, and then you will have victory. Romans 6:11 is the key that unlocks the door of victory over sin within us in Romans 6:6."

If you don't think this is what many have taught and still teach, consider this statement by a wonderful man of God, Stephen Barabas. Although he wrote a generation ago, his work, *So Great Salvation*, admirably summarized the key thoughts of a still existing admirable movement of God. Yet, his statement about how we make Romans 6:6 effective in our lives is a good example of the common misunderstanding of Romans 6:6 and 6:11. Barabas said: "It is judicially true of all believers without exception that they were identified with Christ in His death to sin. The result of this fact is that our bodies are now free from sin's claim, and we need no longer serve sin. But it is not enough to know that historically all believers died with Christ; we must appropriate that truth if it is to be real in our experience. God reckons us dead to sin because of our union with Christ in His death to sin. Now by faith we must enter into God's reckoning. This is not a matter of feeling but of faith. We must claim by faith the freedom from sin's authority which has been secured for us in virtue of Christ's death and our identification with that death. Experimental freedom should follow legal deliverance."[2]

Barabas gets off to a good start by pointing to the judicial nature of our death with Christ to sin. But he quickly succumbs to several typical errors. Confusing the body of sin in Romans 6:6 with our physical body, he says our "bodies are now free from sin's claim." But we all know that sin still seeks to reign over our bodies.

He softens the wording of 6:6 to say that we no longer *need* to serve sin. But Paul doesn't say this. He said the old man was crucified in order to destroy the body of sin so that we *would no longer* serve sin. Paul's wording has the sense of finality while Barabas, with many others, make service to sin in this verse pertain to our continuing struggle and something dependent upon the believer.

Barabas says we must appropriate the truth of 6:6 if it is to be real. He refers to 6:11 by saying we must enter into God's reckoning by faith (something Paul never says). He tells us we must not give in to our feelings, presumably speaking of a believer struggling with the thought, "If I died to my old sin nature, why do I still feel like sinning?" His answer with many others would be: "Don't give in to your feelings. Instead, walk by faith that your old nature died."

Finally, he says we must claim freedom by faith—again, something Paul does not say in Romans 6.

What *does* Paul say? If the common way of thinking about 6:11 is incorrect[3], if I am not supposed to "reckon" an old nature within me dead, what should I do? What does Romans 6:11 mean? This section of our book will answer these questions as we explore Romans 6:11–14. We turn first to Romans 6:11 to discover the meaning of this oft-quoted but little understood admonition: "Even so consider yourselves to be dead to sin, but alive to God in Christ Jesus."

CONSIDER YOURSELVES DEAD TO SIN

The first truth to notice is the important phrase "even so." The Greek word is οὕτως (*houtos*), and one that translators usually render "in the same way."[4] The NIV follows this line of thinking by translating it "in the same way." The NKJV translates it "likewise."[5]

This word shows up in two key places in the immediate context. In 5:15, Paul contrasts the trespass of Adam with the grace of Christ. Just as through the transgression of one man the many died, *in the same way* (*houtos*), the grace of the One, and the gift by that grace, abounds to many.[6]

In 5:18, Paul tells us that just as one transgression brought condemnation to all, *in the same way* (*houtos*), one act of righteousness resulted in justification for all. Paul's point is that just as one man, Adam, affected all humanity, *in the same way* (*houtos*) One Man, Jesus Christ, affected all humanity. Adam's effect was disastrous; Jesus' was life-saving.

The Greek word, *houtos*, is the word Paul uses in 6:11 but with a difference. Whereas in Romans 5 he *contrasted* the work of Adam and Christ, here he wants his readers to *connect* the death of Christ to sin and our death to sin. We have to back up to 6:10 to catch the weight of this connection: "For the death that He died, He died to sin once for all...*even so—houtos in the same way*—consider yourselves to be dead to sin." Whether one translates (*houtos*) with "therefore," "thus," "so," or "even so," the point remains the same: We are to take our understanding of our death to sin from His death to sin. Just as He died to sin, *in the same way*, consider that you died to sin.

Paul has labored for ten verses to explain what His death to sin is about and we have labored for several chapters to understand it. Walking our way through a maze of well-intended but misguided interpretations, we arrive at this truth for Romans 6:11: Just as Christ died to the penalty of sin once for all, in the same way we are to consider ourselves dead to the penalty of sin once for all and alive to God.

But what does this mean for our sanctification? It means that Paul is pointing to our union with Christ in His death and resurrection as the starting point for sanctification.

The rich fruit of sanctification, a changed life that increasingly overcomes sin, does not find its source in self-help remedies, 12-step programs, or even in the time-honored practices of the Christian disciplines. All these can be good and helpful, but they are not the rich, life-giving root that equips, energizes, and empowers.

Paul begins his exhortation to sanctification by pointing to this rich root: We have completely died to sin *even as* (*houtos*)—*in the same way* Christ died to sin. Our old standing in Adam has been crucified and buried. The body of sinful evidence has been cancelled. We are no longer slaves to the penal system because of our guilt. We have been acquitted of all charges, and we stand justified before a holy God because of what Jesus has done for us.

This is Paul's starting point for sanctification. While it is true that he made sanctification references in the previous verses, these were only preliminary thrusts into this important topic to ensure his readers that his theology of death and resurrection with Christ had practical benefits. After a quick statement such as "so we too might walk in newness of life" (6:4), he returned to his main argument: that Christ's death to the penalty of sin brought about our death to the same. But now that Paul has concluded this argument in 6:1–10, he is ready to speak more openly about sanctification.

In previous chapters, I personified these brief phrases as an eager actor just offstage who can hardly wait to come onto the stage and recite his lines. The time has now come for the actor to make his first great appearance. He will make more appearances in the rest of Romans 6 and in 7, and he will make his greatest appearance in 8, but in these verses, 6:11–14, he has some significant lines to recite with some important points to make. And the first significant point is that just as Christ has died to sin, in the same way, we are to consider ourselves dead to sin and alive to God.

When Paul tells us to consider this, he is not telling us to make something happen inside us. He is not telling us that an old sinful nature was somehow mystically crucified with Christ and we have to enforce that death by reckoning it so. Instead, he is telling us what has already happened. Paul uses an interesting word at this place in his discourse. He tells us to *logizesthe* this. The word, *logizesthe*[7], translated "consider" in the NASB[8], is an accounting word referring to the business practice of recording debits or credits on a ledger.

Paul had an assortment of words in his vocabulary to employ if he had only wanted to say "think about this," "meditate on this," "memorize this," "do this," "enforce this," "make this happen," or "practice this." But he used the word *logizesthe*, his word of choice, in the important Romans 4 passage on justification and God *crediting* us with righteousness.[9]

Ancient Greek speakers did use *logizesthe* in many places as a synonym for considering or thinking (see footnote 7), but this kind of thinking was always the result of calculating or reckoning. I believe Paul used it at this place to reinforce his point that because Christ credited His righteousness to our ledger before God, we are therefore to reckon that truth onto the ledger of our minds. We are to make a truth entry on the records of our thought processes—Christ paid completely for our sins and nothing more has to be done to make us right with God. Because He died to sin once for all—in the same way, even so—we died to sin. Count on it. Reckon it. Enter it on the ledger of vital truths for your life. And even though Charles Wesley had a different viewpoint on how sanctification worked out in Romans 6, I cannot improve upon his words to express the meaning of Romans 6:11: "No condemnation now I dread, Jesus and all in Him is mine."

N.T. Wright has some affirming and helpful comments regarding *logizesthe* in 6:11: "The key word here is 'reckon,' the same root as in 4:3 and elsewhere and with the same bookkeeping metaphor in mind. Do the sum, he says; add it up and see what it comes to. The Messiah has died, once for all, and has been raised; you are, by baptism, in the Messiah; therefore, you, too, have died, once for all, and been raised…The point is not, as in some schemes of piety, that the 'reckoning' achieves the result of dying to sin and coming alive to God, any more than someone adding up a column of figures creates the result out of nothing; it opens the eyes of mind and heart to recognize what is in fact true."[10]

Let me explain it this way. Suppose your spouse makes three deposits into your joint savings account over a one-month period—one for $200, one for $300, and another for $500. At the end of the month, you want to review how much your spouse put in, so you take out the deposit slips, *sum them up*, and come up with a grand total of $1,000. Your act of summing them up is a "reckoning." But this reckoning does not create the money in the bank. It only tells you what already exists. In the same way, Paul tells us to consider what Christ has already accomplished on our behalf by His substitutionary death and in which we participate by virtue of our union with Him. We have died to sin completely.

But what does this mean for our lives on Monday morning when we're headed to work? On Wednesday afternoon when we feel pulled in too many directions? On Friday night when we are relaxing from a long week and feel an urge to indulge in forbidden pleasures?

It works in this way: When we feel the pull to sin in that Monday morning moodiness, Wednesday afternoon grumpiness, Friday night fleshliness—or a thousand other ways on any day of the week—*we must first face approaching temptation and sinful problems by recognizing their complete inconsistency with our status before God as one who died and rose with Christ.* Why would we want to indulge in sin when sin is out of character with our status in Christ?

This, actually, is an answer to the question posed in Romans 6:1 where Paul asked, rhetorically, "Are we to continue in sin that grace may increase?" In addition to his historical answer in 5:20–21 (God meeting Israel's increased sin with abounding grace), he gives another answer in 6:11: Sinful behavior does not match your identity in Christ. It is inconsistent with your status as one who died and rose with Christ.

While we are not dead to the pull of sin in our lives, we are dead to the penalty of sin because our standing as a condemned sinner before God has been destroyed and we live as a justified man before God in Christ. When the pull of sin exerts its power in us, we are to think on who we are in Christ—no longer a condemned sinner but a justified man. We must "consider," "reckon" (*logizesthe*) that we died to the old status and rose to a new status. We have a new identity, and sin is inconsistent with that reality.

It is helpful at this point to take an initial look at Paul's statement in 6:12, "Therefore do not let sin reign in your mortal body." Let me paraphrase these verses and show how 6:11 and 6:12 work together:

6:11 – "In light of your status in Christ
6:12 – therefore, don't give in to sin's pull in your life; don't let it reign."

When sin presents itself to you, don't give in to it. If you have a new standing, a new identity before God as a justified man because you died to the condemned status in Adam, then don't let sin have its way with you, because that is inconsistent with what God has done for you and inconsistent with your new standing in Christ Jesus. This answers the question we posed in the beginning of this book from the mouth of a sincere but struggling believer. "I am a follower of Jesus. I want to please Him. I want to advance in my faith, but I have these issues in my life that cause me to stumble. I want to believe I died to sin, but I find myself still living in it. I don't want to continue sinning. May it never be! God forbid! But I do. Can you help me?"

Yes, we can help you, or rather, Christ can help you. In His Word, He tells you that you must learn your new identity in Jesus Christ. Your old identity in Adam is dead and gone. When you sin, when you follow the old patterns of your not-yet-completely sanctified human nature, you are living according to a status that no longer exists before God. You have a new standing, a new status with God, a new identity. Like a street-begging, homeless man someone discovers to be the twin brother of a millionaire and then is brought into a new home and given a generous bank account, you must remain in your new home (your new status) and not return to your moth-eaten blanket under the bridge. You must live according to that new identity.

The first step, therefore, to gain victory over sin is to learn, reckon, and affirm this identity in Christ. The starting point for sanctification is learning to think about ourselves in light of Jesus' accomplishment for us.

HOW DO WE THINK ABOUT OURSELVES?

How do we think about ourselves? Unfortunately, we usually think about ourselves in distorted, skewed images—like the funny mirrors at carnivals that make us too short and fat or too tall and skinny. The way we think about ourselves is conditioned by many things including our upbringing, our personality, and our religious experiences.

Some people grow up in wholesome families and have healthy thoughts about themselves. But many grow up in families where they encounter verbal and mental abuse, being called and then labeling themselves "worthless idiot, ugly duckling, unwelcome intruder, shame-filled failure." And they suffer for it all their lives. Even those who grow up in healthy families suffer from wrong thoughts about themselves, perhaps in a milder form than those just expressed, but they are there. Others suffer from thinking too highly of themselves and living in pride as if life is about them and they are God's unique gift to everyone around. Everyone battles with a distorted idea of his identity in one way or another and its toll on our behavior is incalculable.

Many fine books help believers think about themselves in correct ways. I have in my library a multi-million dollar best seller that encourages me to live to my full potential. In this book, I learn to enlarge my vision, develop a healthy self-image, discover the power of my thoughts and words, let go of the past, and so on. All of these are good and wonderful principles, but divorced from who Christ is and what is now true of me in light of my union with His death and resurrection, they are mere humanistic principles that anyone can use to have a better life. They are not tapping into the rich root of God's power available to them and that Paul talks about in this passage.

A book that hits closer to home is Neil Anderson's *Victory Over the Darkness*. In the early chapters of this book, Dr. Anderson urges Christians to think on, understand, and personalize their identity in Christ. I wholeheartedly agree. He lists 36 biblical ways to think about ourselves such as "I am a child of God, I am Christ's friend, and I am a citizen of heaven."[11] A few pages later, he supplements this list with another list of 31 ways we have received grace in Christ.[12]

Again, a wonderful list, and he includes the grace of Romans 6 in his list. If all believers read and internalized these biblical truths, they would find new power for holy living. But if I could add a perspective to Anderson's lists, it is this: All of these ways of thinking about our identity are rooted in the supreme way we should think about ourselves. I, a guilty sinner in Adam, died to that status before God in Christ and now have a new status before Him—the status of a justified man.

Every other identity I have flows from this identity: I am dead to sin in Christ Jesus but alive to God in Him. Everything revolves around this. And everything *must* revolve around this because the central reality is not a truth about me but a truth about Jesus Christ. He died and rose on my behalf. I must take my cue on how to think about myself, not on some whimsical dream or humanistic self-effort, but solely on who I am *in Him*. This keeps the central figure, Christ, and the central events, His death, resurrection, and enthronement, at the center! I illustrate this in Chart 2.

Chart 2

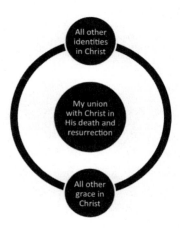

When we keep Christ at the center and take our identity from Him, our lives change. On one level, we were all shame-filled, guilt-ridden, sin-marked associates of the rebel Adam. We stood in solidarity with him and his transgression.[13] But we *were* that! And now we *are* no longer that! We died to the penalty of sin. Our status as condemned criminals before God has been crucified, the charges cancelled, and a new status put in its place—justified, declared righteous.

Paul tells us to reckon this truth in the annals of our mind: "Think about yourself in this way. You are no longer a condemned criminal, a prisoner to sin. You died to that identity once for all when Christ died in your place." And in light of this truth, when sin comes knocking on your door, don't answer it because it will entice you to do things inconsistent with this amazing status you have before God through Jesus Christ.

First Corinthians 6:9–11, one of my favorite passages to teach throughout the years, reinforces this truth: "Or do you not know that the unrighteous will not inherit the kingdom of God? Do not be deceived; neither fornicators, nor idolaters, nor adulterers, nor effeminate, nor homosexuals, nor thieves, nor the covetous, nor drunkards, nor revilers, nor swindlers, will inherit the kingdom of God. Such were some of you; but you were washed, but you were sanctified, but you were justified in the name of the Lord Jesus Christ and in the Spirit of our God."

When I have taught this, I have queried the audience, "What is the most important word in this passage?" Many suggestions come forth and usually one person will get it right: "The most important word in this passage is the word, 'were.'" Such *were* some of you, with the implication that the "were" is no longer valid because of what you now *are*. God has changed our status from one identity to another.

We no longer identify ourselves by one or many sinful habits, but we take our identity from what we now are by virtue of our union with Jesus Christ. We *are* washed, sanctified,[14] and justified in the name of Jesus Christ and by the work of the Holy Spirit in calling us out of sin into a relationship with God. Paul presents the same emphasis in Ephesians 5:8: "For you *were* formerly [once] darkness, but now you *are* Light in the Lord" (italics mine). After he points to our identity, he instructs us to live out our identity: "Walk [live] as children of Light."

How we think about ourselves is crucial. This is not New Age dreaming about becoming gods or a humanistic technique to become something we want to be, but it is understanding what is already true about us because of our union with Christ in His death and resurrection. And out of all the ways to think about ourselves, the first and most important way is to consider that we are dead to the penalty of sin and alive to God. We no longer have any solidarity with the guilty Adam race, but we stand in solidarity with Jesus Christ, with His achievements for us, and with the New Man, the New Humanity that He has created. We are, indeed, *dead men rising!*

It is important that we grasp this as the central way of thinking about ourselves. It is not one of many truths. It is not, for example, insight #17 in a list of 50 insights. It is the core insight, like the hub of a bicycle wheel from which all the spokes radiate.

Paul uses two phrases to emphasize the centrality of this identity. They are phrases that most gloss over in their reading, but they contain life-changing power and eternal significance. I am speaking about the phrases "with Christ" and "in Christ." Douglas Moo identifies more than 30 "with Christ" verses and categorizes them into nine ways that the believer receives something by virtue of his union with Christ.[15]

We,

- die with Christ (Romans 6:5, 8; Colossians 2:20; 2 Timothy 2:11)
- are crucified with Christ (Romans 6:6; Galatians 2:20)
- are buried with Christ (Romans 6:4; Colossians 2:12)
- are raised with Christ (Colossians 2:12; 3:1; Ephesians 2:6)
- come to life with Christ (Colossians 2:13; Ephesians 2:5)
- are seated with Christ (Ephesians 2:6)
- are joint heirs with Christ (Romans 8:17)
- suffer with Christ (Romans 8:17; 2 Corinthians 13:4 weak with Him)
- have our lives hidden with Christ in God – Colossians 3:3)
- will be delivered with Him (Romans 6:5b, 8b; 8:17b, 32b; 2 Corinthians 4:14; Philippians 3:21; Colossians 3:4; 1 Thessalonians 4:14b; 5:10b; 2 Timothy2:11b)
- are with Him after death (1 Thessalonians 4:17; Philippians 1:23)

But we can find an even more extensive listing of verses in Paul's writings if we look at the all-important phrase "in Christ." I have discovered almost 100 verses in Paul's epistles where he speaks of the reality of believers being "in Christ" or similar phrases such as "in Jesus" or "in Christ Jesus." Here is a sampling of this life-changing list:

- We are redeemed in Christ (Romans 3:24)
- Eternal life is in Christ Jesus (Romans 6:23)
- There is now no condemnation for those in Christ (Romans 8:1)

- The law of the Spirit of life in Christ Jesus sets us free (Romans 8:2)
- We have been sanctified in Christ Jesus (1 Corinthians 1:2)
- Grace (for spiritual gifts) was given us in Christ Jesus (1 Corinthians 1:4)
- You are enriched in Him (1 Corinthians 1:5)
- All the promises are yes in Him (2 Corinthians 1:20)
- We are righteous in Him (2 Corinthians 5:21)
- In Christ Jesus the blessing of Abraham comes to Gentiles (Galatians 3:14)
- You are all sons of God in Christ Jesus (Galatians 3:26)
- We are chosen in Him (Ephesians 1:4)
- We are created in Christ Jesus for good works (Ephesians 2:10)
- In Christ we are brought near to God (Ephesians 2:13)
- God carries out His eternal purpose in Christ Jesus (Ephesians 3:11)
- In Him we are completed (Colossians 2:10)
- Our holy calling is in Christ Jesus (2 Timothy 1:9)
- The whole building is growing into a holy temple in the Lord (Ephesians 2:21)
- You are light in the Lord (Ephesians 5:8)

I am sure you can find many more in the New Testament. These lists are not exhaustive but representative to emphasize this great truth: The crucial component for our victory, the crucial truth to turn the "Contradictory Reality" into a consistent reality of pleasing God, is to focus on our standing before God based solely upon who Christ Jesus is and what He has done for us.

Paul labored mightily in 5:12–21 to explain the dire consequences for those "in Adam." But the bleakness of our status in him no longer controls us. We now stand before God in another Adam, the Last Adam (1 Corinthians 15:45) and the Second Man (1 Corinthians 15:47). Because He died and rose *for us*, the topic of 6:1–10, we can say that we joined in these events *with Him* and now stand *in Him* as one who died and has risen.

This, above all other truths, must shape our thinking. It must shape our thinking about what Christ has done for us. It must shape our thinking about who we were. And it must shape our thinking about how we must now live in light of this transfer from the old man, Adam, to the New Man, Jesus Christ. To the degree we "reckon" this reality, to this degree we will live with power for His glory in this fallen world because a new epoch in the history of mankind has emerged. It is the epoch of the Man Jesus Christ and the new humanity of those in Him. In light of this transfer, in light of this status, we can live with hope and purpose. We can put aside the old way of living and find a new way of life.

But let's leave these lofty (and true) ideas aside for a moment and consider how they work for us in the day-to-day routines of life. After all, even the best among us cannot maintain such lofty concepts all the time! Daily challenges and responsibilities relentlessly pursue us, demanding that we focus on earthly things. And with these earthly things we often face our weaknesses, temptations, and failures. Let me provide several examples from my life to show how this has worked for me and how it could work for you.

First, when I have looked at my personality weaknesses, I have learned not to let those weaknesses define my standing with God. I emphasize the phrase "I have learned." I was not always able to do this. For years, I was blind to many character blemishes that others could see clearly (which makes me wonder what people see today that I still don't see!).

As I gained insight into my true nature with its flaws, I would often fall into the trap of comparing myself with others or blaming others for their part in my personal dilemmas. At other times, when the conclusion of my culpability was unavoidable, I'd go to God with a crushed spirit and heart (not necessarily a bad thing) and speak with Him (always a good thing) about my problems. And after speaking with Him, I would sometimes still feel crushed and for days continue with a gloomy disposition because of my weaknesses and sins. I would question myself—my commitment, my love for God, and sometimes even fear that God might not be gracious.

But as I grew in Christ, I learned how to apply the theology of Romans 6:11 in my life. I learned not to let those weaknesses define my standing with God or even with others.

It's not that I now ignore myself or look the other way, refusing to admit to problems, but I have learned that the long-standing issues in my personality that only slowly change have no bearing on the core truth of my status as a justified man before God. I remember that while I am a work-in-progress to become like Christ in my character and behavior, I am a *justified* man who is a work-in-progress.

I may have issues in my life; I may have sinful behavior; but I have died to the penalty of that sinful behavior with Christ, and my issues and behavior have no bearing on my status before God in Christ. My standing is as secure as Jesus Himself at the right hand of God. Therefore, as I reflect on my imperfections (or when they are brought to my attention by others), I don't have to be self-loathing or defensive because I am secure in my core identity as someone who has died and risen with Christ. I am as secure as the crucified and risen Savior.

To loathe myself or to be defensive, rather than to show a teachable, humble spirit can only lead to one place—a place of temptation. If I loathe myself, why should I aspire to a noble life? If I am only a no-good piece of filth, well then, I might as well enjoy the filth for a season. If I am defensive, refuse to admit the obvious—that I have issues and need to work on character areas—I will only blind myself to the infectious sores in my heart and let them run rampant. Either way, greater sin results from a failure to reckon or consider myself according to who I am in Christ by virtue of my union with Him in His death and resurrection.

Years ago, a national company hired me to coordinate the administrative side of its service department. They wanted to hire me at a certain pay level. I wanted a higher starting salary. When I received the call that they agreed to my salary wishes, I was elated! They recognized my worth, and I entered the first few weeks with great enthusiasm and energy.

Then I received my first paycheck. It didn't seem right. I went to the accounting department to tell them of their error only to find out I was the one in error. They had not hired me at the level I thought. Miscommunication with a third party head hunter landed me the position at the lower rate of pay.

My immediate supervisor took me into his office to discuss the issue, and my spirit sank with each new revelation. I wasn't as valued as I had thought. I wasn't such a great, sought-after team member, after all. The opportunities for sin abounded. I could have called people a few choice names. I could have broken out into a rage. I could have walked away in pride—I'm better than this! But I refused to walk those paths that seemed so appealing to me.

Instead, as the image of my status with the company diminished, I rallied my spirit. I reminded myself of my status before God in Christ. I reminded myself of my true value by virtue of what He has done for me, and I retained my composure as we continued to talk. I walked the straight and very narrow path of trusting God while I was walking in humiliation before my supervisors at work. And I might as well add that God rewarded me that same day as my supervisor went to the front office and arranged for the company to pay me what I had asked for!

I was astonished! But more important, I remember that difficult day—difficult because I was not the high wage earner I thought I was. I had a young, growing family to raise while trying to start a church. It was difficult as I grappled with my core identity in this embarrassing episode. And on this day, I chose to walk the path of Christ as I focused on who I am in Him.

I cannot be sure if, on that day, I thought through the logic of Romans 6:11. I cannot be sure if I reviewed the reality that I had died to the penalty of sin and was united with the risen Christ. Life, temptation, and our minds don't always work that way. Often, in the midst of a crisis, our emotions swell up and push aside our reasoning capacities. We often have to make gut-instinct decisions. But I do remember that I reminded myself that their evaluation of me in no way impinged upon God's evaluation of me.

My status with their company was in jeopardy. My more important status with God was not affected in the least because I was in union with Him. This kind of thinking helped me through the day. More importantly, it has changed my life and it will change your life. This is the kind of "reckoning" Paul is telling us to have, and that we must have if we are going to overcome sin. We must consider ourselves in association with Him and what He has done for us. We must take our identity from Him.

In another decade, I was working with another company, this time as a technical writer, and in a city that was maniacal about its football team. As I sat in my cubicle, I was amused as I listened to the conversations of people hovering around the front desk every Monday morning in the fall as they reviewed Sunday's big game. "*We* really put it to them yesterday! *We* have the makings of a Super Bowl team. *We* could go all the way."

I was amused because of the little word "we." I thought, "What do you mean *we*? *We* weren't out on the field. *We* are not part of the team. *We* don't take the heat for fumbles or receive the glory for the winning score. And *we*, especially, don't receive those outrageous paychecks in the mail!" I smugly sat back in my chair, thinking myself superior to such childish behavior…until God reminded me I have lived that way, as well.

It was okay as a child. My team was the Yankees and my player, my hero, Mickey Mantle. If the Yankees lost, that was a day of discouragement, but if they lost in the World Series, well, to be honest, I would cry. But I grew out of that…I thought! Other cities had their teams and the innocent watching of a game became emotional involvement. I found myself using the dreaded word "we" as if I were part of the organization. And though I didn't cry, when some of my teams lost, I have to admit that on more than one occasion I was an emotional mess. Why are we this way?

Last week, a player from a major sport made an announcement that he was leaving one team for another. Such an announcement normally takes about 30 seconds. But this player had to have a one-hour television special to make his "proclamation to the world." Only one thing surpassed the folly of this event—the emotional reaction of people who tuned in to watch the spectacle. In the winning city, the city where this amazing athlete would take his skills to make history (as he stated), the crowd went wild (to use a sports cliché). To watch people cheering, screaming, laughing, and celebrating with tears of joy, one would have thought everyone's personal debt had been erased, or the government had given everyone a million-dollar economic stimulus check. But no, it was only an announcement that this player was coming to town to play for their team!

In the other city, the losing city, the city that lost this gifted athlete, emotions were equally on display. Tears flowed and screaming filled the night, but, since you probably know what I am talking about, you also know they were different tears and the screaming contained different words. A pretty, young woman sat at a bar and cried. A guy sitting close by looked as if his mother had just died. People burned the player's jersey—as if he were a political enemy bent on taking away freedom. Parodies of his name filled the airwaves. Unprintable comments filled blog sites, and city icons—the warehouse-sized poster, for example—started coming down immediately.

Why are we this way? Why do we entangle our emotions, our lives, our identities with people we will never meet and who will never do anything for us? We are this way because we hunger to identify with something larger than our lives. We hunger to be part of something big. We hunger to be part of a family, a movement, or a cause that will fill our lonely, compartmentalized lives with some kind of greater association, thinking that we will find meaning by this association—even if it's only a game.

Certainly, some people give their emotions, lives, and identities to causes with much greater consequence than who wins or loses a contest. All of us could name several examples of people we admire who change lives, or we give to or work with organizations that make a difference in this world. But whether it is an inconsequential game or a humanitarian cause, all of us hunger to identify with someone or something bigger than we are because we want to touch the whole world, make a difference in the whole world, and be part of something great. We are this way because God made us this way—in His image. And our associations, our "unions" with these bigger-than-life people or organizations are often unworthy of the way God has made us and are misdirected efforts to satisfy the hunger within.

Ultimately, only one "union," only one identification, can satisfy the hunger in our soul—our union with Jesus Christ in His death and resurrection. Think of all the heroes in the world. They pale in comparison to Him, the Hero of heroes. Think of what He has done. He has destroyed our guilt. He has defeated death. Look back at chapter three and review the contrasts between Adam and Christ. Think on how He has reversed every consequence of Adam's sin. He has opened the door to life, eternal life. He has restored us to Himself. He is the guarantee that God will one day put all things in order and heaven will return to earth. And as we think on these things, let us remember that these are not things He did only so that we might sit back and applaud. He did them for us, and glory awaits us because we are joined with Him in these epoch-changing achievements.

If we Christians would take one year and reexamine our "unions" and "associations," and if, in that year, we would rethink our union, our association, our "in Christ" status, our death with Him and our resurrection with Him, what difference would that make in our lives? If we would empty ourselves of the garbage and spiritual junk food that litters our soul, if we would ask the Holy Spirit to fill us with the wonder of what Christ did for us in those epoch-changing, earth-shattering, world-changing days of His death and resurrection, we would discover a stronger love for what is right and a distaste for what is wrong.

Why should we give in to the impulses of sinful desires when God is calling us to join Him in a worldwide, history-changing movement with joyful results that will last forever? We should remember the oft-quoted C.S. Lewis illustration: "Why play in a rundown, garbage strewn neighborhood making mud pies when God is calling us to a day at the beach?"

Here is where we find the power to overcome sin: realizing we are united with Him in His death and resurrection by reckoning/calculating ourselves dead in Christ to the penalty of sin and alive to Him with a justified standing.

How we wish for such consistent power and victory in our lives. And the more we reckon (*logizesthe*) such truths, the greater will be our victorious walk with Christ. And when we do fail—what then? This leads to a final personal example—and perhaps the most important.

When I have lapsed into sin because I have forgotten or turned away momentarily from the vision of glory in front of me—perhaps an episode of lustful thinking, envy toward other leaders, gossip, or whining about life—and when I have confessed these sins, I have learned that the most important step I can take is to start obeying quickly and not grovel in my failures.

I'm not saying that I've learned to take sin lightly—that I should continue in sin that grace might abound! On the contrary, I have learned to reflect soberly on my deeds that have brought pain to others, myself, and especially to God. But I have learned to reflect on them as a justified man before God. I've learned to consider that even in the midst of my failures, I am still dead to the penalty of those failures.

Once I admit to my capers and turn from them, I may still feel crummy, or like I have a big "L" stamped on my forehead, but I have learned to speak truth to myself—and not just any truth, but the most important truth of Romans 6:11.

I have learned to say something like this, "Yes, I was stupid and weak to have done that. But I am still a justified man before God. I live under grace. And even though I don't feel very good about myself right now, I must not let my feelings lead me into self-condemnation. If I do, I will only depress myself. That will probably lead me into frenzied efforts to prove myself worthy—to myself or to God—something that I cannot do because only Christ can do that for me and He has already done that for me! My old identity as a condemned man has been crucified. God no longer holds any charges against me. I am freed from the prison house of my sin and live in His favor. So, start obeying. Pick up where you left off. I am alive to God. Start worshiping, and live as a justified man."

This is also the great truth of 1 John 2:1 where John says, "My little children,

I am writing these things to you so that you may not sin. And if anyone sins, we have an Advocate with the Father, Jesus Christ the righteous." Jesus Christ does not stand as our prosecuting attorney but as our defense attorney. He is our legal advocate even in our failure. After all, He is the One who died and rose on our behalf! Paul will put it this way, later in Roman 8:34: "Who is the one who condemns? Christ Jesus is He who died, yes, rather who was raised, who is at the right hand of God, who also intercedes for us."

Recognizing this truth has saved me from greater sin—greater sin that comes from a defeatist attitude that says, "Oh what's the use. I'll never get victory over this, and I'm sure that I have crossed the line this time with God. I might as well indulge."

Recognizing the central meaning of Romans 6:1–11 has restored me to the path of obedience far more quickly as I have thought correctly about who I am in Christ: "Yes, I sinned and it was wrong, but that sinful behavior does not reflect who I really am by virtue of Christ's death and resurrection for me. I am not going to continue in this behavior, and I'm going to get back up on my feet and walk with Christ. I am going to live out the implications of His justifying work for me."

When I do this, I practice the great truth that Paul spoke in Romans 6:11: Just as Christ died to sin once for all, consider that you have also died to sin once for all. I don't live by what I feel about myself at the moment. I live by what I know is true about me at *every moment*—whether times of victory or defeat, joy or sorrow—I have died to sin and stand justified before God.

Discouragement evaporates more quickly now. Healing surges through my spirit with greater force. I walk in steps of obedience with more confidence because I don't measure my identity by my inconsistent record but on Jesus' perfect record. Grace reigns! And God delights to reign over us with His grace! God loves it when we think this way. God loves it when we learn to claim our identity with Christ. He loves it because it honors His great work for us in Christ Jesus and it sets us free!

I might also add this: When we train our minds to think this way, we free our minds from the introspection of trying to figure out how we could possibly sin if our "old sinful nature" has been crucified. We no longer have to figure out if it's our old nature, our new nature, our "flesh" and, if one of those things, why we still sin if we are dead to our sin nature and dead to the flesh.

We no longer have to try to reckon ourselves dead, to keep ourselves dead to sin, to keep the old man on the cross or in the tomb, because Paul is not talking about that. Paul is talking about our status in Adam that died and our status in Christ that defines our relationship with God. We can take our eyes off ourselves. We don't have to analyze ourselves and try to figure out what part of us sinned or how things worked or didn't work. Instead, we can put our eyes on the finished work of Christ and the glorious standing we have in Him.

We are dead men who—miracle of miracles!—have risen. How can a dead man rise? He can rise in Christ! Our next chapter will explore this next concept in detail, our resurrection in Christ.

CHAPTER SEVEN ENDNOTES

[1] Of course, we continue to turn to the Holy Spirit, but we should not expect a once-for-all event to destroy an old nature within us.

[2] Steven Barabas, *So Great Salvation* (Eugene, Oregon: Wipf and Stock Publishers, 2005), 90.

[3] Jerry Bridges, in his classic book, *The Pursuit of Holiness*, identifies this faulty approach to Romans 6:6, 11. He says, "Our dying to sin is not something we do, or something we make come true in our experience by reckoning it so. Some have misunderstood this point. We have gotten the idea that to have died to sin means to somehow be removed from sin's ability to touch us. However, to experience this in our daily lives we are told we must reckon ourselves dead to sin. We are further told that if we are not experiencing victory over our besetting sins, it is because we are not reckoning on the fact that we died to sin. We are indeed to reckon—or to count or consider—ourselves dead to sin, but our reckoning does not make it true, even in our experience." Jerry Bridges, *The Pursuit of Holiness* (Colorado Springs, Colorado: NavPress, 2003), 52–53.

[4] "In this manner, thus, so." Paul used it "with reference to what precedes" in Romans 5:12, 19, 21; and 6:4 or to draw "an inference from what precedes" in Romans 1:15 and 6:11, William F. Arndt & F. Wilbur Gingrich, *A Greek English Lexicon of the New Testament* (Chicago: University of Chicago Press, 1963), 602.

[5] Other translations such as the NLT, ESV, and HCSB simplify with the word "so."

[6] Paul uses *houtos* to make a contrast. He says the grace is not like the transgres-

sion because the grace of God did not match the sin of Adam; grace over-whelmed it!

[7] *Logizomai* shows three uses in Greek: 1) to reckon or calculate; 2) to think about, consider, ponder, or let one's mind dwell on; and 3) to think, believe, be of the opinion of. Arndt & Gingrich, *A Greek English Lexicon of the New Testament*, 476–477. Its meaning of "reckoning or calculating" is its primary meaning with the other two meanings deriving from that usage. Arndt & Gingrich show several NT examples of translating it to "evaluate, estimate, look upon, or consider as a result of making a calculation." They place Romans 6:11 in this category along with Romans 9:8 (to "regard" the children of promise as Abraham's children) and 2 Corinthians 10:2 (Paul's opponents "regarding" him as if he walked in the flesh).

[8] "Count" yourselves dead to sin (NIV); "reckon" yourselves dead to sin (NKJV); "reckon" ye also yourselves to be dead indeed unto sin (KJV); "consider" yourselves dead to sin (ESV); "consider" yourselves to be dead to the power of sin (NLT); "consider" yourselves dead to sin (HCSB).

[9] See Romans 4:4, 5, 6, 8, 11, 23.

[10] N.T. Wright, *The New Interpreter's Bible Commentary, Volume X, Romans* (Nashville, Tennessee: Abingdon, 2002), Romans, 541.

[11] Neil T. Anderson, *Victory over the Darkness* (Ventura, California: Regal Books, 1990), 45–47.

[12] Ibid., 57–59.

[13] And lest we self-righteously point the finger at his failure, we must remember that we have contributed mightily to the cause of our demise and condemnation.

[14] This is one of those verses where sanctification does not refer to our progressive growth in Christ-likeness but to God's once-for-all setting us apart from the world and into His family.

[15] See Moo, *The Epistle to the Romans*, 391–395. Moo states the following about this "with Christ" language: "The theological concept that grounds and motivates the 'with Christ' language of Paul is his understanding of Christ as a representative, even inclusive, figure. Romans 5:12–21 has established that Christ's 'obedience/act of righteousness' affects all who belong to him. Davies refers in this regard to the Jewish teaching that every generation was to consider itself as having taken part in the Exodus" (e.g., m. Pesah. 10). As Tannehill notes, "It is but a 'short step' to the inference that Christ's death is a corporate or inclusive act,

so that his death is at the same time the death of all those who are 'in' him."
393–394

"Even though it has been popular to call this union a 'mystical' one, this language is best avoided as suggesting an ontological or natural union. In the case of both Adam and Christ, the union between them and those whom they represent is primarily—and in Christ's case perhaps exclusively—forensic. Because he is our representative, the judgment or decision that has fallen on Christ falls also on those who come to belong to him. Seen in this light, 'participationist' language of Paul is at the service of, and determined by, his forensic or 'judicial' conception of the work of Christ." 395

CONSIDER YOURSELVES ALIVE TO GOD

Even so consider yourselves to be dead to sin, but alive to God in Christ Jesus.

ROMANS 6:11

WHEN I WAS A LITTLE BOY, I used to collect coins with my older brothers. I had about $100 face-value in pennies, nickels, and dimes. I got away from it when I became a man, but a few years ago, one of my sons inspired me to start collecting the state quarters. I enjoyed picking up my old hobby and found great pleasure in finding quarters that had the mottoes of the 50 American states and distinctive images from those states.

I was happily placing them into my coin folder when I realized the slots called for two kinds of state quarters—50 with a "D" on them and 50 with a "P" on them, denoting which were minted in Denver and which in Philadelphia. Both sides of the coin were important, and I realized I wasn't going to finish the job until I had 50 quarters minted in Denver and 50 in Philadelphia.

In the same way, Romans 6:11 has two sides to it, but only one side has received attention. Just as I focused my attention on one side of the quarters, commentators, preachers, and teachers have focused their attention almost exclusively on only one part of Romans 6:11—that we are to consider ourselves dead to sin.

But there is another part of the verse: "Even so consider yourselves to be... alive to God in Christ Jesus." We are to *logizesthe* ("reckon") that we are alive to God. Clearly, we cannot make ourselves alive to God. And this is where Wright's comment is helpful that the reckoning doesn't make things happen but instead helps us to realize what has already been done to us and for us in Christ. We died with Him—*and we rose with Him.*

It makes perfect sense that Paul would say this. In his Romans 6 argument, he speaks of the resurrection of Christ or our resurrection with Him as much as the death of Christ and our death with Him. It's just that the death part has received all the press. I hope to rectify this. For starters, look at the comparison of death and resurrection statements in Table 9, taken from Romans 6.

TABLE 9	
Death in Romans 6	**Resurrection in Romans 6**
6:2 – How shall we who died to sin still live in it?	
6:3 – Baptized into death	
6:4 – Buried into death	6:4 – Christ was raised from the dead
	6:4 – Walk in newness of life
6:5 – Fused with Him in the likeness of death	6:5 – (Fused) also in the likeness of his resurrection
6:6 – Old man crucified with Him	
6:6 – Body of sin was destroyed	
6:7 – He who has died	6:7 – Is justified from sin
6:8 – If we have died with Christ	6:8 – We shall also live with Him
6:9 – Death no longer is master over Him.	6:9 – Knowing that Christ, having been raised, never will die again
6:10 – The death that He died, He died to sin once for all	6:10 – The life that He lives, He lives to God
6:11 – Consider yourselves dead to sin	6:11 – (Consider yourselves) alive to God
	6:13 – Present yourselves to God as those alive from the dead.

This chart should restore balance to the discussion of Romans 6. As I said, most of the press has gone to the death part with the noble and fervent attempts by our brothers in Christ who have tried to help us make the death part effective.

But as I look at the chart, I find the Christian living part—the new life part—tied with the resurrection side of the verses. For example, in 6:4, Paul says Christ was raised so that "we too might walk in newness of life," and in 6:13, we are to present ourselves "to God as those alive from the dead"—alive to God. We are not to present ourselves to a new death! This chapter will explore how our union with Christ's resurrection empowers us to live for God.

SIDE 2 – ALIVE TO GOD

God has done much more than forgive us, break our solidarity with Adam, cancel the certificate of debt, and remove the body of sinful or fleshly evidence. All of that was necessary, but negative and only half the picture. God has also done a positive work. He has raised Christ from the dead and raised us with Him. God not only wiped away our criminal past, He also applied heroic righteousness to our present and our future. When Christ died to sin and we died to sin with Him, God forgave us and set us free from sin's condemnation. But when He died to sin, that meant He was free to apply His righteousness to our account. We are more than forgiven—much more! We stand with righteousness before a holy God!

Imagine being hauled into court for a terrible crime against humanity— you are charged with an attempt to take the lives of millions through a terrorist act. The prosecuting attorney piles up the evidence against you and a "guilty as charged" verdict with a death sentence seems inevitable. But a dramatic piece of evidence surfaces just before the jury renders its decision. Not only are you not guilty of all charges, you actually were the hero in the story. You risked your life to save humanity from the evil. The judge and jury look over the evidence. It is convincing, irrefutable. You are immediately acquitted of all charges and instead proclaimed the hero of the event!

This is what Jesus did for us. He took the blame for our crimes and died in our place. But He did more than that: He applied His heroic righteousness to our account so that we stand before God much more than forgiven. We stand before Him 100% righteous—all of it a gift from Jesus!

Paul invites us, urges us, in verse 11 to apply this truth to our mind: Consider yourself *alive to God* in Christ Jesus! You do not stand before God with sin and condemnation. You stand before Him with righteousness and justification. You are alive to God because of what Christ has done for you, or, as the text says, you are "alive...*in Christ Jesus*" (italics mine).

In the Galatians 2 passage we examined in chapter two, Paul said the same thing: "Through the Law I died to the Law *that I might live to God*" (2:19, italics mine). The goal of the death of Christ to the Law and sin was to free us from the condemnation of the Law that our sin brought in order to free us to focus on a loving relationship with God. Here, in Romans 6, Paul says, "Consider" (*logizesthe*) yourselves this kind of person, a person who is alive to God with no trace or hint of condemnation or guilt about him.

As we look deeper into the majestic scenery of Romans 6:11, we discover much more than is usually noted. When I think about the trek my wife and I took at Jaffrey Lakes in British Columbia, it would be a terrible oversight to speak only of the difficulty, the arduous walk up, up, and up—the "death part"—and not speak of the lakes, the trees and mountains—the "alive part."

We need to correct this oversight in our understanding of Romans 6:11. It is crucial for our sanctification.

WHAT DOES IT MEAN TO BE ALIVE TO GOD?

So what does it mean to be "alive to God"? Paul provides an explanation for this phrase in the context of his argument. We want to learn what this is because we don't merely want to say no to sin. That's only half the battle. We want to say yes to righteousness. We don't want to be dead to sin only. We want to be alive to God, to experience His power—the same power that raised Christ from the dead. We want to walk in newness of life. What is this explanation? What does it mean to be alive to God?

Paul says. "Even so (in the same way) consider yourselves to be...alive to God." In the same way as what? In the same way as Christ is alive to God. Again, in order to see the context of 6:11, we must look back to 6:10: "For the death that He died, He died to sin once for all; but *the life that He lives, He lives to God.* Even so [in the same way] consider yourselves to be...alive to God in Christ Jesus" (italics mine). Did you catch the point? Just as Jesus now lives to God, *in the same way* consider yourselves to be alive to God.

To understand the full implication of Paul's statement, we must establish some key preliminary points. The first point we note in 6:10 is that the "life of Jesus" Paul refers to is His present, current life. It is His life on this side of His death. Usually, when people use the phrase "the life of Christ," they refer to His life on earth in Palestine, the three and one-half years of ministry that led up to His death and the life that is now finished.

As I have listened to myself and others speak this way, it almost seems as if His life is over and He is still dead, although we don't mean that. But notice that Paul is not speaking of this. He is speaking of His life on the resurrection side of His death. He died to sin once for all but "the life that He lives, He lives to God." Paul is referring to a new life that Christ is experiencing *now* and not to His "finished life" in Palestine.

I once "lived a life in the state of Virginia." There were key people and events in that life. That life is over, but I am "living a new life in the state of Texas" with key people and events. In the same way, Jesus has changed locations and is living a new life with key people and events. This new life has something to do with our walk with God because Paul tells us to consider ourselves alive to God *in the same way that Jesus lives to God with His new life.* This is what we will explore.

A second preliminary point we must make, lest anyone have a heresy hernia, is that when Paul speaks of His life, He is not talking about the resurrection event only. Paul says the life He *lives.* The emphasis is on the life of Christ, beginning not only with the resurrection but also continuing to this moment—the life He is living right now! It almost seems that Paul is saying that Christ's resurrection entered Him into a phase of living not previously experienced.

A final preliminary point we must make is a reaffirmation of the truth that Christ always was alive to God. From eternity past, before the creation of this world and the first man, He lived as the Word of God: "In the beginning was the Word, and the Word was with God, and the Word was God...No one has seen God at any time; the only begotten God who is in the bosom of the Father, He has explained Him" (John 1:1, 18).

No greater words can explain the nearness of Christ to the Father before time began than these words from John's prologue to his gospel. Jesus was "in His bosom, His heart." If you go to the very core of who God is, there you will find Christ. He is the expression of the heart of God. If you penetrate to the depths of the omniscience and wisdom of God, there you will find Christ, the Word. He is the expression of the infinite, eternal mind of God. He was of the same nature as God—with Him and God Himself before time began. My words seem to sag on this paper when I say that He was always *alive to God.* We cannot begin to fathom all that it means! But we can at least agree that He was alive to God before time began.

One day, that eternal life was manifested. John said it this way in the opening words of his first letter: "What was from the beginning, what we have heard, what we have seen with our eyes, what we have looked at and touched with our hands, concerning the Word of Life—and the life was manifested, and we have seen and testify and proclaim to you the eternal life, which was with the Father and was manifested to us" (1 John 1:1–2).

The One who always lived now lived on earth in Palestine in human form. It is also important to acknowledge that He was alive to God during those years. We could think of His adventure in the temple at age 12 when He confounded the religious rulers with His wisdom while causing no small concern to Joseph and Mary who anxiously looked for Him. "Don't you know," He said to them,

"I must be about My Father's business?" Here we have evidence that He was *alive to God* even at this tender age.

When He was baptized by John around age 30 and anointed with the Spirit, the Father said, "This is My beloved Son, in whom I am well-pleased" (Matthew 3:17). Jesus had not yet performed one miracle, yet the Father was well-pleased with Him. From ages 12 to 30, He was alive to God as He lived a God-pleasing, perfect life in submission to His earthly parents.

And during His ministry, He repeatedly affirmed His nearness and "aliveness" to God in His repeated retreats to the wilderness to pray,[1] His determination to do only what the Father gave Him to do,[2] the power of the Holy Spirit to perform miracles,[3] and the compassion of the Father to extend mercy to sinners.[4]

Yet, during this life, a shadow darkened the path between Him and His Father—the shadow of the cross. It was not a shadow of His making or of the Father's making. It was a shadow created by Adam and his children, the shadow of the world's sin that God must put away if He was to provide a way so that we who were dead to Him and alive to sin could die to sin and live to Him.

While this perfect Man lived His perfect life in fellowship with His Father, a day came when the Father had to sever that fellowship and lay His wrath for the sins of the world upon Him. To use Paul's words, Christ became a "curse for us" (Galatians 3:13). But once He made the sacrifice, He rose again to an immortal life and could *live to God* with new possibilities, unhindered by the shadow of our sin. He died to sin, Paul says in Romans 6:10, but He did this once for all. He never has to submit to the ordeal again! It is finished! And now that He has completed that heroic deed, that epoch-changing, sin-shattering, reversal-of-Adam's-transgression act of obedience on the cross, He has risen to a new, immortal life. The shadow has disappeared in the brilliant light of His resurrection, and He can enter into a new phase of ministry.

Jesus hinted at this on the road to Emmaus: "O foolish men and slow of heart to believe in all that the prophets have spoken! Was it not necessary for the Christ to suffer these things and to enter into His glory?" (Luke 24:25–26). I do not think Jesus was merely saying He had to die and once He died and rose He would go back to heaven. If we think this way, we are completely missing Jesus' point. Jesus was talking about something dear to the hearts of the Jewish people—the hope of the Messiah's *glorious reign* that carried with it the promise of exaltation for God's people and deliverance from enemies.

Many hoped Jesus was that Messiah, but His shameful death at the hands of the Roman and Jewish leaders killed that idea—until He rose! And Jesus explained to these men that according to Scripture, the Messiah had to suffer first and then He could enter into His glory—that is, His glorious Messianic reign as the prophecies foretold.

Paul also gives a glimpse of this perspective on the Messiah's current life to God. Standing before Herod Agrippa, he said, "So, having obtained help from God, I stand to this day testifying both to small and great, stating nothing but what the Prophets and Moses said was going to take place; that the Christ was to suffer, and that by reason of His resurrection from the dead He would be the first to proclaim light both to the Jewish people and to the Gentiles" (Acts 26:22–23).

The Prophets and Moses said the Messiah would suffer and then, after the resurrection, He would proclaim light to Israel and all the nations. We do not see a passive Messiah "resting in heaven" after the ordeal of the cross. Instead, we see an active Messiah who is at the forefront of a worldwide mission to all the descendants of Adam—all the nations of the world.

He is active in His glorious reign. But this is getting a bit ahead. I want to return to Paul's statement in 6:10: "The life that He lives, He lives to God." The resurrected Jesus now lives to God, unhindered by any burden with unlimited, eternal potential. It is the truth of this unlimited, eternal potential, this glorious Messianic reign, this living to God I want to unpack. Once we see how He lives to God, we will understand how we—*in the same way*—can be alive to God in this life and have greater resources in our fight against sin.

THE HAND OF EXALTATION

For Jesus to live to God today means He lives under the exalting hand of God. He receives nothing from the hand of His Father except vindication, praise, and exaltation. This is possible because the sin-bearing, curse-receiving part of His life is finished. With the shadow of our guilt forever gone, the Father is free to exalt Christ with unhindered pleasure. How many times during Jesus' earthly ministry did the Father want to exonerate Christ when He had to endure the countless objections of the religious rulers? How many times did the Father want to direct the hearts of His people to the praise and honor of the Son only to hear doubts, the questioning of the multitudes, and the confusion of the disciples?

Jesus said He could call upon His Father and the Father would give Him legions of angels to rescue Him. But the Father never heard that call from His Son, and it grievously pleased the Father not to hear that call as He watched Jesus trudge step by step in self-denial—the steps the Father Himself ordained. How much did the Father endure as He saw His Son agonize over our sin and endure pain and mocking? How did the Father feel when the Son cried out, "Is there any other way? Do I have to drink this cup?"

And the Father could only remain silent, leaving His Son to draw the conclusion: "There is no other way." The Father watched as the Son, His heart of hearts, the eternal Word, the one who was in His bosom before the creation of the world, took one obedient step after another, descending to greater depths of humility. All along, the Father loved the Son and wanted to vindicate Him, but His plan was to humble Him, bruise Him, and punish Him. What was it like for the Father to make the Son to become sin on our behalf—to make the pure, spotless, eternal one impure, tainted, flawed, and worthy of death?

We will never enter the depths of the Father's and Son's thinking on these matters. Surely they are reserved only for God. But one thought we can share with God is that it has all ended. What Christ did was enough, and the Father and the Son never have to do anything in relation to sin and guilt anymore. Death is no longer master over Him! The death that He died, He died to sin once for all! But…the life He now lives He lives to God! Death to sin was a one-time event. The resurrection opened the door to a continuous life with no more shackles, hindrances, shadows, or burdens to pay for the sin of humanity.

The Father is now free to do things for the Son that He could not do until the cross was out of the way. Now, the Father can exalt Him to the highest place and give Him glory. Here is the way the apostles put it:

Peter– "The God of Abraham, Isaac and Jacob…has glorified His servant Jesus" (Acts 3:13).

Paul– "God highly exalted Him, and bestowed on Him the name which is above every name, so that at the name of Jesus every knee will bow, of those who are in heaven and on earth and under the earth, and that every tongue will confess that Jesus Christ is Lord, to the glory of God the Father" (Philippians 2:9–11).

Peter– "[God] raised Him from the dead and gave Him glory" (1 Peter 1:21).

The writer of Hebrews – "Jesus, because of the suffering of death [has now been] crowned with glory and honor" (Hebrews 2:9).

John– "I looked, and I heard the voice of many angels around the throne and the living creatures and the elders; and the number of them was myriads of myriads, and thousands of thousands, saying with a loud voice, 'Worthy is the Lamb that was slain to receive power and riches and wisdom and might and honor and glory and blessing.' And every created thing which is in heaven and on the earth and under the earth and on the sea, and all things in them, I heard saying, 'To Him who sits on the throne, and to the Lamb, be blessing and honor and glory and dominion forever and ever" (Revelation 5:11–13).

Today, heaven resounds with praise to the Lamb. For Jesus to live to God means that He now lives under the praise-giving, eternally exalting hand of God! The hand that once offered a cup of wrath now holds a crown of glory. And here's the joy for us. Paul said, "In the same way, consider yourselves alive to God!" In the same way! In the same way that the risen Jesus no longer lives under the hand of wrath but under the hand of exaltation, you no longer live under the hand of God's wrath but under the hand of His exaltation and joy because you have been crucified with Him, buried with Him, and raised with Him!

A shadow once loomed between the Father and us. Even though He loved us and even though He created us in His image, our sin demanded that we die because the wages of sin is death. But now that He has extinguished the shadow of our sin by the cross of Christ, now that He has severed our solidarity with Adam, now that He has nullified the body of evidence, and now that He has acquitted us, we no longer have to approach God with any hint of condemnation, guilt, or sin.

We are like the three Jewish men who endured the fires of Nebuchadnezzar's wrath. When they walked out of the furnace, their shackles were gone, and no odor or hint of fire, smoke, or singed flesh was upon them. In the same way, as we approach God today, we have no hint or odor of guilt or condemnation upon us because we died to sin with Christ and have risen to live to God in the same way that Christ lives to God.

This sounds like God offers us exaltation in the same way He exalted Christ. Surely this cannot be true. But it is. Many New Testament passages point to our future glory in Christ:

"We exult in hope of the glory of God" (Romans 5:2).

"But we speak God's wisdom in a mystery, the hidden wisdom which God predestined before the ages to our glory" (1 Corinthians 2:7).

"For momentary, light affliction is producing for us an eternal weight of glory far beyond all comparison" (2 Corinthians 4:17).

"It was for this He called you through our gospel, that you may gain the glory of our Lord Jesus Christ" (2 Thessalonians 2:14).

"For this reason I endure all things for the sake of those who are chosen, that they also may obtain the salvation which is in Christ Jesus and with it eternal glory" (2 Timothy 2:10).

Everything we gained in Adam—sin, guilt, condemnation, death—we lost in Christ. God crucified and buried our old solidarity with Adam. God destroyed the body of sinful evidence against us.

Everything we lost in Adam—dominion over the world, glory, honor, the full image of God—we have regained in Christ. God raised us with Christ and seated us with Him in heavenly places (Ephesians 2:5–6). And just as Christ now lives in this way—under the exalting hand of God—we are to consider ourselves as living in the same way—under the exalting hand of God on the road to eternal glory.

No shadow remains between God and us, and just as God exalted Jesus, so He will exalt us some day, and He works in our lives toward that goal. Paul put it this way: "But we all, with unveiled face, beholding as in a mirror the glory of the Lord, are being transformed into the same image from glory to glory, just as from the Lord, the Spirit" (2 Corinthians 3:18). From glory to glory— this means we have not yet arrived. We are in process. We are on a journey, but the final destination is one of praise, honor, and glory from the Father.[5]

But how does this help us today in our fight with sinful desires? How does this help us break deeply ingrained habits? When we consider the truth that we are to consider ourselves alive to God in same way that Christ is alive to God, we realize we don't have to come to God as a troubled sinner. Instead, He expects us to come to Him with the attitude of a justified, exalted, glory-bound image bearer, even though we still have failures and struggles with our sin. This is what it means to present ourselves to Him as ones who are alive from the dead.

It doesn't mean that we hide our sins, deny that we have problems, or try to trick God or ourselves into thinking something not true. We are aware of our issues, and God is even more aware of them, but when we come to Him, we do not come as condemned sinners but as justified family members of God. And when we view ourselves in this way, we will increasingly see that we have no use for those things that are not worthy of Him, not worthy of us, and not worthy of our destiny.

Paul asked, "Shall we continue in sin that grace may abound?" God forbid! How shall we who died to the penalty of sin, who have had our Adam-solidarity broken, who have been set free from death row, who no longer have any evidence against us, continue in a sinful lifestyle? It doesn't make sense.

And God did more than cause us to die to sin. He made us alive with Christ. God raised us with Him to walk in newness of life. Just as Christ now lives to God, we too are to consider ourselves alive to God, completely guilt-free and with a righteous status before Him. Just as Christ now lives to God and can receive God's exalted blessings, we too can approach God to receive His hand of blessing and set off on a journey that will end in glory and exaltation.[6] Why continue in sin? Why indulge in sin? Why eat from the table of the world's processed, fat-filled diet that breeds bad health, bad habits, and a bad heart when God prepares a banquet for us that is nutritious, life-giving, and wholesome?

This, then, is a major reason many Christians have trouble with bad habits and indulge in sin: They don't know the destiny to which God calls them. They don't know their standing before God as guilt-finished, righteous-standing, glory-bound children. And not knowing their status or their destiny, they still hang around the prison yard with old prison buddies because they don't know anything else. They don't know they are free.

In a sad scene from the movie *Shawshank Redemption*, one of the inmates finishes his prison sentence. He is free, but he doesn't know what to do. He doesn't really want to leave prison because that is all he has known for the past decades. His only friends live there. He tries his new life. He has a job at a grocery store but is socially awkward, and being old, he is a little slow on the uptake of his responsibilities. He lives in an apartment by himself with no one to turn to. Finally, he can't take it anymore. He is not allowed back in prison—his only home—and he can't make it on the outside. He ends up hanging himself.

Many Christians live the sad life of that man. They don't know the new life Christ offers. They never quite realize they have a new status with God and are alive to Him—alive to a new purpose of joy, destiny, and glory just as Christ lives to God's purposes of exalting Him. And because they don't realize their new life is to mirror Christ's new life, they find themselves struggling with old habits picked up while they served time in prison.

Some Christians never quite get the point that they are free. They still think God must, in some way or on some point, have something against them. "It can't really be true that I'm completely forgiven, can it? It can't really be true that I'm under no condemnation, can it? It can't really be true that all the evidence against me has been erased, can it? It can't really be true that the Father sees me as alive in Him, can it? It can't really be true that I am to consider myself alive to God in the same way that Christ is alive to God, can it? It can't really be true that God will one day exalt me the same way He has exalted Christ, can it? It can't really be true God has nothing but praise, honor, and exaltation in store for me and that His thoughts for me are always good, can it?"

And so we keep talking ourselves into doubt and unbelief, lingering in an in-between world of shadows and alternating between the lie of condemnation and the truth of justification. Not that such a world exists, except in our mind. We know Christ has done something for us, but we can't quite get our heart to believe that we have been completely forgiven, justified, and commanded to consider ourselves alive to God in the same way that Christ is now alive to God.

But when we do, when we wrap our mind and heart around this truth that we are just as dead to sin as Christ is dead to sin and God invites us to present ourselves to Him as ones alive from the dead, then we will have greater power over sinful temptations, tendencies, and habits. The way to overcome the pull of gravity is to introduce a greater pull that lifts us away from its influence. Like the rocket fuel that propelled the space shuttle into orbit, the death and resurrection of Christ propels us away from the gravity of sin. Paul exhorts us to fill ourselves with this fuel by continually considering ourselves dead to the penalty of sin and alive to the exalting purposes of God in the same way that Christ died to sin and now lives to God.

The Hand of Authority

There is more to the phrase, "the life that He [now] lives"—more that will help us understand the life to which He calls us. Jesus not only lives under God's exalting hand, He also lives under God's empowering and authority-giving hand. Once again, we turn to Paul's classic statement in Philippians 2:9–11: "For this reason also, God highly exalted Him, and bestowed on Him the name which is above every name, so that at the name of Jesus every knee should bow, of those who are in heaven and on earth and under the earth, and that every tongue will confess that Jesus Christ is Lord, to the glory of God the Father."

When God resurrected and exalted Jesus, He bestowed something upon Him—a name. The name is above every other name and will one day cause every knee to bow. What is the name? It is actually a title—the title of Lord. Other New Testament passages and writers express this same truth. To the apostles Jesus said all authority in heaven and on earth had been given to Him (Matthew 28:18). In the first post-resurrection sermon, Peter preached that God made Jesus Lord (Acts 2:36).

God bestowed a name upon Christ after His death and resurrection. God made Him Lord. God gave Him all authority. These verses point to a new experience for Christ or a new status that He gained after His death and resurrection. But didn't Christ have these before the cross? If He was the eternal Word through whom God made the world, wasn't He Lord then? Obviously He was, and obviously He did have power and authority. We see in His ministry in Israel works of power. Jesus attributed these to the kingdom of God—the arrival and inauguration of God's reign on the earth. "If I cast out demons by the Spirit of God, then the kingdom [kingly authority] of God has come upon you" (Matthew 12:28).

When Jesus forgave sinners, He created a stir in Israel. "Only God has such authority the religious," the experts cried. But in order to prove He had authority to forgive, He healed a paralyzed man (Mark 2:1–12). And when He taught, He did not teach like others in His day. His teaching was with authority (Matthew 7:29).

Even the events leading up to the cross and the cross itself were acts of power. Jesus said no one took His life from Him but He laid it down of His own authority (John 10:17–18). And Paul would later gain the insight that the cross—the great event of apparent weakness—was actually an event of power (1 Corinthians 1:18–24). Power and authority—these were hallmarks of Jesus' ministry in Israel.

But something happened after His once-for-all death and glorious rising. When Jesus ascended into heaven, God enthroned Him as Lord of all at His right hand. Two Messianic promises give us insight about this event. The first is Psalm 2. In this psalm, we find the nations of the world rebelling against God's authority (2:1–3). But God laughs at such a ridiculous endeavor. In response to mankind's futile efforts, God installs His Messianic king (2:4–6). Then in 2:7–9 the Messianic king tells us what Yahweh said to Him. Yahweh said He would make Him His Son, He would give Him the ends of the earth, and He would rule over the nations. In light of this reality, all nations are advised to submit to God's reign through His Messianic Son (2:10–12).

The second psalm is Psalm 110:1: "The LORD [*Yahweh*] says to my Lord, 'Sit at My right hand until I make Your enemies a footstool for Your feet.'" Again, we have a conversation between the Messianic king and Yahweh, and again we have a picture of the Messiah receiving authority.

New Testament writers quoted from these psalms extensively, and they pointed to the great truth that after Jesus Messiah rose from the dead, He entered into a new phase of ministry that included receiving authority from God and worldwide dominion. One of the favorite expressions of the New Testament writers is that Jesus is now at the right hand of God.[7] Not only is He at God's right hand but God has subjected all powers to Him.[8]

But that is not all there is to these verses about the Messiah receiving power. These prophecies and their fulfillment are set in a larger context or storyline. They are set within the story of the authority God bestowed upon Adam, the sin of Adam and his race whereby the delegated authority is now misused, and the love of God to pay for the sin of Adam's race and restore mankind to his proper place of ruling over a restored creation.

In Jesus Christ, the Second Adam, man receives dominion again. One perfect man now resides in the presence of God. He is everything Adam was supposed to be—and more! And when Christ finished paying for our sins—once for all—God exalted Him to this place of dominion. The writer of Hebrews put it this way: We do not yet see all things subjected to him [in other words, we still see a fallen world]. But we do see all things submitted to One Man—Jesus—crowned with glory and honor (see Hebrews 2:8–9).

And so, when Paul says, "Christ lives to God," He means that He lives under the empowering, authority bestowing hand of God. God exalted Him to His right hand, and He is enforcing His authority by subduing enemy after enemy just as Psalm 110:1 foretold. The writer of Hebrews presents the same sequence as Paul in Romans 6:10. The writer said, "But He, having offered one sacrifice for sins for all time, sat down at the right hand of God, waiting from that time onward until His enemies be made a footstool for His feet" (Hebrews 10:12–13. Paul said that the death that He died, He died to sin once for all, but the life that He lives, He lives to God.

This means Jesus lives as the perfect man for God's dominion-restoring purposes. God's ultimate plan is for redeemed humanity to rule over a restored earth. One man has attained to this position and He promises to bring the rest of us to it. This is why we find numerous references to our ruling with Christ in the future:

Luke 22:29–30 – "And just as My Father has granted Me a kingdom, I grant you that you may eat and drink at My table in My kingdom, and you will sit on thrones judging the twelve tribes of Israel."

1 Corinthians 6:2–3 – "Or do you not know that the saints will judge the world? If the world is judged by you, are you not competent to constitute the smallest law courts? Do you not know that we will judge angels? How much more matters of this life?"

1 Corinthians 4:8 – "You are already filled, you have already become rich, you have become kings without us; and indeed, I wish that you had become kings so that we also might reign with you."

2 Timothy 2:12 – "If we endure, we will also reign with Him; If we deny Him, He also will deny us."

Revelation 2:26–27 – "He who overcomes, and he who keeps my deeds until the end, to him I will give authority over the nations; and he shall rule them with a rod of iron, as the vessels of the potter are broken to pieces, as I also have received authority from My Father."

Revelation 3:21 – "He who overcomes, I will grant to him to sit down with Me on My throne, as I also overcame and sat down with My Father on His throne."

Revelation 5:9–10 – "And they sang a new song, saying, 'Worthy are You to take the book and to break its seals; for You were slain, and purchased for God with Your blood men from every tribe and tongue and people and nation. You have made them to be a kingdom and priests to our God; and they will reign upon the earth.'"

Revelation 22:4–5 – "They will see His face, and His name will be on their foreheads. And there will no longer be any night; and they will not have need of the light of a lamp nor the light of the sun, because the Lord God will illumine them; and they will reign forever and ever."

But what does this have to do with overcoming sin? Plenty! Just as Christ lives under the empowering, authority-bestowing hand of God with the goal of one day seeing redeemed humanity and a new creation in the same way (*houtos*), reckon yourself as one alive to the same purpose. Present yourself alive to God! You died to the guilt of sin with all its authority-defying, humanity-destroying, and creation-defiling effects so that you could become alive to a new purpose— the purpose of God restoring your full humanity that will one day include dominion over His renewed creation.

God is working on this purpose right now through Christ. God is working among the nations to bring all enemies beneath the feet of Jesus. But He is doing this for us as well. God is working for a day when all enemies will be beneath our feet, including all our sinful habits. God is conquering His enemies one by one throughout the world as He spreads the dominion of Christ. He wants to conquer all our enemies one by one as He spreads the dominion of Christ in our lives and restores His full image in us.

When we realize this life purpose for which Jesus lives today and realize that He calls us to consider ourselves to be alive to the same purpose and to present ourselves to Him as ones alive from the dead, why persist in rebellious attitudes and habits that are not worthy of Him? Christ calls us to nobility, authority, power, and kingship. But when we persist in sin and rebellion, we are like children who want to play with plastic toy soldiers in the mud when He calls us to join in His leadership development program. It doesn't make sense. It's time to put the toys away. It's time to quit playing games and time to present ourselves as dominion-destined children of the king. What Adam lost for us, Christ regained for us!

One of the ways sin works its way into the hearts of many of us is in the area of authority and power. Some people have a strong tendency to control. We call them "controlling people." Often they manifest this in a marriage where one partner wants to control every detail of the other. A co-worker wants to have complete control of a project. A boss micro-manages his employees and drives them to distraction. In worst case scenarios, tyrants like Nebuchadnezzar or Saddam Hussein pursue power and in the process destroy nations. In all of us, the desire to hold on to secret sins or the refusal to relinquish control is the image of God broken and twisted in us.

But when we realize that Christ has come to die to sin and to repair the damage of that sin in our lives, we gain a new perspective. Christ came to restore the image of God in us, and part of that image pertains to the use of power and authority. Christ wants to teach us the true way to use power and the true motivation for the use of power. Power and authority is for serving others. "Let the greatest among you become the servant of all," Jesus said. "I am the Lord and the Teacher, yet I am among you as one who serves!"

I wonder how many of our sinful habits stubbornly hold on because we stubbornly or fearfully refuse to give up control to God? But when we present ourselves alive to God in the same way that Christ presents Himself alive to God, we give up the misuse of authority in exchange for the proper use of authority.

Therefore, just as Christ lives to God, in the same way consider yourself alive to God. As you do, you will enter His sanctifying process of remaking His image in you. You will find old habits falling off and new habits emerging. You will find old motives dying and new motives rising in their place. You will find power for living a holy life. Why continue in sin? Sin seems such a trifling, childish way of expressing our humanity. Step into your restored humanity and become everything for which He created you in the first place. Christ died and rose again to make that possible. You have died and risen with Him.

CHAPTER EIGHT ENDNOTES

[1] Luke 5:16 – "But Jesus Himself would often slip away to the wilderness and pray."

[2] John 5:19 – "Therefore Jesus answered and was saying to them, 'Truly, truly, I say to you, the Son can do nothing of Himself, unless it is something He sees the Father doing; for whatever the Father does, these things the Son also does in like manner.'"

[3] Luke 5:17 – "And the power of the Lord was present for Him to perform healing."
Matthew 12:28 – "But if I cast out demons by the Spirit of God, then the kingdom of God has come upon you."

[4] Matthew 9:13 – "But go and learn what this means; 'I desire compassion, and not sacrifice.'"
Matthew 9:36 – "Seeing the people, He felt compassion for them, because they were distressed and dispirited like sheep without a shepherd."

[5] Paul – "[God will render] glory and honor and peace to everyone who does good, to the Jew first and also to the Greek" (Romans 2:10).
Peter – "So that the proof of your faith, being more precious than gold which is perishable, even though tested by fire, may be found to result in praise and glory and honor at the revelation of Jesus Christ" (1 Peter 1:7).

[6] This is not to say that we can demand health and wealth – "to live like a king" – as some erroneously teach today. This side of glory, we are called to a sacrificial life, and it will sometimes involve suffering. We are to pick up our cross and follow Him in a life of service to others. We are to say "no" to sin in light of the destiny that is before us because of our status as ones who are alive from the dead.

[7] See Luke 22:69; Acts 7:55; Romans 8:34; Ephesians 1:20; Colossians 3:1; Hebrews 1:3; and 1 Peter 3:22.

[8] See Ephesians 1:22 and 1 Peter 3:22.

DO NOT LET SIN REIGN

> Therefore do not let sin reign in your mortal body so that you obey its
> lusts.
>
> ROMANS 6:12

WE HAVE TRAVELLED SO FAR AND LEARNED SO MUCH. We have learned that Jesus
Christ died and rose for us. We have died and risen with Him.

We have learned that when He died for us, He put away the guilt of our sin
forever. When we died with Him, we died to that guilt and our old status in
Adam. God destroyed the body of sinful evidence accumulated against us and
freed us from the prison house of our sin.

We have learned that when He rose, He entered into a new phase of ministry in His relationship with God. Now that He has once for all dealt with sin,
He can live completely, in an unhindered way to God's exalting and empowering
hand. The work started in Israel can spread to the whole world.

We rose with Him, and just as Jesus completely lives to God for His worldwide kingdom purposes, we are to present ourselves alive to God—alive to the
same goals and the same exalting and empowering hand. He has forever
destroyed sin, darkness, death, and guilt. No shadow stands between God and
us. We are to consider ourselves alive to Him in the same way that Christ is
now alive to God.

In light of this great truth, what next step can we take? Paul tells us in
6:12:"Therefore do not let sin reign in your mortal body so that you obey its
lusts."

I like the word "therefore." A thousand times I have heard the corny saying,
"If you see the word "therefore," you have to find out what it is *there for*." Let
me make it 1,001 even though, in addition to corniness, I am going to have to
commit the grammatical sin of ending the next sentence with a preposition.
What is the "therefore" in 6:12 there for? And we know the obvious answer. It
is there to connect Paul's previous thought with his next one.

Here is the connection: *In light of this great truth* that you have died to sin and are alive to God in the same way that Christ died to sin and is alive to God, *you must not let sin have its way in your life.* This is what we are looking for, praying for, and hoping for—an answer to the dilemma that plagues God's people— sinful tendencies and habits that bring grief to us, not to mention grief to the Holy Spirit, and grief to our loved ones. Paul tells us we are not to let sin reign in us, but notice where he grounds this exhortation. He grounds it in the death and resurrection of Christ and our crucifixion and resurrection with Him. We are not to let sin reign (6:12) because we have died and risen with Him (6:11).

One of the ways sin gains mastery over us is that we keep hanging around the prison yard of guilt where we lived for so long. I have read material and heard firsthand, eyewitness reports of prison life. It is a foretaste of hell. We must not think men and women receive a prison sentence and then dutifully report to cheerful guards and a helpful system that will watch over them until their time is up when they can walk free as newly reformed, educated, productive citizens. Prison is full of sinful people often mistreated by sinful guards who work for an institutionalized form of abuse that spirals people downward into further despair and degradation.

Life without Christ is this way. Our sin locks us up in the prison of our guilt and while locked up, we learn some nasty habits and ways of living in order to survive in that dark world. But Christ set us free from the sentence that hung over us and broke down the prison door so that we could walk out to a new life.

But as we walk out of the darkness and into the light of our new life, we carry with us some old habits that we picked up in our years of slavery to sin's penalty. Paul says, "In light of the truth that you died to sin with Christ, stay away from the prison yard, the other prisoners who won't walk out, the abusive guards, and the system that destroys people. And not only are you to stay away, don't let those old habits, when they resurface, dominate your life. If you hang around the prison yard, you will reinforce those habits. If you stay away, you will have a better chance of resisting the old habits and forming new ones."

What is the prison yard? And why do some Christians continue to hang around it? The prison yard is our old guilty status in Adam where guards pick up the fragments of the shredded certificate of debt, the body of sin, and attempt to piece it to together to read to us how sinful and guilty we are. "You must come back in. You are not really free," they cry. "Yield to the system and give in to your old way of surviving here with us."

But when we realize we are not guilty anymore and that we are no longer in solidarity with Adam and his disobedience, we don't have to listen to those lies and give in to the deception that we really deserve to go back to prison. Instead, we can think about ourselves in a new way, as ones who are now justified and alive to God.

And so Paul says, "Therefore." In light of your new status as a justified family member of God, don't let sin reign in your mortal bodies that you should obey it. I find Paul's exhortation insightful for several reasons and in this chapter, I hope to unpack those reasons and share with you what I have learned and how it has helped me not to let sin reign. But first, let me share two more truths from this passage we must not ignore. They reinforce the main premise of this book.

Insight #1 – Sinful Tendencies Still Exist Within Us

I find it interesting that just one sentence after Paul said we died to sin, he says we still must not let sin reign in our mortal bodies. This reinforces one of the primary points in this book: When Paul says in Romans 6:2 and 6:11 that we died to sin, he is not talking about dying to temptation or sinful impulses arising from within. This has confused many. "If I have died to sin, why do I still feel like doing these wrong things, and why do I sometimes give in?" The answer is, "You didn't die to sinful impulses; you died to the penalty of sin."[1]

Paul's exhortation is also just a few sentences after his famous statement about the crucifixion of the old man and the destruction of our body of sin. Again, in the popular exposition of 6:6, preachers, pastors, and commentators equate the old man with something inside us, an old nature, an appendage, something ungodly and unnatural that we inherited from Adam and that will never improve. Somehow, that old nature or old thing got nailed to the cross.

In addition, our body of sin, commonly interpreted as a synonym for our old nature,[2] or the totality of our sinful nature,[3] or the sinful tendencies in our physical body[4] was nullified or cancelled so that we could have freedom over the tyranny of sinful habits. But then, if God nullified the body of sin, what happened? Why do I still feel these lustful urges, give in to gossip, feel jealous, pout, or lose my temper? The answer is: Nothing inside you was crucified. Your body of sin is not a synonym for the old man and has nothing to do with your physical body and the temptations you can feel in it.

Notice, instead, according to Romans 6:12, Paul expects sin to raise itself within us so that he must warn the believer. Hardly a breath passes between Paul's telling us to reckon ourselves dead to sin and then telling us not to let sin reign. This doesn't seem to produce any anxiety within Paul—the fact that people will still have to say no to sin and that sin might gain such a foothold in the lives of those who have died to sin that sin could still be said to reign! But that is because Paul understands the difference between justification and sanctification and (obviously) he knows the meaning of 6:1–11.

One of the great misfortunes of the incorrect interpretation of Romans 6:6 and the surrounding verses is that many Christians, having thought they had extinguished sin in their lives through a new experience (usually the Eradication Theory with its accompanying second blessing) or a new understanding of the passage (usually the Counteraction Theory) have come to grief and disillusionment when they realized that sin was still there.

Consider this example from the life of one of the greatest preachers and pastors in Christian history who thought that by receiving a second blessing, he could eradicate all sinful impulses within him.

"Dr. H.A. Ironside…paints a sorry picture of his own inner torture, and that of other Christian workers, brought up during earlier years in the eradication doctrine. If ever a young man sincerely handed himself over to Christ, and reverently 'claimed the blessing,' and intensively persevered to experience the eradication of inbred sin, he did. Yet at last, exhausted after years of painful trial and re-trial, he knew that any further pretence was sheer hypocrisy: and at the same time he discovered that others around him who professed 'the blessing' were similarly heartsick with secret agony of disillusionment."

Dr. Ironside tells how he continually sought the blessing, until: "At last, one Saturday night…I determined to go out into the country and wait on God, not returning till I had received the blessing of perfect love. I took a train at eleven o'clock, and went to a lonely station twelve miles from Los Angeles. There I alighted, and leaving the highway, descended into an empty *arroyo*, or water-course. Falling on my knees beneath a sycamore tree, I prayed in an agony for hours, beseeching God to show me anything that hindered my reception of the blessing. Various matters of too private and sacred a nature to be here related came to my mind. I struggled against conviction, but finally ended by crying,

'Lord, I give up all—everything, every person, every enjoyment, that would hinder my living alone for Thee. Now give me, I pray Thee, the blessing.'

"As I look back, I believe I was fully surrendered to the will of God at that moment, so far as I understood it. But my brain and nerves were unstrung by the long midnight vigil and the intense anxiety of previous months, and I fell almost fainting to the ground. Then a holy ecstasy seemed to thrill all my being. This I thought was the coming into my heart of the Comforter. I cried out in confidence, 'Lord, I believe Thou dost come in. Thou dost cleanse and purify me from all sin. I claim it now. The work is done. I am sanctified by Thy blood. Thou dost make me holy. I believe! I believe!' I was unspeakably happy. I felt that all my struggles were ended."

From then onwards, young Ironside was an earnest testimonial and advocate of the doctrine. The wilderness was past; he was in Canaan; he was "entirely sanctified"; inward sin-bias was now "destroyed"—or so he thought. But as time went on, evil desires began to reassert themselves. He was nonplussed. However, a leading teacher assured him that these were only "temptations," not actual sin; so that pacified him for a time. During those years there were tormenting relapses, full nights of prayer, renewed struggles after self-crucifixion, with inescapable evidence that the supposed eradication of his "sinful nature" was a delusive sophism.

He writes: "And now I began to see what a string of derelicts this holiness teaching left in its train. I could count scores of persons who had gone into utter infidelity because of it. They always gave the same reason: 'I tried it all. I found it a failure. So I concluded the Bible teaching was all a delusion, and religion was a mere matter of the emotions.' Many more (and I knew several such intimately) lapsed into insanity after floundering in the morass of this emotional religion for years—and people said that studying the Bible had driven them crazy. At last I became so troubled I could not go on with my work…Finally, I could bear it no longer, so I asked to be relieved from all active service, and at my own request was sent to the Beulah Home of Rest, near Oakland."

I cannot help bowing my head in reverence at such an example of a man seeking God! Yet, what a struggle, and it almost ended in disaster, and for some, it did lead to emotional breakdown and spiritual bankruptcy as they tried to align a spiritual experience with an incorrect view of Romans 6 and with the reality of sinful impulses rising from within. Thankfully, his story had a happy ending as Ironside realized that sin was not eradicated within him. Ironside came to learn this: "Quiet, unassuming Christians, who know their Bibles and their own hearts too well to permit their lips to talk of sinlessness and perfection in the flesh, nevertheless are characterized by intense devotion to the Lord Jesus Christ, love for the Word of God, and holiness of life and walk."[5]

The same is true for the Counteraction Theory—the more popular teaching of Romans 6 today. I have heard glowing reports from people having experiences where their supposed sin nature was crucified with Christ and their subsequent new walk of victory over sin. Here is an example:

"For a couple of agonizing hours I lay on the floor behind my desk. It was almost 2 A.M. and I had no tears left. The pressure of anxiety that had built up over the previous year had been released in this unexpected burst of emotion. Now I just felt tired and empty. In the stillness of the early morning hour, my thoughts turned to a piece of paper that someone had given me a few weeks earlier. I reached up to my computer desk, took the sheet, and began to read it. It was a quotation about absolute surrender to God. On one side was a list of things to commit to God. On the other side was a list of rights to give up…I took that paper and began to pray my way down the list. 'Lord, I'm tired of struggling for victory in my own life and I am tired of striving for success in my ministry.'

"As I continued to pray, I chose to lay aside everything that had brought me a sense of worth: my efforts to have a growing church, my hunger for affirmation in ministry, my education, and my experience. As I came to the bottom of the list, I read this paragraph:

'I give God permission to do anything He wishes to me, with me, in me, or through me that would glorify Him. I once claimed these rights as mine, but now they belong to God and are under His control. He can do with them anything He pleases.'

"Although I didn't understand the full implications of absolute surrender, I signed my name below that paragraph. I sense that this night was a turning point in my life and ministry. Before I finally went home to sleep, I wrote these words in my spiritual journal:

'On this morning between midnight and 2:00 A.M., God's Holy Spirit has done a redemptive work in my heart by consuming me with Himself. Details are too personal and sacred to even write, but it is a work of His grace in me like nothing I have ever known in over eighteen years. May this be my 'Ebenezer' to mark the moment of a life altering encounter with Him.'"[6]

I have a love/hate relationship with the above stories. I love them because I read about men of God who earnestly sought the Lord. They are examples for all of us. I love McVey's story because I read of a God who met with him and blessed him in great ways. God is full of grace! I have no doubt his experience was a genuine encounter with the Holy Spirit and it changed his life and, as he said, was a turning point. I wish all of God's people would seek God this earnestly!

But I have a problem with the stories. I have a problem with their explanation of what happened to them. Listen to how McVey explains his: "Within days after that night of absolute surrender in my office, God began to reveal the truths of my identity in Christ. I understood that when I was saved, He had given me a new nature. For the first time I knew that my old man really was dead."[7]

There it is. He has a genuine experience with the Spirit of God, but he wrongly interprets it as a revelation that an old man residing inside him really was dead and that God gave him a new nature. Earlier, he stated this about his experience: "When God began to teach me about my identity in Christ, the truth about the death of my old nature was the most difficult thing for me to accept…I thought that my old nature *felt* very much alive. But the truth is that the old Steve—the person I was before I was saved is dead. I really wrestled with this fact. And even when God revealed the truth to me, I couldn't understand *how* it could be true."[8]

"Paul says that the old has 'passed away.' You know what it means when someone has 'passed away.' To put it plain, they're dead. That's what happened to our old sin nature. It passed away and is never coming back."[9]

It sounds like all of his problems were solved; yet, just a few pages later, lest anyone think that he was claiming sinless perfection, McVey says, "Does this mean that Christians will enjoy sinless perfection? Of course not. Our old nature was put to death with Jesus at the cross, but there is another obstacle to a victorious lifestyle that we must understand. While the old man is dead, the flesh is still an enemy to be reckoned with every day."[10]

What? I thought sin came from the old man, but now there is another enemy we have to fight called "the flesh"? McVey defines the flesh as "the techniques we use to try to meet our needs, independent of Jesus Christ."[11]

definition of "the flesh"

I have no problem with that definition—I think it is a good one. But, I ask, if Scripture teaches that the old man is crucified based upon such passages as Romans 6:6 and Galatians 2:20, what about Galatians 5:24 that says "those who belong to Christ Jesus have crucified the flesh with its passions and desires"? If the cross of Christ dealt with the old man, why did it not deal with "the flesh"? If the old man is completely dead because of crucifixion with Christ, why do we still have to fight the flesh if it has been crucified with Christ?[12] Why do we still find present, in McVey's words: "techniques to meet our needs, independent of Jesus Christ"?

I want to repeat that I honor such men who seek God for His full blessing and who surrender everything to Him, and I do not doubt for one moment their experience with God and the greater victory in life. But I do not accept their interpretation of what happened and their linkage of their experience with Romans 6 and other co-crucifixion verses. I myself tried for years to "reckon my old man dead." I did this sincerely and with faith, but still found that "old man" stubbornly hanging around long after I thought he had died and been buried!

I share these stories for two reasons. First, they illustrate the truth that even the best among us still have sin residing within. No eradication of the old sin nature experience, second-blessing experience, or reckoning-my-old-nature-dead experience can nullify the fact that sin still resides inside us and will threaten to reign over us if we are not careful, *as Paul says in 6:12.*

Second, I share it because even though some, like H.A. Ironside, eventually learned the truth of God's Word, some people never do and they end up disillusioned or walking away from the faith as he described.

I don't want that to happen to anyone. And for this reason, even though at this moment in this chapter all may sound rather bleak as if Christ only paid for our sins and has nothing more for us to empower us, I share these stories and these preliminary points to protect us from such disillusionment. Stott warns that this faulty teaching causes believers, eventually, to be "torn between their interpretation of Scripture and their empirical experience. As a result, some of them begin to doubt the truth of God's Word, while others, in order to maintain their interpretation, resort even to dishonesty about their experience."[13]

I also want us to be honest with the text. If those old interpretations and second blessing experiences or counteraction experiences are correct, why would Paul say what he says in 6:12: Don't let sin reign in your body? How redundant would that be? "Reckon yourselves dead to sin and alive to God, and, oh, by the way, don't let sin reign in you."

That would be like a father telling his young children, "Kids, don't be afraid. I killed that ugly, old monster in the back yard. I threw him in the garbage can, and the city picked him up and buried him in the landfill far away. And, oh, by the way, when you go to bed tonight, look under your bed to make sure he isn't waiting there for you. And if he does come out from under the bed tonight to bother you, just believe that he doesn't exist, "reckon" him dead, and he'll go away and leave you alone." What?!

Insight #2 – Paul Speaks About the Physical Body

Notice what Paul says in 6:12: "Do not let sin reign in your **mortal** body." Why did Paul think it necessary to use an adjective to describe what kind of body he was talking about in 6:12? Throughout his letters, Paul frequently uses the word "body" to refer simply to our physical body. For example, in 1 Corinthians 6:19 Paul says, "Don't you know that your body is a temple of the Holy Spirit?" Every reader knows he is talking about our physical body, and he has no need to define it. In just a few chapters from Romans 6, Paul will urge the believers to offer their bodies as a living sacrifice to God. Again, there is no need to define what body he is talking about.

But when he wants to use "body" in a different way, in a metaphorical way, or to refer to Christ's body, he often adds an adjective or phrase to give it a new meaning. Thus, we have in the New Testament, these uses for "body":

- *the body of Christ* to refer to the church,[14]
- *the body is of Christ* to refer to the totality of who Christ is and what He has done, i.e., the substance that casts the shadows and types in the Old Testament,[15]
- *the body and blood of the Lord* to refer to Christ's physical body.[16]
- And, of course, as we have learned in this book, we have *the body of the flesh* in Colossians 2:11 and *the body of sin* in Romans 6:6 to refer to the legal document, the certificate of death that charged us with our crimes against God and humanity.

Here in Romans 6:12, we find one of the few places[17] where he uses an adjective to describe the physical body, using the word "mortal."[18] And why does he do so? Because he wants to distinguish our physical body from the metaphorical body of sin in 6:6. And when he speaks of our mortal body, he presents the strong exhortation that we who have died to sin must not let sin reign in our fallen, decaying, susceptible-to-temptation bodies.[19] This now brings us to the important question: How do we not let sin reign in us and over us? *We must learn to consistently and firmly say "no" to our sinful desires.*

I wish I could say that I have a magic pill or a principle that once swallowed or applied will give us complete victory for the rest of our lives. In my own struggles with sin, I have had to learn a hard and bitter lesson: There is no magic pill that will give me effortless victory over temptation all the time. There is no verse I can quote that will quickly and powerfully expel the enemy as soon as I say it, all the time. There is no experience that will lift me above every vice so that it will never again have any pull on me.

That was a hard lesson to learn because I kept hoping that someone or something would help me attain to a level of effortless, consistent obedience. And the ensuing lesson was equally hard: Sometimes I just had to say "no" in spite of every fiber of my body or heart saying, "indulge." It doesn't feel good to say no. It doesn't feel good to give up that extra helping of food when I know to pile it on my plate means the sin of gluttony. It doesn't feel good to turn my eyes away from a beautiful woman when I want to linger over her face and form. Sometimes, it's just hard to say no. But we must do it.

Please don't misunderstand. I'm not saying it's always like this. I experience wonderful seasons of victory when sin doesn't have any hold on me. During those times, the desire to fulfill my God-given needs in unrighteous ways seems ludicrous. Sin is distasteful, illogical, and a dishonor to God. I turn away from it with ease on many occasions. And I see progress in my life in numerous ways for which I praise my Savior and His grace. I have had mountaintop experiences with the Holy Spirit where I have completely surrendered. These experiences have lifted me to new levels of obedience to Christ, relying on Him, and walking in the power of the Spirit. But I have learned never to think that I have arrived.

And I have learned from God's Word, contrary to centuries of teaching, that my "old man" and "flesh" are not some entities inside me that were somehow mystically crucified with Christ by a second blessing or that I have to keep dead by reckoning them dead. Because I have learned what the old man and the flesh are, I have also learned not to be surprised when sinful desires rear their ugly head within me. I have learned God is still sanctifying my human nature and conforming me to Christ. The job is not done, and God is still at work within.

I have learned that just as I have seasons of victory, I can still have new seasons of temptation where I have to fight sinful desires and sometimes I just have to say "no" to sin. And in times like this I have learned that it is a benefit not to have to question my Holy Spirit experiences or to ask, "What's wrong with me? I thought my old man was dead?"

When you're in hand-to-hand combat, you really don't want to waste energy wondering why you're in hand-to-hand combat. You just want to fight for all you're worth! Saying no is often unsatisfying and can even be painful, but I have learned to say "no" in faith that there will be a greater "yes" in the future. If I say "no" to unrighteousness in the present, I say it in the faith that something better is waiting for me in the future. And after I make the hard choices, I discover that the pain of denying myself diminishes, and in time God fills me with greater joy.

Paul presents this step to those he is teaching in Rome. Christ died to sin. So did you. Christ lives to God. So do you! In light of this amazing truth that you are legally free from sin, justified, and alive to God, when sin raises its ugly self within you, do not let it have its way with you. Do *not*! Say "no" to it because you have a greater purpose in your life.

We see that Paul's first command, actually his first two commands, when he deals with the reality of sinful temptation that arise within us, are negative commands:

1. *Do not* let sin reign.
2. *Do not* present the members of your body to sin.

Paul gives us some down-to-earth, simple wisdom: Say "no" to sin. Do *not* let it have its way in your life. And with this, many other passages in the New Testament agree.

- Romans 13:14 – Put on the Lord Jesus Christ and *make no provision* for the flesh in regard to its lusts.
- 1 Corinthians 6:18 and 2 Timothy 2:22 – *Flee* immorality. *Flee* from youthful lusts.
- 1 Corinthians 15:34 – Become sober-minded as you ought, and *stop sinning.*
- Titus 2:11–12 – The grace of God has appeared, bringing salvation to all men, instructing us to *deny ungodliness* and worldly desires.[20]
- Hebrews 12:4 – You have not yet resisted to the point of shedding blood in your *striving against sin.*
- 1 Peter 2:11 – Beloved, I urge you as aliens and strangers to *abstain from fleshly lusts* which wage war against the soul.
- 1 John 2:15 – *Do not* love the world.

"Make no provision," "flee," "stop," "deny," "say no," "strive," "abstain," "do not." We could add other verses and phrases to this list that indicate we must fight sinful desires in our body and in our soul, but these are enough to show the consistent witness of the New Testament: Sinful desires have not been eradicated or counteracted once-for-all by some experience. They are still within us, and only a daily growth in the Spirit, learning to walk with Him, and learning to fight with the weapons He provides will give us victory. One of these weapons is to learn to say "no."

DON'T LET SIN REIGN

When Paul says, "do not let sin *reign*," he is using the verb form for the word "king." Don't let sin *act as king* in your life. This provides another important lesson in overcoming sin–we can't play around with it. Sin isn't a friend. Sin is a tyrant. Sin will not be an ally. Sin will seek to dominate us. Sin will not be our servant or be a friend who lets us in the back door of an establishment so we don't have to pay the admission price. Sin will exact a full price, and more. Sin will rule over us. To employ the old proverb: If we give it an inch, it will take a mile.

The Bible presents many stories, verses, and words that show sin's dominating power. One of these is in the opening pages of the Bible in the story of Cain and Abel. After God told Cain that He did not approve of his sacrifice,

Cain became angry and depressed. God approached him asking, "Why are you angry? And why has your countenance fallen? If you do well, will not your countenance be lifted up? And if you do not do well, sin is crouching at the door; and its desire is for you, but you must master it" (Genesis 4:6–7).

What a picture! Sin is crouching at the door like a ravenous beast ready to consume. In the opening pages of his classic novel *White Fang*, Jack London presents such a picture where two men and a team of sled-pulling dogs are journeying in the wilds of Alaska. The men have only three bullets left, and hungry wolves are following! One by one, the wolves cleverly pick off the dogs during the long nights of their journey. Then, they kill one of the men and only one remains to fight off the wolves. Out of ammunition, his only weapon is fire and he surrounds himself with it, but the fire burns lower and lower and he can only stay awake for so long. Closer and closer the wolves approach, ready for the right moment to pounce and satisfy their hunger.

That is the way sin is. Sin is not a friend. Sin is a ravenous beast, always devouring—never satisfied—and its desire is to master us. Years ago a friend told me one of his favorite lines in deceiving himself about the nature of sin was: "Just one more time. I will do this only one more time." With sin, there is no "one more time." And this is why Paul said, "Do not let sin reign in your mortal body." It may approach as a friend, but it will not remain as a friend; it will dominate you and reign over you.

The middle of the Bible presents another picture of sin. It does it through the description of idolatry. Listen to how the psalmist pictures idols with their deadly results in Psalm 115:3–8:

> But our God is in the heavens; He does whatever He pleases. Their idols are silver and gold, The work of man's hands. They have mouths, but they cannot speak; They have eyes, but they cannot see; They have ears, but they cannot hear; They have noses, but they cannot smell; They have hands, but they cannot feel; They have feet, but they cannot walk; They cannot make a sound with their throat. Those who make them will become like them, Everyone who trusts in them.

God, the God of Israel, the true God, does whatever He pleases, but the idols of the nations, what can they do? They have mouths but cannot utter a word. They have eyes but are blind. They have ears, noses, hands, feet but cannot hear, smell, feel, or walk. They are nothings. And here is the shocker: Those who make them and worship them will become like them! Those who worship nothings will become nothing. Man, who is made gloriously in the image of God with amazing capacities to see, feel, hear and create, becomes just like the images he worships. He becomes nothing.

This is what sin does to us. Sin strips us of our humanity. Sin shatters the image of God within us into smaller and smaller pieces until the image is unrecognizable. We have ears but cannot hear. We have eyes but cannot see. We have mouths but cannot speak. The amazing capacities with which God has endowed us diminish until we are blind, mute, and deaf to what really matters in life. Sin destroys us. This is why Paul says, "Do not let sin reign in you." If you do, you'll find yourself in slavery to its lusts where you are doing the obeying rather than the commanding.

In a great piece of writing, Ray Bradbury pictured the work of sin in our lives. In his novel *Something Wicked This Way Comes,* he tells the story of a carnival that would mysteriously appear in different locales throughout the country. The lusts of men called it to their borders. A man named Dark ran the carnival and he paraded through the city compelling people to come to his shows. And what would he promise? He would give people whatever they wanted—for a season.

A man who lost a leg during the Great War constantly reminisces about the glory days of college when he was a football star. Another man longs for unlimited sexual encounters with exotic women. An old woman looks at her wrinkles and weeps over lost beauty. They all go to the carnival and get their wish, but with a price. The man gets his leg back, but he is no longer a man or even a college student. He becomes a little boy with a toy football and will remain that way forever. The lustful man gets his women, but then he turns into a woman himself. The old hag receives her youthful beauty and then loses her eyesight. They got what they wanted, but with a heavy price. They are Mr. Dark's slaves and they lose their humanity. The Dark Carnival preyed upon their lusts and consumed them.

Such is the nature of sin. And this is why Paul says, "Do not let sin reign in your bodies." Things may start well, but they will end in disaster. Your pleasures that you are satisfying—whether they are physical or emotional—will, in the end, make you their slave so that you will find yourself obeying those lusts, even though you don't want to. Do not present the members of your body to sin as instruments of unrighteousness. Do not!

The final picture of sin is found near the end of the Bible in 1 Peter 4:3–4: "For you have spent enough time in the past doing what pagans choose to do—living in debauchery, lust, drunkenness, orgies, carousing and detestable idolatry. They think it strange that you do not plunge with them into *the same flood of dissipation*, and they heap abuse on you" (NIV, italics mine).

The key phrase is "flood of dissipation." This is an oxymoron because dissipation means to disperse or drive away, to spend wastefully, to squander. Such things do not gain in power and create floods but do the opposite—they disperse. But Peter puts these words together to create an unforgettable picture. Sin causes dissipation in our lives, a flood of dissipation. The unraveling of our lives grows until it becomes a flood of unraveling. We break apart into ten pieces, a thousand, a million pieces, a flood of broken fragments cascading from what used to be a glorious picture of God Himself. Sin will do that to us. Sin will cause us to break apart and become something less than we wish.

No wonder Paul gives us such stern warning. Don't give in to it because it doesn't want to be your friend. It wants to be your king and dominate you so that you have no choice but to obey its lusts. Sin becomes the great narcotic, and we become slaves to its addiction.

I hope the dismal and frightening pictures of sin remain with you and help you say no. They have often helped me to say no to sin. I wish I could say that I always have said no. I haven't. But God has been gracious, forgiving, restoring, and empowering so that I say no with greater frequency. I don't want to dissipate, become a nothing, or be devoured. I want to live to God. I want to make progress in my God-given destiny as one who is alive with Christ.

Paul then gives us a helpful step in saying no when sin comes knocking on our door demanding entrance and the right to rule in our lives. Don't present the different parts of your body to sin. Keep your body away from sin. Keep your hands away from sin. Keep your eyes away from sin. Don't present your bodily organs to activities that lead to sin or that indulge in sin.

My wife once asked me if I liked the haircut of a woman who was on TV. I said yes. My wife said, "Don't you think she looks cute with it?" And I replied, "Yes, I do. And that's why I don't watch this show!" I walked away and didn't present my eyes to sin. Both of us were happy.

✳ ✳ ✳

Years ago, I won an award at work and my supervisor presented me with two tickets to a football game. During the third quarter, I watched the opposing team march up and down the field on offense. The defense couldn't stop them, until they were backed up to their own 20-yard line. Then, they stiffened and repeatedly denied the other team a touchdown or field goal. Everyone cheered for the defense. But I noticed something. I could see the defensive players sitting exhausted on the bench and some receiving oxygen. They were depleting themselves of energy, and if the offense didn't get a drive going, they would eventually allow the other team to score.

It's the same way in the Christian life. We must say no to sin, sometimes frequently. We must not let it reign in our bodies, and we must not present the members of our body to sinful thoughts or activities. We must have a good defense and know how to shut down the opposition. But we can only say "no" for so long. We must learn to have a good offense. A good offense, spiritually, is learning how to say "yes" to God and learning how to present ourselves to Him for His purposes.

This will form the focus of our next chapter: presenting ourselves to God.

CHAPTER NINE ENDNOTES

[1] "But this freedom from the dominion of sin is not the end of our struggle against sin. In fact, it is the beginning of a new conflict with it …. It remains and still is sin. What has changed is not its presence within our hearts, but its status (it no longer reigns) and our relationship to it (we are no longer its slaves)." Sinclair Ferguson, *Know Your Christian Life*, 138.

[2] Charles Hodge, *Commentary on the Epistle to the Romans* (Grand Rapids, Michigan: Eerdmans, 1976) – "The body of sin is only another name for 'the old man' or rather for its concrete form," 197.

[3] Joseph A. Fitzmeyer, *The Anchor Bible: Romans* (New York: Doubleday, 1992) – "The 'body of sin' is not merely the material part of a mortal human being, as opposed to the soul, but the whole person as considered earth-oriented, not open to God or his Spirit, and prone to sin," 436.

[4] Leon Morris, *The Epistle to the Romans*, (Grand Rapids, Michigan: Eerdmans, 1988) – "On the whole it seems that Paul is here referring to the physical body

which so easily responds to sinful impulses," 252.

[5] This story quoted by Dr. J. Sidlow Baxter, *A New Call to Holiness* (Grand Rapids, Michigan: Zondervan, 1973), 50–52. After telling this story, Baxter reports on some of John Wesley's exasperation over believers who have received the second blessing, yet who lapse back into sin. "Although many taste of that heavenly gift, deliverance from inbred sin, yet so few, so exceeding few, retain it one year; hardly one in ten; nay, one in thirty," 53.

[6] Steve McVey, *Grace Walk* (Eugene, Oregon: Harvest House, 1995), 27–28.

[7] Ibid., 65.

[8] Ibid., 56.

[9] Ibid., 59.

[10] Ibid., 92.

[11] Ibid.

[12] In this book, I do not provide a lengthy explanation of Galatians 5:16–25 and the meaning of "the flesh." However, in Appendix D I have provided a brief overview of my thoughts on "the flesh" and how it fits with the legal interpretation I propose for Romans 6:1–10.

[13] John Stott, *Men Made New* (Grand Rapids, Michigan: Baker Book House, 1988), 41.

[14] See Romans 12:5; 1 Corinthians 10:17; 11:29; 12:13, 18, 27; Ephesians 1:23; 2:16; 4:4, 12, 16; 5:30; and Colossians 1:18. Sometimes Paul will use "body" in a metaphorical way without the adjective but the context is very clear that he is using "body" in this way. For example, in 1 Corinthians 12:18 Paul says God has placed members in the body as He has desired. It is obvious from the context he is referring to the body of Christ.

[15] Colossians 2:17.

[16] 1 Corinthians 11:27

[17] The other places being 1) 1 Corinthians 15:42, 44 where he contrasts our current fallen body with our resurrection body. Our current body is perishable and natural. Our resurrection body will be imperishable and spiritual. 2)Romans 7:25 where he refers to the body of this death. Here he speaks of the body refusing to obey the good intentions of the will that desires virtue. The body indulges in sin and experiences death.

[18] "Mortal," from the Greek word, (*thneto*). Often, the NT writers use this word to refer to people who have died or are dead as in Matthew 2:20; Mark 15:44;

Luke 7:12; and Acts 14:19; 25:19. In addition to 6:12, Paul uses it to refer to our mortal bodies in Romans 8:11; 1 Corinthians 15:53–54; and 2 Corinthians 4:11; 5:4.

[19] I believe it important to say, at least in a footnote, that sin also affects our soul/spirit. Sin can reign over our minds, our emotions, and our will. Paul is not giving exhaustive treatment of human nature and the integration of the material and non-material parts of our humanity, but is merely pointing out the obvious, and often most troubling part of our human nature that falls to sin, our bodily needs.

[20] I like how the NIV renders these verses: "The grace of God…teaches us to say 'No.'"

PRESENT YOURSELVES TO GOD

And do not go on presenting the members of your body to sin as instruments of unrighteousness; but present yourselves to God as tose alive from the dead, and your members as instruments of righteousness to God.

ROMANS 6:13

ONE OF THE FRUITS OF VIEWING the concepts "old man," "body of sin," "dead to sin," and similar phrases in a legal framework is that it has helped me view myself properly. I have been able to eliminate confusion in my thinking, to devote myself to Christ and His grace, and to focus on the challenge before me to walk with Him instead of becoming introspective, distraught, and bewildered. When I speak about eliminating confusion, I'm referring to the popular teaching, alive for centuries and continuing in our day, that I have presented in this book. This teaching has promoted confusing ideas that have caused me to raise questions such as the following.

good questions:

- What sinned, my old nature or my new nature?
- If my old nature is dead, why do I still sin?
- If God gave me a new nature when I was born again, and this new nature is the life of Christ, how can that sin?
- If my new nature sins, have I reenacted the fall of Adam?
- If it is not my new nature sinning (and my old sinful nature is dead), and if it is my flesh causing me to sin, why didn't Christ deal with the flesh, also, on the cross?
- But wait, Galatians 5:24 says those who belong to Christ Jesus crucified the flesh with its passions and desires! But if we crucified the flesh, why do we still have ungodly passions and desires?
- Is the flesh still on the cross, lingering in pain—not quite dead, but still causing problems from the cross of Christ?"

I could add a few more that illustrate the confusion this way of thinking generates. And it is confusing. I have seen charts on the Christian life so complicated I wonder how anyone could even think this stuff up or figure it out!

Consider these sample statements with my questions and comments.

SAMPLE STATEMENTS: Our old nature was put to death with Jesus at the cross, but there is another obstacle to a victorious lifestyle that we must understand. While the old man is dead, the flesh is still an enemy to be reckoned with.[1]

MY QUESTIONS AND COMMENTS: Sin has two sources? The old man and the flesh? If God took the trouble to crucify the old man—one source of our sin—why didn't he crucify the other source, our flesh? But wait! The flesh with its passions and desires was crucified with Christ according to Galatians 5:24. If so, why are we not delivered from this as well as the old man?

SAMPLE STATEMENTS: But at salvation God changed our very essence; we became "partakers of the divine nature, having escaped the corruption that is in the world by lust" (2 Peter 1:4). You are no longer in the flesh; you are in Christ. You had a sinful nature before your conversion, but now you are a partaker of Christ's divine nature. You are neither eternal nor divine, but you are eternally united with Christ's divinity.[2]

MY QUESTIONS AND COMMENTS: God changed our very essence at salvation? Isn't that confusing justification and sanctification? Isn't *God changing our very essence* sanctification and a process? If I *had* a sinful nature before conversion, do I no longer *have* a sinful nature after conversion? If my nature isn't sinful, then, is it perfect? If I have partaken of Christ's divine nature, what happened to my *self*? Does my human identity still exist?

SAMPLE STATEMENTS: The new man is born in Christ's resurrection from the grave. The power of sin is now limited to the body. Flesh is a function of the brain.[3] Sin rules the spirit, soul, and body of the unregenerate person, but sin only indwells the body of the new creature in Christ.[4] Sin resides in the body. It is not in the soul or the spirit. Those two parts are the righteous new man.[5]

MY QUESTIONS AND COMMENTS: Sin is limited to the body? Sin only indwells the body of the Christian? If so, why are we to cleanse ourselves from all defilement *of the spirit* in 2 Corinthians 7:1? Why are many of the works of "the flesh" non-bodily sins such as jealousy and envy? Flesh is a function of the brain? Now we have the old man who is dead, the flesh, and the flesh working through the brain!

SAMPLE STATEMENTS: The "old man" is the old, sinful life which we inherited from Adam; all that we were before we were born again. It is the old, corrupt nature, with which we were all born and which is the cause of all our sinning, that was crucified with Christ. Christ, thus, not only deals with our sins, which are the effect of our sinful nature, but with the very cause of sinning. This is not a matter of feeling, but of fact. It is just as much a fact as that Jesus Christ was crucified.[6]

MY QUESTIONS AND COMMENTS: The old, corrupt nature was crucified with Christ, but evidently that wasn't enough because believers can still *feel* the old nature within them and must live by fact rather than feeling. Isn't this denying the obvious: we still have sinful desires within us, as the epistles clearly teach?

SAMPLE STATEMENTS: If she is to attain victory over her unique version of the flesh, she must recognize that, based on the reality of God's Word, those are not her thoughts. They are coming from her enemy, sin, waging war against her mind. No! Those are not my thoughts. I am dead to them. They're being fed to me. I choose to act dead to them because God's Word tells me that I am dead to sin.[7]

MY QUESTIONS AND COMMENTS: So…the flesh works through my brain and "sin"—to which I am dead—is feeding me with thoughts? My thoughts are not my thoughts? They don't originate from my human nature, from my own mind, but from "sin" within me? How does "sin" generate a thought and feed it to my brain? Why does Paul tell us to be transformed by the renewing of our mind in Romans 12:2?

So now we have the old man, the flesh. The old man is dead, and the flesh is not dead. Sinful thoughts do not have their source in the real me but in something called "sin personified." Sin works through the brain. Sin only resides in my body. My spirit and soul have no sin.

What is this? This is what I call *spiritual anatomical madness*. Is it really this hard to understand sin within our human nature? Do the apostles really present such a confusing picture of sin within us, yet not within us? It's here but not there. It's dead, but we have to keep it dead. It's dead, but we still have feelings from it, and we must ignore them. It works through my brain and body but not in my soul and spirit. And does it take a mystical experience or believing something in spite of the evidence so that people have to exhort us in the following way:

> When we find a promise in the Bible, we claim it. When we come to a commandment, we obey it. But when we read a truth, we believe it. The verses in Romans 6:1–11 are not commandments to obey; they are truths to be believed. Christ already died to sin, and because you are in Him, you have died to sin too. You cannot die to sin because you are already dead; you can only believe it. I've met many Christians who are still trying to die to sin, and their lives are miserable and fruitless as a result because they are struggling to do something that has already been done.[8]

> It doesn't matter whether you feel dead to sin or not; you are to consider it so because it is so. People wrongly wonder, "What experience must I have in order for this to be true?" The only necessary experience is that of Christ on the cross, which has already happened. When we choose to believe what is true about ourselves and sin, and walk on the basis of what we believe, our right relationship with sin will work out in our experience. But as long as we put our experience before our belief, we will never fully know the freedom that Christ purchased for us on the cross.[9]

crazy

Did you catch the point of this exhortation? This supposed truth of our supposed old man dying is not a promise to claim or a command to obey but a truth to believe whether we *feel dead to sin or not* and *whether our experience says so or not*. And if you don't feel it or experience it, then you are guilty of putting your experience before your belief and you must be lacking in your faith or lacking in your life or lacking in something!

I don't believe these teachers are mean-spirited and only have our best in mind, but I must protest! I must say, "Enough of this confusing, spiritual-sounding gibberish that continues generation after generation, compelling us to accept it as 'Gospel truth.'" Let us step back from it. Let us look at it objectively and see that it is not scripturally supported, is not experientially true—and not just experientially in a young, immature believer but in the lives of seasoned, godly saints—is full of inner contradictions, and it doesn't even make good sense.

How can we say to people, "It doesn't matter how you feel? You may think your old man still feels alive, but it's really dead and you must accept this by faith" when these people are struggling with sinful desires, lusts, and addictions. This is not a matter of an intermittent temptation that causes one, politely, to question his faith or a fine point of theology. We are dealing with people who struggle with sinful desires that rise up within them, and when we tell them to disregard what is really going on inside them, we are charting a course for spiritual wandering.

But we have followed these explanations and this line of thinking so long that we glibly go along with them, never stopping to ask, "Are these things really so?" We have created theological confusion and we are unwittingly harming God's people. And I must re-insert John Stott's corrective exhortation on precisely this point: [This line of thinking] "is incompatible with Christian experience…Scriptural and historical biographies, together with our own experience, combine to deny this. Far from being dead, in the sense of quiescent, our fallen nature is so alive and active that we are urged not to obey its desires, and are given the Holy Spirit to subdue and control them.

"A serious danger of this popular view is that it can easily lead to disillusion or self-deception. If we struggle to 'reckon' ourselves to be 'dead to sin' (i.e. unresponsive to it), when we know full well that we are not, we feel torn between Scripture and experience, and may then be tempted either to doubt God's Word or, in order to maintain our interpretation of it, to resort even to dishonesty about our experience."[10]

We have created confusion because the man-made theology does not match human experience and the clear teaching of the Word of God. When people detect and admit the obvious—sin is still working inside them!—and we tell them to put God's Word above their experience, or we tell them, "You don't have enough faith or you are not sincere or you may not be saved,"[11] then we are doing a great disservice to them and the rest of the Body of Christ. We did not die to sin's power inside us. Our "old man" is not something within us that the Holy Spirit crucified. We must still fight a war against sin.

The problem with this line of thinking it that it has so compartmentalized human nature that it takes a road map or a chart to figure out what goes where, what died when, and what part of us is still a problem in spite of our supposed death to sin. And then, in spite of contradictory and confusing statements by teachers, we tell our parishioners who fight against sin on a daily basis that they died to it. And when they say, "How could I have died to it? Just last night you would not believe the temptation I went through and I gave in! I thought I was dead to sin," and then we tell them, "Put the Word above your experience. You must believe!" It sounds pious. But when we say such things, we are blind guides of the blind and all of us will fall off a cliff on our journey.

However, another explanation exists that will give sight to the blind. Another path exists that will avoid the dead ends and lead to the destination of our journey: victory over sin. A simple approach exists that will sweep away the confusion of charts and the spiritual anatomical madness. It exists in black and white on the pages of Scripture in Romans 6. Look again at these portions of Romans 6:11–13: "Even so consider your*selves* to be dead to sin, but [your*selves*] alive to God in Christ Jesus.… Do not [go on] present[ing] *the members* of your body to sin…but present your*selves* to God as those alive from the dead, and *your members*…to God" (italics mine).

I italicized a few words in the preceding paragraph because I want to emphasize something we easily overlook in our familiar reading of these great verses. The "selves" that died to sin are alive to God, and we are to present these same "selves" to Him. The "selves" that are dead to sin in 6:11a are the same "selves" that are alive to God in 6:11b. The "selves" of the believer that are dead to sin in 6:11a are the same "selves" that believers are to present to Him in 6:13. Notice that we can present the members of our body to sin or present *those same members* to righteous living in 6:13.[12] Paul does not say "present your new man" or "present your new nature" to God; he says to present your "selves" and your members to God.

What is all this about? It is about understanding human nature, the way God made us, what sin did to us, and the remedy for our sinful, fallen human nature. This is the focus of this chapter to which we now turn.

ONE HUMAN NATURE

We must clear up the confusion about our human nature if we are to gain victory over sin and live a holy life for God. Let me share several clarifying points:

- Every person on the planet—saved and unsaved—has one nature. The difference between the saved and unsaved is that one has the Holy Spirit residing in his human nature because he is justified by faith and the other does not.
- Sanctification does not bring death to any facet of human nature (death to "the old man" or death to "the body of sin" as popularly interpreted). Instead, it brings life to our fallen nature and restores it for God's glory.
- Sanctification is a progressive work of God's grace that renews human nature and transforms it into the original image in which God made it.

Let me elaborate on these points. First, let's describe our human nature. God created us body, soul, and spirit.[13] We all know what the body is. The soul, I learned years ago, consists of the intellect, the will, and the emotions. The spirit is the innermost part of what we are that can commune with God at a level deeper than the mind can understand.[14] Other than these things, I don't know what human nature is. But when we start talking about our old nature and our new nature as some types of separate appendages or internal parts of us, and when we add "the flesh" to the mix, working through the brain and our body but not in our soul and spirit, have we not so fractured our understanding of how God made us that we can no longer identify what we are as humans?

In a similar vein, I must quote Dr. Baxter's refutation of this popular, but misguided and confusing teaching, which he faced in his day and which we still face in our own. First, I will present the quote that Baxter presents and then his refutation. It is worth the read! (Italicized words are Baxter's.)

THE QUOTE: "But let me now very earnestly entreat you to mark the distinction between the *heart* and the *nature*. The evil heart is not the evil nature. It is in this connection that thousands of people are making a great mistake. No wonder they get confused in the matter of sanctification. The heart is capable of passing through varying conditions. The nature remains unchanged. The heart may be cleansed, sanctified, and made the dwelling-place of God. But you cannot sanctify the evil nature. Therefore let us not confuse the heart, the evil heart, with the evil nature."

BAXTER'S REFUTATION: "Now surely this distinction here between the "heart" and the "nature" is artificial and misleading. We have looked up the 958 instances where our Authorised Version has the word "heart," and in its singular, plural, and compound forms, also the Hebrew and Greek usage; and if one thing stands out it is this: that when used in its figurative sense the heart represents, more often than anything else, either the whole mental and moral being, or the centre-point of thought, desire, will, and feeling. In a representative sense, the "heart" is the "nature," the living, self-aware human person. In a moral sense, what I am in my heart, that I am in my nature. Yet we are told that the heart may be cleansed, but not the nature!

"The speaker rightly defines the heart as 'the place within you where three things are focused—your thoughts, your desires, and your will.' On another line he calls it the inner world of intellect, emotion, volition. Now if all our thought, desire, will, intellect, emotion, volition, are the 'heart' (as he himself says) but not the 'nature,' then what can the 'nature' possibly be? What else is there in our mental and moral being beside intellect, emotion, volition, desire, and conscience? If the 'nature' is some vagary outside all these, is it worth even noticing?"[15]

Well-stated, Dr. Baxter! And I would add this point: The Bible employs all kinds of words to describe our inner experiences such as our heart, our kidneys, and our bowels. But these are expressions of the inner working of our human nature, of who we are. Different words describe the same person, but the object is always to view them in a holistic way. The Hebrew way of thinking does not radically compartmentalize us, but presents us a whole that can do evil and slide downward into corruption or do good and become godlike.

Second, what happened to us when Adam sinned? Two catastrophic consequences occurred. First, the human race became legally guilty before God. Adam's sin rendered him and us judicially unrighteous before a holy God and doomed us to judgment by the same God who cannot allow sin to prevail in His universe.[16] We have already seen in chapter three how Paul expressed this consequence of Adam's sin in Romans 5 in his extensive contrast between Adam, the old man, and Christ, the new man. This is the external result of the Fall: Man became judicially guilty before God.

The second consequence of the Fall is that our first parent's human nature (and ours by inheritance)—though fearfully and wonderfully made by God—was marred, damaged, broken, and polluted with the poison of disobedience. Man's nature did not become completely corrupted *at that moment*, but his nature in every aspect (body-soul-spirit) was severed from the life-giving grace of God. Severed from God, and having tasted the sweet but poisonous fruit of rebellion, it became highly likely that humanity would continue to indulge in the fruit of rebellion. The result is that human nature continued a downward slide away from God's holiness. This is the internal result of the Fall: man's body-soul-spirit increasingly lost its reflection of God's image and became increasingly unholy.

A mirror serves as a good illustration of human nature. A mirror reflects the image of the one standing before it. But throw a rock into the mirror and it shatters into pieces with the result that the mirror now distorts the image. It still reflects an image, but the image is now difficult to see. You can pick up shards of glass and see a portion of the original image, but only a portion. The image-producing function of the mirror no longer works as intended, and the one standing before it cannot perfectly see himself.

In the same way, human nature does not function as originally intended. It gives a distorted picture of God's nature. At best, bits and pieces provide a slender resemblance of the original. Its only hope is for a master craftsman to put the pieces together. But some do not allow the Master Craftsman to do this, and they complicate matters by continuing to throw rocks into the already broken mirror. The pieces of glass become smaller, the image harder to detect, and the work of restoration increasingly complicated. Sinful human nature is like such a mirror. For some, the mirror may only be broken into several pieces; for others, their mirror may be shattered almost beyond recognition. But whether the pieces are few or many, all of us possess a broken human nature imperfectly reflecting the image of God.

This leads to a third clarifying point: Jesus came to reverse the double effect of the Fall. First, He paid the penalty of our sin and thereby took away the con-demnation that resulted from Adam's transgression. In Romans 5, Paul contrasts the effects of Adam's sin with the effects of Jesus' obedience. He states in 5:18 that "through one act of righteousness there resulted justification of life to all men." This is the glory of the doctrine of justification. Condemnation is gone. Justice has been satisfied. God has not compromised His holy nature. He main-tains His justice, yet He is able to declare ungodly men righteous in His sight through the work of His Son, Jesus, if they will put their faith in Him![17]

Paul continues this theme in chapter 6 where he says we died to sin in the same way that Christ died to sin, God crucified our old sinful standing with Adam, He destroyed the body of sin, set us free from slavery to sin, and acquitted us.

Because we are justified, God can reverse the second effect of the Fall. Because faith-filled, baptized men are now judicially righteous before Him, God, without compromising His eternally holy nature, can reenter their fallen human nature and put together the pieces of their shattered humanity—shattered not only by Adam's transgression, but also by their own choices, rebellion, and sinful addictions. We can walk in newness of life.

This is sanctification. It is the *renewing* of our once-fallen human nature. It is the refashioning of human nature back to its original state. It is the Master Craftsman delicately putting the pieces of the mirror together. It is not a new nature given us to combat an old nature, like a new kidney put into a body where old kidneys don't work. Instead, sanctification is God coming to live within that which He created, which became distorted and polluted, but which He now reclaims by the blood of His Son.

Sanctification is the life of God reentering man so that He might put the pieces together, bit by bit, so that it might once again function as He intended. Sanctification is the sweet, life-giving, healing balm of the Spirit of Jesus that works its way through our system, cleaning out the effects of the disease of sin and reinvigorating our soul and spirit so they become healthy, functional, and, once again, image-bearing.

This is what Paul had in mind when he stated, "Now may the God of peace Himself *sanctify you entirely*; and may your spirit and soul and body be preserved complete, without blame at the coming of our Lord Jesus Christ" (1 Thessalo-nians 5:23, italics mine). Notice that Paul speaks of the totality of our human-ity—our body-soul-spirit.

He does not say these are intrinsically evil. He does not say we have two souls, two spirits, or two natures—an old one dead and buried that we must keep dead and buried and a new one "in Christ." Instead, he looks at our one human nature from various angles—body, soul, and spirit—and prays that God would do His sanctifying work on all aspects of what we are, realizing that each part of our nature will have various temptations and struggles.

Our will may struggle with wrong choices or weakness of will, our intellect may struggle with incorrect thinking or a tendency to be gullible or believe lies, our emotions may struggle with feelings unworthy of our high standing in Christ, our body may struggle with bad deeds. But the Spirit's work is to change all that. His work is to strengthen our will to stand firm for Him and make right choices. His work is to renew our minds to think right thoughts. His work is to change our emotions, ridding us of weighty baggage and liberating us to experience love and joy. His work is to teach us to yield our bodies as a living sacrifice. His work is to renew our human nature.

Several verses in the New Testament emphasize the *renew*ing of who we are by the *transformation* of our nature (italics mine).

Romans 12:2 – And do not be conformed to this world but be *transformed* by the *renewing of your mind*, so that you may prove what the will of God is, that which is good and acceptable and perfect.

2 Corinthians 3:18 – But *we* all, with unveiled face, beholding as in a mirror the glory of the Lord, *are being transformed* into the same image from glory to glory, just as from the Lord, the Spirit.

2 Corinthians 4:16 – Therefore we do not lose heart, but though our outer man is decaying, yet *our inner man is being renewed* day by day.

Ephesians 4:23 – And that you be *renewed in the spirit of your mind*.

Colossians 3:10–11 – [You] have put on the new self who is being *renewed* to a true knowledge according to the image of the One who created him— a *renewal* in which there is no distinction between Greek and Jew.

Let's make some observations on these verses. In Romans 12:2, Paul exhorts us to be transformed by the renewing of the mind. How many minds do we have? We have one mind that that we can use in different ways. With our one mind we can think as the world thinks or think like God. If we think as the world, our nature will become more like the world. If we think like God and choose His good, holy, and perfect will, we will transform our lives. The mind can move in one of two directions—downward, earthly, and sinful or upward, heavenly, and holy. But whichever direction it goes, it is our one God-given mind that is changing, and God's desire is to restore it.

Ephesians 4:23[18] speaks of an even deeper transformation. It is not merely an intellectual transformation where we replace, for example, bad theology with good theology, but a deeply spiritual transformation—*the spirit* of your mind. This is the deeper spiritual part of human nature that apprehends the nature of God in contrast to the mental part of the mind that apprehends facts. Paul speaks of it as being renewed.

Second Corinthians 3:18 says we are being transformed into Christ's image. It is a gradual process and a glorious one as we go from one degree of glory to another. God views the whole process as glorious as we increasingly reflect the image of Christ. Using the broken mirror metaphor, if the mirror is broken into 100 pieces, it is still God's mirror and is in one sense glorious. As He puts two pieces together, a new expression of God's glory emerges. When four pieces come together the glory increases, and so on, until all pieces are together, the mirror is completely functional, and the full glory of the image reveals itself.

The day-by-day process of transformation is reinforced by Paul's statement in 2 Corinthians 4:16 that the inner man is being renewed daily, and Colossians 3 speaks of a renewal in the image of the Creator. What was lost at the Fall, the Holy Spirit restores through Jesus Christ. This is the sanctification of human nature.

What is the value of seeing sanctification from this perspective? I see three benefits.

First, this view affirms God's creation. We know all things God made are good. When we look at human nature made in His image, fallen, and now in the process of restoration, we are saying God's creation is worth saving. He did not come to destroy human nature, but to save it because of the precious way He originally made it. This is quite a contrast to a teaching long ago that has continued to pervade modern thinking. The old teaching sought to emphasize that our "old nature" was not savable. Listen to this statement from a famous, godly woman: "But do not expect, dear boy, ever to find thy old nature any better or any nearer thy ideal; for thee never, never, will. Thee thyself, that is, thy old nature, will always be utterly vile, and ignorant, and corrupt; but Jesus is thy life now.[19]

But this is not what Scripture teaches. It teaches that our human nature was made in the image of God, and even though sin has grossly distorted it, God has come to redeem it and change it into the likeness of His image.

Second, this viewpoint enables us to value our humanness. If human nature is valuable to God and worth saving, it should be valuable to us as well. Rather than look upon ourselves with dread or disdain, we can look upon all aspects of our humanity and cherish how God has made us. God made the *body* and is for the *body*.[20] He is the Father of our *spirits*[21] and the God of the *spirits* of the prophets.[22]

In four closing benedictions in his epistles, Paul blesses the believers by asking that the grace of the Lord be with their *spirit*.[23] We are encouraged to do the will of God from our *soul*.[24] John prays that in all respects the believers would prosper and be in good health just as their *soul* prospers (3 John 1:2). And the greatest command is that we would love God with all our heart, soul, mind, and strength (Matthew 22:37–39). Every part of human nature is a recipient of God's saving and sanctifying grace.

Third, this view places sin as the culprit. Sin, to be sure, has infiltrated the entirety of human nature, but *sin* is the enemy, not human nature. We need to attack sinful behavior, not some "old man" or "old nature" or "old whatever" part of us that supposedly is the source of sin.[25]

To disparage or fight against any aspect of our humanity is like the old, misguided medical practice that drained blood out of sick people thinking this would affect a cure. The problem was not the blood that God made. The problem was that something in the blood needed to be overcome! Sin is like this. It is like an invading virus coursing through the bloodstream and spreading its sickness. Sin is like a smothering weed wrapping its tendrils around a plant and slowly choking it. The goal is to get rid of the weed, not the plant. The goal is to kill the invading virus, not drain the blood. There is no part of human nature that God "kills" or "crucifies." Paul stated it clearly in Romans 8:3: "He condemned *sin* in the flesh" (italics mine), but not the flesh (the body).

Sin has tainted every aspect of our nature, but His will is to restore every aspect of human nature because sanctification is the restoration of human nature. It is the renewal of the image of God in our body, soul, and spirit. Sanctification makes human nature what God originally intended it to be. And because all of it is valuable, we must honor all of it. We must strengthen the intellectual part by filling it with the truth of God's Word. We must strengthen the volitional part by learning to stand on principles and convictions and by resisting the allurements of temptation. We must heal the emotions by ridding ourselves of unhealthy practices we inherited and learned and become emotionally whole. We look forward to the restoration of our body into conformity with the glorified body of Jesus (Philippians 3:20–21), and we cleanse ourselves from all defilement of our body and spirit, perfecting holiness in the fear of God (2 Corinthians 7:1).

I believe this approach to be far simpler than the two-nature view, the view that one has an old sinful nature residing inside that somehow got crucified and buried with Christ yet still causes problems. It is simpler than the view that we received a new nature when we were born again. Not only is it simpler, it is scriptural. When we were born again, we received the Holy Spirit. The Holy Spirit came to live inside our human nature. It is in this sense that we have "become partakers of the divine nature" (2 Peter 1:4).

Our nature does not become divine, but the Divine One has come to live inside our human nature. His life now courses through us as He lovingly and patiently puts the pieces of our fallen nature back together for His glory.

This perspective shuts down many ideas that teachers have presented through the years such as your old nature is not renewable, something inside you died, you received a new nature, and the two natures war against each other. Now, when I sin, I don't have to resort to spiritual anatomical madness trying to figure out why I am still sinning if my old nature died.

I still sin because my human nature has not yet been completely sanctified. I am still a work in progress. My mind doesn't always think correctly. My will doesn't always choose the right path. My emotions sometimes get mixed up and betray me. But as I present myself to God, I find that my mind learns to filter out error and focus on truth, my will grows stronger to choose what is right and shun evil, and my emotions settle down into true joy and avoidance of extreme mood swings. God is changing my human nature. But we have to present ourselves to God, and that is the subject of this chapter.

PRESENT YOURSELVES TO GOD

Paul's counsel for us to overcome sin is to present our "selves" to God.[26] The same "self" that is dead to sin's condemning finger is now alive to God's justifying and exalting hand. We are to present what we are to Him. We do not present ourselves to Him for crucifixion with Christ. That is done. We died once-for-all to sin with Christ. But we present ourselves as ones who are alive from the dead, and the members that we once presented to sin, those same members we present to God for righteous living.[27]

Present yourself to God.[28] Present your mind, your heart, and your will to the counsel of His Word. Present all that you are to His service. Present all that you are to His people. Pray that His Word would teach your intellect, strengthen your will, and saturate your emotions. As you present yourself, say something like this:

"Lord, here I am. I present myself; I offer myself to you. All that I am—my hands, feet, eyes, ears, all my senses, my legs, arms, and every part of me—I present to You for Your purposes. I realize that I died to sin's penalty with Your Son. I thank You that even though I struggle in some areas and have had recent failures, I have no condemnation. You cancelled the certificate of debt. My old status as a condemned criminal is dead and buried. Thank You! I come to You as one who is alive from the dead. I come to You as a justified person. I stand before You with a righteous standing through Christ, and I can come boldly. Because of the position You have given me through Christ, I present myself to You. I give You every part of who I am. Change me. Sanctify me. Make me holy. Make me a new man. I want to live to You as Christ lives to You. I want Your exalting hand in my life. Just as You exalted Christ, lift me up into a new life. I want Your empowering hand in my life. Just as You gave Him power and authority, grant me power to live for You and teach me to use that power to serve others for Your glory."

In the previous chapter, I used a football story to explain that we have to do more than say no to sin. A team cannot play only defense—otherwise the players will exhaust themselves and eventually give in to the other side. Instead, we have to say yes to the right things. We must not present ourselves to sinful things but present ourselves to good, wholesome things. If we present our bodies to good, nutritious food, we will become healthy. If we eat junk food all the time, we will get sick. In the same way, if we present ourselves to good, wholesome activities that please God, we will find ourselves growing stronger and we will have greater power over sin.

Actually, I learned the above illustration from Dr. Baxter in his book *A New Call to Holiness*. I remember reading this illustration more than 30 years ago and it made a lasting impression on me. Again, I will quote him. Again, it is lengthy. And again, you will find blessing by thinking deeply about his illustration of holiness. (And again, the italics and ALL CAPS are Baxter's emphasis!)

> Here is a man with ailing health and diseased body; anaemic and toxic blood, symptoms of tuberculosis in the lungs, enfeeblement of limbs, fits of languor through nervous exhaustion, pallid face and pasty-looking skin. He dwells in a dank, unhealthy slum. His daily diet not only lacks the required freshness, proteins, vitamins, minerals, but consists of debilitating substitutes. He dodders round, an abject specimen of inanition and emaciation. Then, one day, owing to a sudden turn of circumstance, he is transplanted from that malodorous hovel to a lovely villa on a high hilly slope, with glorious mountains stretching away in the rear, and the wide rolling ocean away in front. The purest air in the world begins to fill those shrunken lungs. The best of nourishing food is now supplied to those starved organs; fresh fruits, rich milk, honey, good bread and butter, plenty of vital vegetables, lean meats and well-prepared fish-meals; and all this week and after week. Soon, what a change in our man! There is new vigour. He now climbs those hills, and exercises on that beach. As he now breathes deeply, the invigorating air of sea and mountains expands those lungs. The pallor gives place to rosy countenance and ruddy physique. Inertness of limb gives place to normal mobility, then to developing muscle and sinew and exuberant energy. Some time later, a medical examination reports, "*Thoroughly healthy.*"

> Is it the same body? There are new corpuscles, new membranes, new nerve-cells, new tissues and tendons, new blood, new protoplasm, new

lungs, new reflexes, new co-ordination and organic functioning. It is the same body; yet decidedly *not the same*. New life has invaded and permeated that body, through oxygenation, rich nutrition, and regenerative metabolism. The new energy has interpenetrated every part of the organism, transforming disease into fullness of health. Can we say, then, that through this metabasis the body now has *absolute* heath? No, for there is no such reality as "absolute health" on earth. What we can say is, that this body now has *HEALTH ABOUNDING*.

Yes, "health abounding"; and, by parallel, that indeed is what *holiness* ~~defining~~ is in our *moral* being, [HOLINESS] *IS MORAL AND SPIRIUTAL HEALTH* ~~holiness~~ *ABOUNDING*. It is not absolute sinlessness or moral perfection, for there is no such reality as "absolute holiness" on earth. Holiness is the life of the Holy Spirit transfused and interpenetrating every part of my moral and spiritual being, transforming diseased impulses and responses, impure desire and inclination, unholy thought, motive, purpose, temper, imagination, into fullness of moral health; so that hatred becomes love; anger becomes kindness; impure desire becomes holy aspiration; selfishness becomes Christlike otherism; jealousy becomes sincere affection; perverted motive and purpose change into earnest ambition to fulfill only the will of God; evil temper and carnal imagination give place to equanimity and spiritual mindedness; pride becomes humility; egocentricity becomes Christocentricity. The whole inner life becomes pure, gracious, *healthful*.[29]

How I wish I could write like that! But I can't, and it doesn't matter all that much, because I hope that through his words and hopefully a few of mine you can see that when we present ourselves to spiritually nourishing activities and habits, when we present ourselves to the living God of life, love, and light, we will change, become like Christ, and find increasing victory over sin.

When I walked away from the show my wife was watching, I could have gone to my study, turned on my computer, and presented my eyes to internet images of the same woman, but I chose not to. Instead, I presented my mind and my eyes to other things that built me up and brought health instead of debilitating spiritual disease.

And when you do this, you will change! You will not find yourself groveling in despair over your sin. You will not be afflicting yourself with guilt trips because you died to the penalty of sin and no guilt and condemnation exists in your life. And when we do this, all of us can stop making incorrect statements like the following:

- "I just need to get out of the way and let Christ do His work." I understand what this means and I have often said it. What we really mean is that we need to stop resisting God's will and start doing His will. But God never wants us to "get out of the way." He wants us to be "in the way," i.e., He wants to work through us and use the image-bearing humanity He has made as the vehicle through which He works to accomplish His purposes on earth.

- "He must increase and I must decrease." I also understand the godly sentiments behind this statement that I also once made, but which I never say anymore. The godly sentiment is that God's will must increase in my life and my selfishness and wanting my own way must decrease. I agree with this completely. John the Baptist is the one who originally made this statement (John 3:30), but he was not referring to his human nature. He was saying that his ministry must decrease and Jesus' ministry must increase. Concerning our human nature, God does not want to decrease it but to increase it! The writer of Psalm 119 confidently stated that he would run the way of God's commandments because God would *enlarge his heart* (Psalm 119:32). Paul prayed that God would *strengthen us in the inner man* (Ephesians 3:16). Paul said God's will for the Church was for it to *grow into the full stature* of Christ (Ephesians 4:13). God wants to remove the debris of sin from our human nature and transform us so that our human nature becomes stronger and more Christ-like. The more we grow, the more we increase in Christ, the greater He is able to show Himself through us.

- "Christ is my life." Well, yes, of course! But this does not mean that Christ supplants our personality. This kind of thinking comes from the faulty interpretation of Galatians 2:20: "I have been crucified with Christ; and it is no longer I who live, but Christ lives in me." Many have sentimentally but superficially interpreted this to mean that "we should stop living" and let "Christ live through us." If, by this we mean that we should stop sinning and being selfish, I concur completely. Alas, many go beyond this and speak as if God's plan was to override our humanness whereby we become mere tubes through which His water of life flows. But we are far more than "tubes" or "straws" through which He breathes. He has made us "fearfully and wonderfully" (Psalm 139:14) He has made us with complexity and majesty. He has made us in His image, and His will is for us to function fully in that image as He transforms us from a broken person into a whole person.

Besides, we discovered earlier that Galatians 2:20 is not about sanctification but justification, and we see in the latter part of the verse that Paul says, "And the life which *I now live* in the flesh *I live* by faith in the Son of God" (italics mine). Christ does not suppress Paul's "I-ness" but makes it alive. Christ indwells the person and energizes the person to present his God-given capacities to Him for renewal.

When we learn to think and speak correctly about our human nature and what Christ is doing in us, we will also learn not to let sin surprise us whenever it shows up on the trail like a wild animal. We know we are on a long journey and the battle against sin is a lifelong process that God graciously understands. He invites us to come to Him for grace in this lifelong battle. We know that He looks upon us as His justified children; He is committed to make us glorious; and He will one day have us rule with Him. He encourages us to keep walking toward our ultimate destiny when He will completely restore through Jesus Christ all that we lost in Adam.

All this should be reason enough to live for Christ and overcome sin. We have died to guilt. We are alive to Him and His purposes. We don't have to be surprised or disappointed by sin and temptation but can learn to stand fast against it and say no to it, knowing that relief is ahead with renewed desires for righteousness. And we can present ourselves to God with confidence as those alive from the dead. We don't have to resort to spiritual anatomical madness and confusion to figure things out. We know we are fallen humans, but redeemed, justified, born again, and recipients of the Spirit who is graciously renewing our humanity day by day to glorify Him.

But Paul isn't through. He has one more resource He wants to make available for us. It is the greatest resource of all. It is the grace of God and this is the subject matter of the next chapter and the last verse of this majestic section of Scripture.

CHAPTER TEN ENDNOTES

[1] McVey, 92

[2] Anderson, *Bondage Breaker,* 45.

[3] Gillham, 97.

[4] Gillham, 103

[5] Gillham, 123

[6] Barabas, So Great Salvation, 91. Barabas is summarizing the thought of the Reverend E.L. Hamilton, a popular preacher of the counteraction theory that set the stage for so much misunderstanding today.

[7] Gillham, 115

[8] Neil T. Anderson, *The Bondage Breaker* (Eugene, Oregon: Harvest House, 1990), 46.

[9] Ibid., 47.

[10] John Stott, *The Message of Romans* (Downers Grove, Illinois: IVP, 1994), 170–171.

[11] Consider this statement from the Reverend Hamilton quoted in *So Great Salvation* by Steven Barabas: "To people who say that they do reckon their 'old man' crucified with Christ but do not find it true experimentally, he answers that they are not reckoning with a living but with a dead faith. A dead faith is an intellectual assent to the truth; a living faith, a heart grasp of it. If we have trouble with faith in this matter, let us remember that there is almost always a moral cause of unbelief." Steven Barabas, *So Great Salvation* (Eugene, Oregon: Wipf and Stock Publishers, 2005), 92.

[12] When we read "members of our body," we must not think only of the physical body but of those internal parts of us, all of our human faculties that we can use for good or evil. Stott says, "Since the body seems again to be our material frame, its parts (*mele*) are likely to be our various limbs or organs (eyes and ears, hands and feet), although probably including our human faculties or capacities, which can be used by sin as instruments of wickedness. *Hopla* is a general word for tools, implements or instruments of any kind, though some think sin is here personified as a military commander to whom it would be possible to offer our organs and faculties as 'weapons.'" Stott, *Romans*, 180–181.

[13] Whether you are tripartite or dipartite doesn't matter. The important matter is that humans have a material and a non-material part to them. The tripartite position holds that the soul and the spirit express distinct parts of human nature while a dipartite position is that the soul and spirit are two ways of looking at the same thing.

[14] 1 Corinthians 14:14: "For if I pray in a tongue, my spirit prays, but my mind is unfruitful." Whether you are a cessasionist or not in regard to tongues is irrelevant at this point. My purpose in quoting this verse is to show that there is an aspect of human nature deeper than the intellect. Perhaps this is the part that experiences the peace that surpasses (mental) comprehension (Philippians 4:7) and the part that comprehends that which surpasses (mental) knowledge (Ephesians 3:18–19).

[15] J. Sidlow Baxter, *A New Call to Holiness* (Grand Rapids, Michigan: Zondervan, 1973), 62–63.

[16] Romans 3:9: "What then? Are we better than they? Not at all; for we have already charged that both Jews and Greeks are all under sin."

[17] This is the beauty of the following two verses: Romans 3:26 – "For the demonstration, I say, of His righteousness at the present time, so that He would be just and the justifier of the one who has faith in Jesus" and 4:5 – "But to the one who does not work, but believes in Him who justifies the ungodly, his faith is credited as righteousness."

[18] See Appendix A: "The Old Man and New Man in Ephesians and Colossians" for a brief explanation of Ephesians 4:22–24.

[19] Hannah Whitall Smith, *Record of a Happy Life*, p. 88, quoted by Baxter, *A New Call to Holiness*, 117.

[20] 1 Corinthians 6:13 – "The Lord is for the body."

[21] Hebrews 12:9 – "Shall we not much rather be subject to the Father of spirits, and live?"

[22] Revelation 22:6 – "The Lord, the God of the spirits of the prophets."

[23] Galatians 6:18; Philippians 4:23; 2 Timothy 4:22; Philemon 1:25.

[24] Ephesians 6:6 – "Doing the will of God from the heart [literally, soul]"; Colossians 3:23 – "Whatever you do, work at it with all your heart" (NIV).

[25] Note that Paul tells us in Romans 8:13 to put to death *the deeds* of the body.

[26] Present yourselves to God is an aorist imperative. "Some commentators think that Paul therefore pictures this 'presenting' as a 'once-for-all' action, or as

ingressive ('start presenting'), or as urgent. But the aorist tense in itself does not indicate such nuances; and nothing in the context here clearly suggests any of them. In fact, the aorist imperative often lacks any special force, being used simply to command that an action take place—without regard for the duration, urgency, or frequency of the action. This is probably the case here. However, we may surmise that, as the negative not presenting ourselves to sin is constantly necessary, so is the positive giving ourselves in the service to God, our rightful ruler." James D.G. Dunn, *Word Biblical Commentary, Vol. 38A, Romans 1–8*, (Nashville, Tennessee: Thomas Nelson Publishers, 1988), 384.

[27] "Those natural capacities and abilities that God has given us are weapons that must no longer be put in the service of the master from whom we have been freed." Douglas Moo, *The Epistle to the Romans* (Grand Rapids, Michigan: Eerdmans, 1996), 384–385.

[28] "Present yourselves is *paristemi* which can be used as a military metaphor but also was used in the LXX as service to the king (1 Kings 10:8)." Moo, 384.

[29] Baxter, *A New Call to Holiness*, 134–136.

You Are under Grace

For sin shall not be master over you, for you are not under law but under grace.

Romans 6:14

If I subscribed to the theology that I have sought to refute, the theology that says that we died potentially to some old sin nature inside us that we have to keep dead experientially by reckoning it dead, and if I were to pick a place in Paul's letter where I would give one good, final reminder before I moved to a new topic, verse 14 would be the place. I would say, "For sin shall not be master over you for your sin nature died with Christ and by an act of faith in reckoning it dead, you can keep it dead." But Paul did not say that or anything resembling it.

When Paul closed this section, he said something very different: Sin shall not be master over you for you are not under law but under grace. Paul sees sin gaining its mastery over us through the Law.[1] He will expound on this fully in Romans 7. Unfortunately that falls outside the limits of this volume. In Romans 7, he will be careful not to put the blame on the Law. We are to blame. Our fallen human nature is the problem, such a problem that sin will use even the good gifts of God such as His Law to find a way of gaining mastery over us! But Paul is confident that sin shall not and cannot hold mastery over those in Christ because they are not under Law but under grace.

For three verses, Paul has spoken in plain terms about how to overcome sinful desires that continue to rise up within the mortal bodies of God's justified people. Let's review his teaching:

- 6:11 – Think about and consider yourself dead to the penalty of sin just as Christ died to the penalty of sin.
- 6:11 – Think about and consider yourself alive to God, as one risen in Christ, and one who lives to God's purposes just as Christ now lives in a new way to God's purposes.[2]

- 6:12 – Say no to sin.
- 6:13 – Present your entire self, all the members of your body, to God as one raised from the dead.

Now in 6:14, Paul gives the rationale for it all. He begins his sentence with the word "for," showing that he is going to give the basis for why we can, with confidence, present ourselves to God as ones who are alive to God. What is the rationale? "For...you are...under grace."

Paul finishes his discourse by returning to the judicial basis for victory: Sin shall not be master over those in Christ because those in Christ are not under Law, which brings repeated failure, frustration, and condemnation. They are under grace. One can hear a tone of definiteness and finality in Paul's words. When he says sin shall not be your master, he means that sin is now no longer our master, similar to his wording in 6:6 when he said our body of sin was destroyed so that we would no longer be slaves of sin.

An irrevocable divide separates our old status from our new. We *were* under Law. We *are* under grace. Therefore, sin shall not be, cannot be, and is not our master any longer because an epoch-changing event occurred when Christ died and rose. Humanity's solidarity with Adam, expressed in the idolatry of Gentile nations, and strangely, in the failure of God's elect nation to keep the Law, was broken by Christ's death and resurrection. God created a new humanity with those who through faith/baptism align themselves with the New Man, Jesus Christ. This new humanity finds the old alignment broken through death and burial and a new solidarity established through resurrection to newness of life. We are no longer under sin, under death, under law, or under condemnation. We are under grace.[3]

Paul introduced grace as the great remedy for our lives earlier in his presentation. In 5:15, he talked about the grace of God and the gift of righteousness by the grace of God abounding. In 5:17, he talked about believers receiving the abundance of grace. In 5:20, he said that even though the Law came in increasing transgression, God met that increased transgression with abounding grace. He explained in 5:21 the goal of it all, grace reigning, grace being king and master instead of sin being master and king in our lives.[4]

Then, in 6:1, Paul answers the objection that his opponents presumably threw his way: "If God met Israel's increased sin with abounding grace, then what keeps us from following the same pattern? Let us sin so that we will get abounding grace! We can have our fun with sin but still find the grace of God!"

Paul shows the illogic of this statement and the misunderstanding of his argument by showing God's work in Christ in 6:1–10. Christ came to deal with sin in a decisive, once-for-all way. He died to the penalty of sin that we might die to it also and be free from the slavery of condemnation. Christ then rose from the dead and entered into a new phase of living for God's purpose in which we can have a role for we died and rose with Him.

By dying and rising with Him, we have entered into a new relationship with God. We can reckon that we died to sin's penalty with Christ and rose to a new relationship with God in Him. Therefore, we now say no to sin and present all that we are to God for His healing, transforming grace. He then summarizes it all in 6:14 where he tells us: Sin shall not be master over you; grace is master is over you. Sin does not own you anymore. Grace owns you. We are no longer under sin and the Law, but we are under grace. We are dead men rising. We have experienced the death of sin and the rise of grace in Christ.

Under grace is the focus of our final chapter and the final leg of our journey that has brought us through some difficult terrain. In this chapter, I hope to fill out the picture of what it means to be under grace and to live a grace-filled victorious life. In our Reformation zeal to exalt a right standing with God by grace, we sometimes have missed the full teaching of grace. Grace is not just the starting point. Grace is the continuing point and the ending point. Grace abounded so that grace might *reign* in our lives.

Our Best Introduction

We need to go back to Romans 5 again. But we need to back up further than 5:12–21, which offered so much insight for our study of 6:1–11. We need to back up to the first two verses of this great chapter: "Therefore, having been justified by faith, we have peace with God through our Lord Jesus Christ, through whom also we have obtained our introduction by faith into this grace in which we stand; and we exult in hope of the glory of God."

Paul tells us that our justification has brought us two things. First, it brought us peace with God through Jesus Christ. No more condemnation and no more judgment hang over our head. We are not in a state of war with God. We are in a state of peace with Him.

But justification brought us a second gift. Paul says through Christ we have also "obtained our introduction by faith into this grace in which we stand." The grace that saved us was just the introductory greeting of the grace of God in our lives.

I have been introduced to many people in my life. One year, I met up with a friend in Washington, D.C., who was attending a conference at a downtown hotel. The conference was over and the keynote speaker was in a receiving line greeting people. My friend wanted to meet him and I tagged along. When my turn came, I shook his hand, told him my name, and expressed how his books and ministry had benefited me. But that was my last contact with him. I never saw him again in person. He never called me and I never called him. The introduction led nowhere, except that I regularly received a letter from him along with millions of others.

Let me tell you another "introduction story." In October of 1945, a gruff woman who ran a boardinghouse had just finished preparing dinner for the men and women who were renting rooms in her home. The table was set and a pretty, 23-year old woman by the name of Stella sat down at dinner. It was her first night at the boardinghouse. She was in for the introduction of her life. The owner shouted out to one of the men lingering in another part of the house, "Hey Red! Come here. There's someone I want you to meet."

Stella's embarrassment showed up in her face, which turned the color of Red's hair. In strode Red, 35 years old and single as well. The owner of the boardinghouse made the introduction and Red, suddenly interested in dinner, took a seat by Stella.

During the course of their dinner as they came to know each other, Red asked Stella the first of what would be three questions: "Would you like to go to a movie?" And Stella said "yes." So off they went to a movie.

After the movie, Red asked Stella a second question: "Would you like to get something to eat?" Again, Stella answered, "Yes, I would," and so the two of them went to a neighborhood restaurant for a bite to eat and a drink.

When they finished, Red and Stella walked back to the boardinghouse and Red asked a third question: "Will you marry me?" And Stella answered, "Yes, I will!" Four days later, Red and Stella were married and remained husband and wife until Red died in 1982, 37 years later! Together they had three sons and ten grandchildren.

This is not a story on dating, courtship, love, and marriage. But it is a story of making the most of an introduction. I was introduced to a famous man in 1988 and never saw him again. Red and Stella were introduced to each other, married, and raised a family. They made the most of their introduction.

Which of these stories better describes your introduction to grace? Have you met the grace of God in salvation, but then wandered off and never become best friends with grace, only occasionally reading a form letter that doesn't seem personal? Or, have you become intimately involved with grace and made the most of this introduction? Your justification, according to Romans 5:2, was your introduction to the grace of God. It was the all-important starting point to a relationship with God, but only a starting point. God intends for you to become intimately acquainted with grace.

The Greek word translated "introduction" is most often translated "access."[5] *By faith we have access to this grace in which we stand.* God has made His grace accessible to us for whatever we need.

In Volume I of *The Chronicles of Narnia: The Lion, the Witch and the Wardrobe*, Lucy is playing hide-and-seek with her sister and brothers and runs to a wardrobe to hide. She burrows as deeply into it as she can, walking through rows of coats until something strange happens. A branch pokes her, the solid sound of the wooden floor gives way to the crunch of snow, and as Lucy continues to walk through this enormous wardrobe, she discovers that she has gained access to a new world, the world of Narnia. She looks back and can still see the door of the wardrobe, slightly open with the light of the room shining through, but she looks ahead and sees a forest of snow covered trees…and adventure. For those who have seen the movie or read the book, we know what Lucy chose. She walked forward into this new world and started an adventure that would change her life and the whole world of Narnia.

We have entered a new world. It is a world of grace. Through Jesus Christ we have peace with God and we have also obtained our access by faith into this grace. God invites us into His world of grace to explore the rivers, valleys, mountains, people, and adventures that the world of grace offers. The question is: how deeply do we choose to move into His world of grace? In the story, Lucy chose to walk into her new world, and when her sister and brothers discovered it, they chose to walk in it also and changed the course of Narnian history and their own lives. They didn't have to. They could have remained at the edge, just looking at the beautiful snow-filled trees.

What do we do? Do we remain at the edge of grace, just looking and wondering but afraid to venture too far from the comfort of the familiar wardrobe? God invites us to walk deeply into His world of grace. Christ died so that we might access His world of grace because His grace will enable us to become everything He created us to become. Remember, He not only died so that we might die to sin, but He rose to a new life with God that we might one day rise to a new life with God. Just as He lives under the exalting, empowering hand of God, we live under that same exalting, empowering hand for a new life now.

Many Christians, unfortunately, see grace only as the power of God in forgiving and justifying. But grace is much more. Grace has two other functions in our lives. Grace cleanses and heals, and grace empowers and restores.

Grace Cleanses and Heals

Sin did a doubly damaging work on us. Sin made us guilty before a holy God and sin corrupted our human nature. Sin was like a poison that spread its damaging effect on our human nature. Our human nature is made in God's image, but sin has infiltrated every facet of the image of God and polluted it.

Sin has polluted our intellect. Instead of a truth-filled mind, we find our minds often filled with lies, heresies, exaggerations, and false ideas about God.

Sin has polluted our will. Instead of using our God-given volition to choose righteousness, we have built-in habits of turning away from God, even when we know it is the wrong thing to do.

Sin has polluted our emotions. We are filled with insecurities, shame, prideful feelings, anger, selfishness, greed, and a host of other issues that weigh us down.

When a man or woman comes to Christ and finds the liberating message of grace that releases us from our condemnation and alliance with Adam and brings us into a new family and a new humanity, we are forgiven and declared righteous before God. We are indeed dead to sin and alive to Him.

But the purpose of this new solidarity with the New Man, Jesus Christ, is so that we can, as Paul put it in 6:4, "walk in newness of life." The Holy Spirit enters into our lives and into the mess of what we are—people with intellects that have a mixture of right and wrong ideas, people with stubborn wills or weak wills, and people with emotional baggage inherited from their ancestors and piled on by their upbringing and circumstances in life.

It is the grace of God that He is even willing to enter such a mess! But enter He does and He begins to work at putting the pieces of our lives together. He starts cleaning up the dirty areas of our lives; He finds the areas that are broken and wounded; and He starts mending and healing those areas that are in the depths of our hearts. This is a work of grace.

It is sometimes a painful work and sometimes a slow work. If God made us with the simplicity of a mousetrap, we could imagine the work of healing and sanctification to be a relatively quick and simple process. But He did not make us this way. In Psalm 139, King David said that we are fearfully and wonderfully made. God made us with great complexity and care, revealing His majesty in our image-bearing human nature.

We are more like a complex software program with millions of lines of code invaded by a virus. The code writer must go in and remove line-by-line the invading force that causes the glitches in our performance. We are more like a great piece of art defaced and disfigured by vandals. An expert must come in and painstakingly remove the offending marks so that the glory of the original masterpiece can once again be displayed for all to see.

God is Code Writer and God is the Artist. His master work has been invaded, disfigured, and broken. But in love, He takes the time painstakingly to put the pieces of our lives together. He doesn't just forgive; He cleanses and He heals. When we were introduced to His saving grace, we were introduced so it might become cleansing and healing grace so that we could once again reflect the great mind and the great heart of the Creator.

GRACE EMPOWERS AND RESTORES

God's grace has another function. It does more than cleanse and heal. His grace also empowers and restores. Reflecting His image means more than having His character developed in us; it also means restoration to the position of ruling the world and using our God-given abilities to glorify Him with our creativity and with our mission in life. That, after all, is why God originally made us.

Genesis 1:28 tells us that after He made the first humans in His image He then blessed them and said to them, "Be fruitful and increase in number; fill the earth and subdue it. Rule over the fish of the sea and the birds of the air and over every living creature that moves on the ground" (NIV). Rule the world! Rule over God's creation! And that is why so many New Testament verses hold out the prospect of ruling with Christ some day.[6] Ruling with Christ will be the full expression of our humanity made in His image.

To think about such an experience and existence exceeds our imaginations and wildest dreams while we live on this earth. We are struggling to rule our own souls, let alone rule the world with justice! But all this points to grace. The grace that helps us overcome sin now is also equipping us for the future work of reigning with Christ.

Paul let such a view of the future shape his life, and this is why he became the man that he was. We could say that he was a man who made the most of his introduction to grace. Look at these examples of grace powerfully working in him.

- PAUL BECAME WHAT HE WAS BY THE GRACE OF GOD. "But by the grace of God I am what I am, and His grace toward me did not prove vain; but I labored even more than all of them, yet not I, but the grace of God with me" (1 Corinthians 15:10).

- PAUL'S MINISTRY OF TEACHING, PREACHING, AND APOSTLESHIP WAS A GIFT OF GRACE. "Through whom we have received grace and apostleship to bring about the obedience of faith among all the Gentiles for His name's sake" (Romans 1:5). "Of [this gospel] I was made a minister, according to the gift of God's grace which was given to me according to the working of His power. To me, the very least of all saints, this grace was given, to preach to the Gentiles the unfathomable riches of Christ" (Ephesians 3:7–8).

- GRACE ENABLED HIM TO DO THE AMAZING THINGS THAT HE DID. "But I have written very boldly to you on some points so as to remind you again, because of the grace that was given me from God, to be a minister of Christ Jesus to the Gentiles, ministering as a priest the gospel of God, so that my offering of the Gentiles may become acceptable, sanctified by the Holy Spirit. Therefore, in Christ Jesus I have found reason for boasting in things pertaining to God. For I will not presume to speak of anything except what Christ has accomplished through me, resulting in the obedience of the Gentiles by word and deed, in the power of signs and wonders, in the power of the Spirit; so that from Jerusalem and round about as far as Illyricum I have fully preached the gospel of Christ (Romans 15:15–19).

- GRACE GREW HIM UP, EQUIPPED HIM, AND EMPOWERED HIM TO SERVE GOD IN THE WORLD. "I thank Christ Jesus our Lord, who has strengthened me, because He considered me faithful, putting me into service, even though I was formerly a blasphemer and a persecutor and a violent aggressor. Yet I was shown mercy because I acted ignorantly in unbelief; and the grace of our Lord was more than abundant, with the faith and love which are found in Christ Jesus" (1 Timothy 1:12–14).

The grace of God is available to grow us up, equip us, and empower us for service. God not only gives us grace to clean us up and heal us of deep personal issues, grace also enables us to serve Him, to love others, and to make a difference in this world. Grace is restoring us to our God-given destiny to become rulers. We are kings and priests who will one day function in this world as He created us to function all along.

ACCESSING GRACE

But how do we access this grace? How do we take steps to ensure that our introduction becomes intimate experience? We receive grace in two ways. We receive it by faith and by humility. "By grace through faith" is the familiar phrase I heard growing up—a heritage from the Reformation—and a direct quote from Ephesians 2 where Paul said that salvation was not by works, but by grace through faith.

But the entire Christian life is to be a life of grace through faith. Paul said that while we are in this world we walk by faith and not by sight (2 Corinthians 5:7). The author of Hebrews said that without faith it is impossible to please Him (Hebrews 11:6). As we exercise faith in Him through the journey of life, what comes to us is grace. If we come to a circumstance that requires we trust Him, and if we do trust Him, we receive grace. But if we turn away in unbelief, we forfeit the grace of God for that situation.

Stephen, one of the seven chosen by the Jerusalem congregation to care for the feeding of widows, is an example of a grace-filled life because he was a man with a faith-filled life. We know he was grace-filled because the apostles recognized his character to be worthy for the task of caring for the feeding of widows.

We also know he was grace-filled because of the miracles God worked through him and his powerful preaching. Acts 6:8 sums up his life well when it says that he was "full of grace and power." But how did he get the grace? Acts 6:5 gives the answer. It says he was "full of faith and of the Holy Spirit." He was full of power because Stephen was full the Holy Spirit. He was full of grace because he was full of faith—grace comes through faith.

The world of grace into which God calls us contains many trails that are traversed only by faith. I have hiked many paths with my wife and sometimes the trailheads will rank them as beginner paths, intermediate, or advanced paths. Sometimes God's paths are similarly marked—this one is for the beginner in faith, this one for those who are making progress, this one for advanced faith.

Sometimes the paths to which He calls us are dark and dangerous. Sometimes the path is winding or clouded and we cannot see far ahead. We walk by faith and not by sight. But eventually, the sun burns through the fog and we can see where we are going. Eventually, the path straightens out and we arrive at our destination. But these glorious days are only possible if we continue on the path of trusting Him. And as we grow in our faith, we will find empowering and restoring grace and find ourselves becoming people we thought only the spiritually elite could become, or we will find ourselves doing things we never thought possible. We experience increasing measures of grace.

Peter put it this way, "Grow in the grace and knowledge of our Lord and Savior Jesus Christ" (2 Peter 3:18). Grow in grace. Grow in your capacity to experience the grace of God. The way you enlarge your grace container is to enlarge your faith container.

John put it this way, "Of His fullness we have all received, and grace upon grace" (John 1:16). I like to think of "grace upon grace" as the waves of the sea coming to the shore. Wave after wave after wave—never stopping, continuously bringing its refreshment. Grace is that way with us. God brings wave after wave of grace into our lives if we will trust Him because grace comes by faith.

Grace comes to us a second way. Grace comes through humility. Here is how Peter put it: "You younger men, likewise, be subject to your elders; and all of you, clothe yourselves with humility toward one another, for God is opposed to the proud, but gives grace to the humble " (1 Peter 5:5). There it is in black and white: grace to the humble.

Humility is one of those words we easily misunderstand or misapply. Some think humility is thinking lowly of ourselves. But Jesus described Himself as humble of heart, and I don't think He thought of Himself as a lowly worm with no value. *— definition of humility*

Humility is simply knowing who we are before God and knowing who God is—and not getting the two confused! God did not make us lowly worms. He made us in His image. We are significant. We are important. We are the prize of His creation. But we are still created beings.

Our pride is that we have sought to be more than we are—to place ourselves on an equal footing with God. This was the sin of our first parents, and we repeat it throughout our lives. Rather than being content with who we are in Him and how He has made us, we strive to make ourselves something else or make ourselves out to be more than we are.

In our search for significance in a world that demeans our worth, we want to know that we are special. This is a God-given desire within us, but we have to learn to go about discovering our God-given worth in the right way. We do it by humbling ourselves before God, remembering that He is God and He has made us. We are His people, created for His pleasure and glory. God does not exist to please us. We exist to please Him. This is a lifelong lesson for us, but as we learn true humility, we discover grace pouring into us.

Jesus demonstrated humility by obedience to His Father's will. He emptied Himself of outward glory and then humbled Himself by obeying His Father every painful step to the cross as Paul so aptly described in Philippians 2. In the same way, we grow in humility as we grow in obedience to the Father. We are not trying to earn grace through our obedience because then it would not be grace. But God is working to break our stubborn, self-centered, rebellious, Adam-like tendency to exalt ourselves. He therefore brings us to places where we must make choices, choices to continue walking in our old Adam-like trait or choices to identify with the New Man and walk in obedience as He walked in obedience.

Humility has nothing to do with beating ourselves up, thinking lowly of ourselves as if we are worthless wretches, but it means learning to take our rightful place before Him as His redeemed creatures being restored. In other words, "Consider yourselves...alive to God in Christ Jesus...Present yourselves to Him as those alive from the dead" (Romans 6:11–13).

And as we learn this humility, we receive grace. The world of grace is filled with paths that are labeled humility. No one wants to walk this path. I have seen thousands of thought-provoking street names in my life, but I have never seen one called Humility Lane! In God's world of grace, paths of humility stretch out before us, and as we walk them, we find grace pouring into our lives.

These paths come to us in three ways. First is the path of circumstances. God brings humbling circumstances into our lives. Peter refers to this in his great humility passage in 1 Peter 5:5–7 when he tells us to "cast all our anxiety on Him." Anxious, debilitating times come to us all, and all we can do is cast ourselves upon Him. These times are humbling. But with humility comes grace.

The path of humility comes to us through our peers. Peter tells us to "clothe ourselves with humility toward one another." He wants to remove from us desires to conquer others, defeat others, and make ourselves look better than others. In the family of God, we are not in a competition to see who can be the holiest saint, the wisest counselor, the deepest teacher, or the most passionate preacher. God calls us to humility of mind toward one another and to regard others as more important than ourselves. And when we walk this path, sometimes a painful path because it seems like others undermine us or ignore our God-given importance, we find grace because grace comes to the humble.

The path of humility comes to us through our leaders. "You younger men, likewise, be subject to your elders" (1 Peter 5:5). How I wish I had fervently obeyed that verse when I was a younger man The self-inflicted pain I would have avoided! But I thought I knew more than my elders, my father, and my pastor, and I made bad decisions that have remained with me throughout my life. God is opposed to the proud—but, but He gives grace to those who learn to walk the path of humility toward their elders, their peers, and their circumstances.

WHAT IS GRACE?

We have talked about grace throughout this book and especially in this chapter. But what is grace? "Grace" is one of those words we throw around a lot but without stopping to think about what it means. I grew up with this definition of grace: the unmerited favor of God. I like that definition, and it worked for me for a while, but as a young Christian man and pastor, I found that it did not embrace all of my experiences and it grew stale. It was only a password of sorts that Christians would use to assure other Christians that they knew what grace was and they were not heretics.

Through the years, as I meditated on God's Word and had my experiences of walking with Him, I came to describe grace in this way: Grace is the personal work of God in my life to do for me what I cannot do for myself and which I will never deserve to have done for me.

Defining Grace

I would like to unpack this description of grace line by line. First, grace is the personal work of God in our lives. This means that He customizes His grace to our particular needs. This means that He is paying attention to us and knows our unique needs. He knows about our circumstances. He knows about our upbringing. He knows about our challenges, our temptations and our secrets, and He fashions His grace to minister to us in the particular ways that sin has distorted us. Grace is not a square-shaped object He tries to fit into a round hole. Grace is malleable, flexible, and adaptive to reach into the deepest corners and crevices of our dark hearts to bring light and healing.

In what particular ways does sin show up in your life? Sin has a unique presence in all of us because each of us is unique before Him, but none of our sins and image-distorting practices is too difficult for the grace of God. God can shape His grace to minister to each of us. I think of the great prophetic words of Isaiah where the voice calls out, "Let every valley be lifted up, and every mountain and hill be made low; and let the rough ground became a plain" (Isaiah 40:4).

Each of us has a unique terrain of valleys, mountains, hills, and rough ground in our hearts. Our internal topography, while similar because we are all sons of Adam, is still somewhat different for each of us because of our unique makeup, upbringing, circumstances, and choices. But the prophetic voice assures us that God is able to reduce the mountainous problems to rubble, lift up the valleys of depression and despair, and smooth out the rugged, rough ground of character. His grace can do all of that for each of us so that the glory of the Lord will be revealed.

God's grace is His personal work for us because He is not a cookie-cutter God. God is not interested in cloning a bunch of look-alike zombie religious people. Rather, He is infinitely creative, and part of that infinite creativity is the way He made you with your particular blend of personality, needs, desires, and experiences. He knows the specific way you need grace. He customizes His grace for your needs because He wants to be personally involved with you to bring out the best in you for His glory. A friend of mine once said, "God's grace is His 'givingness' to us, whatever we require." It is His love in action.

The second feature of grace is this: It is *His involvement in our lives to do for us what we cannot do for ourselves*. At the risk of your thinking that all I do is watch movies, I will use another illustration from one of my family favorites we watched when my kids were growing up, *Ernest Goes to Jail*.

Ernest was a janitor in a bank and with his skill set, honestly, a janitor was about all he could ever hope to be. But he had ambition! In an unforgettable scene (at least for me), Ernest, with mop in hand, had that faraway, visionary look in his eyes. He opened his mouth and eloquent words poured out about his dreams. "I won't always have this job. I'll be able to wield the financial muscle of this institution. I'll be able to move assets around like chessmen on a financial chessboard. Someday corporate managers will shudder in their wingtips at my approach for I will become...a bank clerk." This buildup to the revelation of his life ambition matched the humorous letdown as we listened to him reveal his great life goal was to become a bank clerk!

When my daughter, who is now in her 20s and married, was a little girl, she wanted so much to scan the groceries at the grocery store. We would go to the store together and those bigger-than-life privileged people who ran those products over that laser to ring up our grocery bill mesmerized her. That was one of her great goals in life. Well, she reached her goal when she was 15, and the thrill of scanning products at a grocery store lasted for about...oh, three days. Needless to say, her dreams are a lot bigger than that now.

What are your dreams? Are they cashier-sized? Are they bank-clerk sized? My apologies to anyone reading this who may be working as a bank teller or as a cashier at a grocery store, but I doubt if anyone graduating from high school said to a counselor, "I have great ambition for my life. One day I want to be a bank teller or scan products in a supermarket." Those are temporary, entry level stepping-stones to greater things in life.

God wants to open your eyes to those greater things. If He opened your eyes and showed you what He really had in mind from the start for you and what He still has in mind for you, you might faint, run away in fear, or say, "impossible—there is no way that could ever be true for me." And you know what? You would be right. There probably is no way that it could ever be true for you, and that's where grace comes into play, because grace is the personal involvement of God in our lives *to do for us what we could never do for ourselves.*

Do you remember the verses we looked at earlier for Paul? He said, "I am what I am by the grace of God." He said that God's grace enabled him to serve as an apostle. He said that God's grace empowered him to preach in ever-expanding regions to bring the Gentiles into obedience. And all this in spite of the fact that he was the least of all saints. Yet, that was the point. God's more-than-abundant grace raised him up to do what he never would have thought possible.

In the same way, God comes into our lives like a personal trainer and says, "Let me work with you. Let me develop you. You have Olympic-sized capabilities. I'll take you to places you never dreamt possible." This is grace: God doing for us what we can never do for ourselves. This is not something reserved for the so-called spiritually elite. This is His plan for every one of His children. And this is part of what Paul had in mind when he told us to consider ourselves alive to God and to present ourselves and our members as those who have been raised from the dead. God is not in the process of preparing you for eternal janitorial service. God is preparing you to rule.

But some may say, "Look, Jonathan, I know God can do that. I mean, after all, He is God and God can do anything. But you don't know me. I've messed things up really bad. There's no way God would ever do anything for me—would He?"

Maybe you had at one time big goals and then somebody crushed them. Maybe you have experienced failure and now a bigger-than-life dream seems impossible to achieve because of your bad choices. Maybe you've never had dreams. Or maybe you've had selfish dreams and now you are wondering if God can ever forgive you and replace your dreams with His.

This brings us to the third part of the definition: Grace is the personal work of God in our lives to do for us what we cannot do for ourselves and *which we will never deserve to have done for us.*

If the whole truth were known about every one of us, we would see that no one is worthy of God's personal care and involvement. But that's why it's grace.

When we see that we don't measure up and that we don't have what it takes, that is when God steps in and says, "But I am the God of all grace. This is what separates Me from all other so-called gods. They are tyrants. I am gracious. They are furious. I am forgiving. They are weak. I am all-powerful and able to hurl galaxies into existence and care for those in need."

The sooner we realize that, the sooner we get out of the bad habit of trying to earn God's favor and realize that it is already earned through Jesus Christ and that we are fully accepted on the bad days as well as the good days, the sooner we will experience more grace in our lives.

When we learn God's grace in this way, why sin? If God wants to be personally involved in my life and shape His grace to bring healing and empowerment, why sin? If God wants to make things happen that I cannot cause to happen and do things in me and through me that I would not dream possible, why sin? And if God does it all in spite of what I have been, and in spite of my current issues, and in spite of the possible lapses in the future, why sin? Why not cast yourself upon His grace! Why not enter fully into the new world and explore His grace for you. Why not allow yourself to be surprised, amazed, and awed by the ever-increasing cascade of grace because of His inexhaustible, greater-than-your-problems love for you.

No wonder Paul says that sin shall not be master over us because we are under grace. God has opened a world of grace for us through the death and resurrection of Jesus. The death of Jesus broke our solidarity with our old man, our old standing in Adam. It cancelled the body of sin that held us captive. It acquitted us of all charges and set us free. In a phrase, His death to the penalty of sin affected our death to the penalty of sin.

But He also rose from the dead. He lives to God. He and His Father are free to embark on a world-conquering quest to reclaim ruined sinners, reconcile them to Him, and change them into image-bearers who will glorify Him in this age and in the glorious age to come. We are alive to God in Christ Jesus, and He asks us to mark this indelibly upon our minds and hearts and to present ourselves confidently to Him as those who are alive from the dead. All of this is true and sin shall not be master over us because we are not under Law or under sin—we are under grace.

Shall we continue in sin that grace might abound? What a foolish question and what a foolish way of thinking. Of course not! God forbid! To think and live in this way is to think and live with distortion and miss completely the point of what He has done for us and the goals He has in mind for us—goals so glorious that even the best this world has to offer is nothing compared to them.

It is a life we may not be able to imagine now, but if we walk with Him in faith and humility, we will see it unfold gloriously in front of us and we will see that its offer is far greater and far more satisfying than the promises of sin. It is a life in the world to come that is so glorious we can only catch glimpses of it through a glass darkly.

We will live in a world where righteousness and peace abound, where sorrow, suffering, pain, tears, and death are banished. We will live in a world where every aspiration of our heart will be only godly and will be attained as we live in the presence of our glorious God. Everything we will be and everything we will do will glorify Him, please others, and bring joy to our hearts. And sin will be but a distant memory.

✳ ✳ ✳

Red and Stella could not have imagined the adventures that awaited them when they were introduced to one another on an October night in 1945. After they married, they quickly conceived two boys who were born in 1946 and 1948. Life was good, but life was hard. Red worked as a steam-shovel operator in a rock quarry to make cement. Stella stayed at home with the kids, and worked hard to keep the house clean and prepare good meals.

But restlessness grew in her heart as her two sons grew older. She wanted another baby. She talked to Red about it, but he repeatedly said no. Resources were scarce. Work outside and inside the home was too demanding. But Stella would not take no for an answer. She prayed and told the Lord that if He gave her another baby she would dedicate him or her to His service and raise that baby to be devoted to His purposes in the world. And God heard her prayer. She conceived and gave birth to a son.

I am that son, and as I look back on my years, I am amazed by the abundance of grace in my life—the grace of a mother who would not take no for an answer but who persisted in faithful, fervent praying until the answer came. The grace of parents who taught me Bible verses and praying from the time I could walk and talk. The grace of parents who cared for my eternal destiny and who one day knelt with me beside their big bed as I asked Jesus to come into my life and be my Savior.

Grace has come to me in countless ways through leaders and peers who encouraged me to walk in those paths of faith and humility. Grace came to me when I realized with great shame and disappointment that I would not grow up to play for the Yankees, but found that misplaced ambition replaced with a love for God's Word and a desire to teach it to others.

Grace has come to me through the hardships of life. Yes, some of the hardships came to me because of what others did to me. But, honestly, most of my hardships have been my own fault. But I have found grace in the hardship and discovered a patient God who is determined to teach me to quit wrestling with Him, to let go of the old-Adam ways, to rest in His love, and to anticipate His purposes for my life.

Grace has come to me through an astonishing abundance of forgiveness—astonishing because of all my failure and astonishing because His grace is greater. And His grace has come cleansing, healing, restoring, and empowering me to do what I never would have thought possible. For example, writing a book like this that began when I looked deeper into His Word after hearing some well-intended but questionable teaching.

I look back on a life of grace and realize that what I am, I am by that grace. I look to the future and realize that whatever I will become or do, I will become or do it by the grace of God. I have explored many parts of His world of grace. I want to explore more. I hope you will come into this world and explore it deeply, too!

Shall we continue in sin that grace might abound? What a ridiculous question!

CHAPTER ELEVEN ENDNOTES

[1] "To be under law is to accept the obligation to keep it and so to come under its curse or condemnation. To be under grace is to acknowledge our dependence on the work of Christ for salvation, and so to be justified rather than condemned, and thus set free" John Stott, *The Message of Romans: God's Good News for the World* (Downers Grove, Illinois: IVP, 1994), 181.

[2] "We are to recall, to ponder, to grasp, to register these truths until they are so integral to our mindset that a return to the old life is unthinkable. Regenerate Christians should no more contemplate a return to unregenerate living than adults to their childhood, married people to their singleness or discharged pris-

oners to their prison cell." Stott, *Romans*, 180.

[3] Remember that the Law had a sin-producing, sin-intensifying function. It brought the knowledge of sin (3:20), wrath (4:15), transgression (5:13–14) and an increase of the severity of sin (5:20). In 1 Cor. 15:56, the Law is the power of sin. Moo says, "This means there can be no final liberation from the power of sin without a corresponding liberation from the power and lordship of the law," 389.

[4] Notice the contrast of rulers – Death reigned (5:14); sin reigned in death (5:21); grace reigns (5:21); those who receive the gift of righteousness reign (5:17).

[5] The Greek is *prosagogen* and is found here and in Ephesians 2:18 – "for through Him we both have our access in one Spirit to the Father" and in 3:12 – "in whom we have boldness and confident access through faith in Him." Most translations render it "access," including the NIV, NKJV, KJV, ESV, and HCSB. The NLT renders the passage "this place of undeserved privilege." The verb *prosago* means "to bring forward or to come near or approach." 1 Peter 3:18 speaks of Christ bringing us to God.

[6] For example, Luke 22:28–30; Romans 5:17; 2 Timothy 2:12; Revelation 2:26–27; 3:21; 5:10; 22:5.

JOURNEY'S END

WE HAVE COME TO THE END OF OUR JOURNEY and arrived at the destination that we sought—a place where we can find victory over the sinful desires and failures to which we sometimes still succumb and that grieve us. We know that we have often lived a contradictory reality, but we have continued to pursue Christ with the hope of gaining a consistent reality of living in a manner pleasing to Him.

As we arrive at our journey's end, we look at the view that unfolds before us and we discover a breathtaking landscape dominated by the grace of God. Grace is everywhere. Its fragrance fills the air. It beckons us to breathe deeply of its fresh, sweet, life-giving spirit. Like the four children, playing hide-and-seek on a rainy day, we realize that we have indeed walked through a magic wardrobe into a new country that beckons us to come in fully and explore its rivers, mountains, valleys, and all the adventures contained within them.

Through Christ we have entered a new world, a world of grace, a world everyone desperately needs to see but are blind to without Him. It is a world whose brilliant light can still blind us as our eyes adjust to its overpowering beauty. But as we grow, as our eyes adjust to the light of grace, we discover that we are in the land that ensures victorious living, joy-filled hearts, a Christ-honoring life, and ultimate triumph. We discover the brilliant light of grace doesn't actually blind us; instead, it helps us see what we need to see.

I wrote *Dead Men Rising* because I wanted to do two things. I wanted to explain God's Word carefully, consistently, and clearly, and I wanted to apply that word to my life in a manner true to human reality, but also true to the great reality of what Christ has done for us.

It is a journey I started for myself, yet I became aware that I would be taking it for many others who would read this "journal" and walk the path I have discovered. And so I wrote *Dead Men Rising* for you also, with the hope that you would trace the path I have walked. It has not always been easy. For many chapters we had to examine side trails that many of our brothers have taken—trails that only led to steep cliffs or impenetrable brush. We learned that many of the ideas they have presented have not matched Paul's intent or his doctrine. Nor have they matched human experience. For this reason, we had to spend a long time examining them and explaining why we should avoid them.

I hope in these chapters that I have not offended anyone still living. I say "still living" because many who have written on Romans 6 are now with the Lord and must smile at us as we continue on our journey to follow Christ, and though we see better each day, we still only see through a glass dimly. I don't think they mind at all if I don't agree with them since they live in the presence of the Lord whose favor is all that matters. I hope all of us who dwell in the beginning reaches of the eternal country of grace can maintain such a heavenly perspective as we seek to learn from one another and discover fully what Paul is talking about in this important section of Scripture.

We have covered a lot of ground. Perhaps it would be good, having walked such a great distance together, to reflect on the path we have taken and to view carefully the landscape that now surrounds us. As we do so, we will discover the key features Paul describes for every believer in Romans 6:1–14 to live in a manner pleasing to God.

1. Live in and explore the land of grace. You are not under Law but "under grace." Realize His grace is much more than for forgiving you—the forgiveness you first experienced when you placed your faith in Him and walked into your new solidarity with the New Man, Jesus Christ and away from your solidarity with the old man, Adam. His grace is for cleansing, healing, restoring, equipping, and empowering. You live under grace, not under sin, not under Law, but under the matchless, never-ending, impossible-to-exhaust grace of God. He beckons you to explore this world and to strengthen your body, soul, and spirit—your entire self—with His energizing expression of constant kindness.

2. With such a world surrounding us, with such a destiny ahead of us, take all that you are and all that you have and present it to Him. He understands that you are still learning to breathe in grace. He understands that your human nature still has the corroding effects of sin, but He brought you into this world so that His grace might sweep away the old in your life, fill you with the sweet, life-giving air of grace, and renew you in His image. Therefore, present yourself to God *as one alive from the dead.* You are a dead man who has risen, a dead man who by the

miracle of grace is alive in Him! Walk toward Him! Present your mind, your will, your emotions, your heart, your soul, your spirit, every part of your body, and whatever other way you choose to describe or think of your human nature, to Him.

3. As you present yourself to Him, do so knowing that you are presenting yourself for change, and that change means you will have to start saying no to some things to which you have been accustomed to saying yes. But say "no." Say no to sin. Do not let sin rise up within you and present itself as your friend or as your solution to your needs because it is not your friend or your help. It is your enemy and it will reign over you if given the chance. Do not let sin reign over you and do not present the members of your body to sin the way you once did. Instead, keep on presenting yourself to God—daily, moment by moment, as the needs arise, and especially if you lapse back into an old behavior. If you do, re-present yourself to Him for fresh grace.

4. You now live to God as Christ lives to God. In the same way that Christ rose from the dead and now lives to God's exalting and empowering hand, you too have risen to a new status with God—a justified man who lives under the exalting and empowering hand of God. Understand your status, think on it, reflect on it, calculate it, and reckon it on the ledger of your mind. You have a new identity and a new destiny. Pursue them.

5. Remember that you are a *dead man* who has risen. Reflect on, calculate, and reckon on the ledger of your mind what God did for you on the cross of Christ. He crucified your old standing with Adam, the old man. He rendered null and void, cancelled, and destroyed the body of sinful evidence compiled against you. He freed you from the prison house of death so that you are no longer a prisoner to your guilt. Remember that there was a once-for-all event. Not a once-for-all experience of the Spirit that frees us from all sinful tendencies within, but a once-for-all dealing with your sin on the cross that destroyed your solidarity with Adam so that you could have a new solidarity with a far better Man. Therefore, just as Christ died to sin once for all and death is no longer master over Him, in the same way consider that you died to sin once for all and death is no longer master over you.

6. Keep the central person and the central events—the cross and resurrection—at the center of your life. What we reckon is not some mystical experience for something internal to us, but we reckon what the central person did for us in the most important events in the history of the world. Keep focusing on Him and what He did for you.

7. The greatest step anyone can take to gain power over sin is to think about and internalize what it means for us to be united with Christ. With this, I am sure no member of Christ's body will disagree. His death and resurrection is the central event of history, and His death and resurrection for us should be the central event of our lives. This union with His death to sin and resurrection to God should remain at the forefront of our Christian awareness and conviction.

John Stott said: "If Christ's death was a death to sin (which it was), and if his resurrection was a resurrection to God (which it was), and if by faith-baptism we have been united to Christ in his death and resurrection (which we have been), then we ourselves have died to sin and risen to God. We must therefore 'reckon' (AV), 'consider' (RSV), 'regard' (NEB), 'look upon' (JBP) or *count* (NIV) ourselves *dead to sin but alive to God in*, or by reason of our union with, *Christ Jesus*. This 'reckoning' is not make-believe. It is not screwing up our faith to believe what we do not believe. We are not to pretend that our old nature has died, when we know perfectly well it has not. Instead we are to realize and remember that our former self did die with Christ, thus putting an end to its career. We are to consider what in fact we are, namely *dead to sin and alive to God* (11), like Christ (10). Once we grasp this, that our old life has ended, with the score settled, the debt paid and the law satisfied, we shall want to have nothing more to do with it."[1]

Having nothing more to do with it. That is what we want: nothing more to do with sin. As we fix our gaze on Christ and His great work for us, we will find the greatest reason of all to say no to sin and not let it reign in our mortal bodies. As we fix our gaze on Christ and His great work for us, we will find every reason to present all that we are, body-soul-spirit, to Him as those who have been justified and raised. As we fix our gaze on Christ and His great work for us, we will realize that we are not under law, sin, condemnation, or any other dehumanizing element that robs us of joy and God of His rightful glory as our Creator and Redeemer. We are under grace. And we will live under grace for the duration of this life and for the life to come.

Like Peter, Edmund, Susan, and Lucy who ran into the New Narnia after Aslan destroyed the old, and who discovered that the deeper in they went the bigger and more glorious it became, we too will discover that the deeper into grace we go, the bigger and more glorious it will become.

What shall we say to these things?

CHAPTER TWELVE ENDNOTES

[1] John Stott, *The Message of Romans: God's Good News for the World* (Downers Grove, Illinois: IVP, 1994), 179.

THE OLD MAN AND NEW MAN IN EPHESIANS AND COLOSSIANS

MANY PEOPLE HAVE MISSED the meaning of Ephesians 4:22–24 and Colossians 3:9–10. Some look at these verses and say, "See, here is an old man and a new man that is internal. It's not just referring to status. Furthermore, we are commanded to put off the old man and put on the new man." Here are the verses.

> That, in reference to your former manner of life, you lay aside the old *[Greek tense is important]* self, which is being corrupted in accordance with the lusts of deceit, and that you be renewed in the spirit of your mind, and put on the new self, which in the likeness of God has been created in righteousness and holiness of the truth (Ephesians 4:22–24).

> Do not lie to one another, since you laid aside the old self with its evil practices, and have put on the new self who is being renewed to a true knowledge according to the image of the One who created Him (Colossians 3:9–10).

The misinterpretation usually arises from a casual reading that seems to suggest that *we* are to lay aside the old self and put on the new self, as if Paul is commanding us to do this. This comes out most strongly in the Ephesians passage. However, the Greek tenses and moods do not allow this. "Lay aside" and "put on" are aorist indicatives, which indicate past completed action. Paul is not commanding believers (this would require an imperative) to do the job of laying aside the old man and putting on the new man. Instead, he is reminding them that it already occurred when they gave their lives to Christ. This coincides with the union with Christ theology of Romans 6:3–4. When we expressed faith/were baptized, we died and were buried with Christ, or to look at it in anthropological terms, we laid aside the old self and put on the new self. We laid aside our union with Adam and entered into our union with Christ.

The middle verse of the Ephesians 4 passage is a present passive (or middle) imperative and is the only command in the verses. It emphasizes the continued work of God's Spirit to renew us at the deepest level of our humanity—the spirit of our mind. Because we already had our old man put away in Christ and have already put on the new man in Him, we are to renew ourselves at the deepest core of who we are—in the spirit of our minds. Perhaps, also, Paul is thinking that in order to have victory over our continued sinful desires, we must focus on renewal at the deepest levels of our identity, to renew ourselves in accordance with our new identity and status God has given us in the New Man, Jesus Christ.

A second misinterpretation is to use these verses to promote a two-nature theory in believers. We have an old man (self) and a new man (self) that war with each other. But the tenses in Colossians 3, an aorist ("you laid aside") and a perfect ("have put on the new self"), emphasize past completed action (aorist) and past completed action with continuing results (perfect), make this unlikely. Thus, the old self has once for all been laid aside (Colossians 3:9) and the new self has once for all been put on (3:10). God does not view the believer as an old man and a new man at the same time but only with the status as a new man in Christ. Similar to Ephesians 4:22–24, the only present tense in the passage is the part about the renewal of the person in the image of God.

The best way to interpret these passages, therefore, is to view them in a legal way, showing our solidarity with Adam. Our old self, our old life in Adam with all its evil practices (Colossians) and corruption (Ephesians) has been once for all laid aside through our union with Christ. Our new self is our solidarity with Christ, our union with Him. This standing in Christ is one of legal righteousness and holiness of truth (Ephesians) whereby we are set apart as belonging to Him (sanctification used in a forensic way). This enables us to experience renewal in the image of God who created this legal position in Christ for us (Colossians).

Notice also that all of this happened to "you." Paul does not compartmentalize human nature but explains what happened to *the whole person* before God. "You" laid aside the old self and put on the new self, and the same "you" must now be renewed. Your ties with Adam, with his downward spiraling corruption in culture and in the person, were severed. Your ties with Christ, the New Man, were established in something called "the putting on of the new man," which enables an upward spiral into holiness and righteousness, a true renewal of your humanity. Therefore, we are to engage in behavior consistent with Christ, the New Man.

THE USES OF *KATARGEO* IN ROMANS 6 AND BEYOND

PROPONENTS OF THE SUPPRESSION THEORY have sought to advance their position by resorting to an interpretation of Romans 6:6 that runs like this: "Our old nature was crucified with Christ so that our sinful impulses (body of sin) might be subdued or weakened so that we would no longer be enslaved to those sinful impulses."

The key word is "subdued" or "weakened" and is a translation/interpretation of the Greek word *katargethe*. It works hand-in-hand with the idea that the old man is something internal to us.

The reasoning runs this way: "We know that our sinful desires can never be completely eradicated until we go to heaven or receive our resurrection body. Therefore, when Paul speaks about our old nature being crucified with Christ, he says that it did something to our 'body of sin' (interpreting this as sinful impulses working within us). Because we know that we still have sinful tendencies within us, Paul could not have meant that our body of sin was destroyed. Therefore, we have to render it with an alternative word such as subdue or weaken. Then, as we reckon our death to sin, we keep the 'body of sin' under control and live in victory."

I picture this interpretation like a wrestling match. As we reckon our old man dead, the body of sin remains pinned to the floor in a helpless state. But if we don't reckon our old man dead, the body of sin can rise up and pin us to the floor. Our job is to keep it pinned so that it will be in that helpless state.

But does the Greek word *katargethe* allow for this interpretation? Does it have the sense of making weak or subduing? How does Paul use this word elsewhere in Romans, and in what context?

In this appendix, I will show that we have to go beyond word choices and synonyms and view the context in which Paul employs the word. Once we understand the context of the verses and how they fit into the overall theme of Romans, we will see the appropriateness of the word, the proper translation, and the proper interpretation. The English word translating the Greek word from the katargeo word family, will be in bold.

Romans 3:3 – What then? If some did not believe, their unbelief will not **nullify** the faithfulness of God, will it?

Paul is trying to explain a riddle to his readers. He had been preaching that God was faithful to His covenant promises and brought salvation to His people through Messiah Jesus. But, if the Messiah has come and brought the promised deliverance in fulfillment of the promises, why do so many of His people not believe? And if so many do not believe, would this nullify God's faithfulness to His covenant promises? Paul answers, "*Me genoito* (God forbid)," and he explains (eventually in chapters 4–11) that the promises find fulfillment in Jesus Messiah and in those who unite with Him through faith/baptism. The ones who exercise faith are the promised remnant, and the covenant faithfulness of God is fulfilled through them rather than through the whole nation.

"Nullify" appears to be a good translation, therefore, as it is a word that would correspond to contracts, agreements, covenants, vows, and promises. When any of these social conventions are terminated, we say they have been nullified, which means they have no more binding force.

Other translations of Romans 3:3:
NIV – nullify
NJKV – without effect
ESV – nullify
NLT – unfaithful
HSCB – cancel

Romans 3:31 – Do we then **nullify** the Law through faith? May it never be! On the contrary, we establish the Law.

Paul answers a Jewish objection to his gospel. If God establishes His covenant promises through faith in the Messiah and not by works of the Law, then you have just nullified the single most important event in the history of Israel, the giving of the Torah on Sinai and the people entering into a covenant relationship with God. You have nullified the Law! Paul's answer is, "*Me genoito!* (may it never be!). Through faith in the Messiah, we establish the Law, i.e., we arrive at the goal of the Law (Romans 10:4), something that the Law never had power to do (Romans 8:3). We come to the same place, the same wonderful end that the Law wanted to achieve but could not through the weakness of our sinfulness. We don't nullify the Law, but we establish it through faith.

"Nullify" appears to be a good translation choice for the same reasons as with 3:3, the topic pertains to covenant purposes. God establishes His covenant purposes through faith, the same covenant purposes to which the Law pointed. But faith, rather than nullifying God's covenant plans makes them reality. The Law was an expression of God's covenant, the stipulations that His covenant people were to perform. But finding an inability to perform them, they found themselves in a desperate plight. Faith arrives at the goal of the Law, a righteous standing for the believer within the covenant and the covenant faithfulness for God.

OTHER TRANSLATIONS OF ROMANS 3:31:
NIV – nullify
NJKV – make void
ESV – overthrow
NLT – forget about
HSCB – cancel

ROMANS 4:14 – For if those who are of the Law are heirs, faith is made void and the promise is **nullified**.

The same theme continues in Romans 4 but with a fuller explanation. Paul establishes faith as the means by which God has always advanced His purposes in the world. He puts forth Abraham and David as key examples of God using faith to move His covenant purposes forward and shows that faith, and not circumcision, is the key identifier for those belonging to the covenant and therefore the family of God.

The pattern he sets forth with those men is the same pattern with the nation of Israel. God promised Israel an inheritance (the land), but the fulfillment of the promise does not come through the Law but by faith. If the promise comes by law-keeping, faith has no place in God's agenda, and the promise will be nullified because law-keeping (as he will show later in 5:13–14, 20–21 and chapter 7) cannot possibly succeed for any individual or for the nation to achieve covenant blessing.

OTHER TRANSLATIONS OF ROMANS 4:14:
NIV – worthless
NJKV – made of no effect

ESV – void

NLT – pointless

HSCB – canceled

ROMANS 7:2, 6 – For the married woman is bound by law to her husband while he is living; but if her husband dies, she is **released** from the law concerning the husband.

But now we have been **released** from the Law, having died to that by which we were bound, so that we serve in newness of the Spirit and not in oldness of the letter.

Here we have the most unusual translation of *katargeo* (released), but the idea of nullification is everywhere present and one can also see the covenant emphasis as Paul uses marriage to illustrate the believer's past relationship with sin and the Law and his present relationship with Christ. Before we met Christ, we found ourselves bound to one husband (sin) by the Law. But when that husband died, we were free to be bound to another husband, Christ. Our union with sin and Law terminated "through the body of Christ" so that we could be joined to the resurrected Christ (7:4). Because we died to sin (6:2), we also died to the Law (7:4).

Because Paul pairs the verb with the person (she is released, we have been released), it would be awkward to translate *katargeo* as "nullified" because the person is not the one nullified, but the binding agreement is nullified. Perhaps we should translate these as middles instead of passives and render them "she finds nullification from the binding force of the law" and "we have found and now experience nullification from the Law's demands." Whatever way we translate them, we find another example of a formal, binding relationship brought to an end.

These are the uses of *katargeo* in Romans besides our key verse, 6:6. In every case, Paul employs this word in a formal, binding covenant context. *Katargeo* speaks of the severance of such an agreement. When we employ this nuance in Romans 6:6, we find a perfect fit and see why Paul would use it. We had a binding agreement with sin. A certificate of debt, a body of sinful evidence, kept us imprisoned before a holy God. But God nullified the "body of sin," the formal evidence against us that kept us legally bound. *Katargeo*, then, becomes the perfect word choice for Romans 6:6 since it matches Paul's careful use of it in other key places in Romans where he employs it as the word to express contract nullification.

Paul, then, is not talking about some mystical death to a force inside us, and we do not have to resort to word games to express how something can be dead but not dead, or rendered powerless but still able to exert great power. Paul is not saying that our sinful impulses have been weakened but that the formal relationship with the legal body of sin against us has been irrevocably severed.

OTHER TRANSLATIONS OF ROMANS 7:2, 6:
NIV – released/released
NJKV – released/delivered
ESV – released/released
NLT – no longer apply/released
HSCB – released/released

OTHER NEW TESTAMENT VERSES
Paul uses *katargeo* in many other contexts, which is why we find a host of translations including: passing away (1 Corinthians 2:6), doing away with (1 Corinthians 6:13; 13:8, 10–11), abolished (1 Corinthians 15:24, 26; Galatians 5:11; 2 Timothy 1:10), fading (2 Corinthians 3:7–14), severed (Galatians 5:4), and bring to an end (2 Thessalonians 2:8). But he also uses it in covenant passages such as Galatians 3:17 and Ephesians 2:15 where translators use words that correspond to contract nullification.

GALATIANS 3:17 – What I am saying is this: The Law, which came four hundred and thirty years later, does not invalidate a covenant previously ratified by God, so as to **nullify** the promise.

OTHER TRANSLATIONS OF GALATIANS 3:17:
NIV – do away with
NJKV – annul
ESV – annul
NLT – cancel
HSCB – cancel

EPHESIANS 2:15 – By **abolishing** in His flesh the enmity, which is the Law of commandments contained in ordinances, so that in Himself He might make the two into one new man, thus establishing peace.

OTHER TRANSLATIONS OF EPHESIANS 2:15:
NIV – abolish

NJKV – abolish
ESV – abolish
NLT – ending the system
HSCB – do away with

We find one non-Pauline usage of *katargeo*:

Hebrews 2:14–15 – Therefore, since the children share in flesh and blood, He Himself likewise also partook of the same, that through death He might **render powerless** him who had the power of death, that is, the devil, and might free those who through fear of death were subject to slavery all their lives.

Some could point to this verse and say, "See, here is a rendering powerless of a person who continues to exist and cause havoc. In the same way, our 'body of sin' (interpreting it internally) continues to exist and we must continue to reckon it defeated."

I would argue in this way: Even though the devil continues to live and will not find his final demise until Christ returns, his great weapon—death—has been destroyed. The next verse says that it was the fear of death that made us subject to slavery all our lives. The writer says Christ rendered Satan powerless that He might free us from this bondage to death (condemnation). Satan's great weapon was our guilt, our awareness that something is not right—that we are on the road to judgment. He manipulated this awareness of our doom to create different forms of slavery.

But when Christ died, He satisfied the Law's demands so that condemnation and judgment no longer hang over the head of believers. He destroyed Satan's great weapon. This is exactly Paul's argument in the highly forensic Colossians 2 passage where He says that in cancelling our certificate of debt, He disarmed the powers, made a public display of them, and triumphed over them through the cross where He forgave all our transgressions and removed the body of the flesh.

Other translations Hebrews 2:14–15:
NIV – destroy
NJKV – destroy
ESV – destroy
NLT – destroy
HSCB – destroy

Options for the Body of Sin in Romans 6:6

W‌HILE MANY COMMENTATORS have rightly interpreted "dead to sin" and "old man" within a legal framework, no one, to my knowledge, has correctly identified the meaning of body of sin that I have proposed in this work. To interpret it as I have done, to consider it a legal term referring to the "body of evidence against us," brings the pieces of the Romans 6 puzzle together. No longer do we have to force the pieces together and make the passage say something that neither makes sense nor works in life. Every phrase comes together.

Having said this, I realize other interpretations will persist. For this reason, I offer two other viewpoints and their strengths and weaknesses (from my perspective). These are the Future Glorification interpretation and the Present Sanctification interpretation. After I present these, I then present the Legal interpretation, believing it to be the soundest and most reasonable explanation of Paul's thought as it makes all parts of 6:6 come together and in harmony with the clear judicial reading of 6:7:

Future Glorification Interpretation

> *6:6a – knowing this, that our old self was crucified with Him,*
> *6:6b – in order that our body of sin might be done away with,*
> *6:6c – so that we would no longer be slaves to sin;*

The old self—our legal status before God in Adam—has been crucified in order that our physical body that is fallen with its continued propensity to sin might be done away with at the resurrection so that in the future we would no longer be slaves to sin.

S‌TRENGTH #1 – Romans 6:5 speaks of the resurrection, although some find this interpretation questionable and prefer to see the resurrection in 6:5 as referring to our new life and a parallel phrase to our "newness of life" in 6:4. Our new walk with God is a "likeness" of His resurrection.

WEAKNESS #1 – If 6:6b is future and speaking of the resurrection, then 6:6c loses its force. It would read logically: Our old standing in Adam was crucified with Christ that we might one day have a new resurrection body so that we would no longer (then?) be slaves of sin. That doesn't give much hope for conquering sin and having a victorious life now. The purpose of 6:6a, b points to the slavery ceasing now in this life.

WEAKNESS #2 – If 6:7 is the rationale for it all, it doesn't make sense that 6:6b points to the future. 6:7 points back to the cross and our justification rather than pointing to the future. If he is pointing to the future, it should read, "For he who has been raised is freed from sin" rather than "he who has died is freed from sin."

PRESENT SANCTIFICATION INTERPRETATION

6:6a – knowing this, that our old self was crucified with Him,
6:6b – in order that our body of sin might be done away with,
6:6c – so that we would no longer be slaves to sin;
The old self—our legal status before God in Adam—has been crucified in order that our physical body that is fallen and has propensity to sin might have these sinful effects rendered powerless in this life so that we would not be in slavery to sinful impulses in this life (so that we can serve in newness of life).

STRENGTH #1 – It follows the emphasis of 6:4–5 of walking in newness of life.

STRENGTH #2 – 6:6c makes better sense than the Future Glorification interpretation. The evil desires of the body have been nullified so that our slavery to sin *in this life* might cease.

WEAKNESS #1 – It weakens the sense of *katargeo*. See Appendix B for more on this.

WEAKNESS #2 – It doesn't flow into 6:7. Paul says that the one who dies *is freed* from sin, not, is "potentially freed" or "mostly freed," but *is freed* from sin.

WEAKNESS #3 – It tends toward redundancy. If 6:6c is about freedom from slavery to sinful habits, why would he say it again in 6:7?

Weakness #4 – It doesn't take into consideration that the proper translation of "freed" is "justified."

LEGAL INTERPRETATION

6:6a – knowing this, that our old self was crucified with Him,
6:6b – in order that our body of sin might be done away with,
6:6c – so that we would no longer be slaves to sin;
The old self—our legal status before God in Adam—has been crucified in order that the "body of sin," i.e., the accumulated evidence of sin might be destroyed so that we would no longer be (legal) slaves to (the penalty) of sin.

WEAKNESS #1 – "Body" isn't used this way in the immediate context (6–8).

STRENGTH #1 – It lines up with Colossians 2 where Paul employs the similar phrase, "body of flesh." Flesh and sin become synonyms and both make the same theological point–the legal body of evidence against us has been nullified. Whether we call it the body of sinfulness or the body of fleshliness, the point is the same.

STRENGTH #2 – It fits perfectly with the forensic nature of 6:6a, allows a forensic interpretation of 6:6c, and fits perfectly with the forensic vocabulary and tenses of 6:7.

STRENGTH #3 – It fits with the flow of the argument of Chapter 6. Verses 1–10 provide the legal and logical basis upon which Paul makes his appeal not to let sin reign in our mortal bodies in 6:12. It is in 6:11–14 that the practical outworking (the sanctification part) begins.

STRENGTH #4 – In 6:12, Paul feels the necessity to identify the body as our *mortal* body. He could have said, "Do not let sin reign in your body that you should obey its lusts," but he adds a qualifier, an adjective. Why does he do this? Is it to make sure that his readers distinguish it from a very different kind of body in 6:6, the "body of sin"?

STRENGTH #5 – 6:6b does not say *our* body of sin but *the* body of *the* sin. The body of the sin has a more impersonal flavor to it.

STRENGTH #6 – It matches uses of the word "body" in English and in ancient Greek, the uses of totality or mass and the legal use of body.

What about the Flesh?

In *Dead Men Rising*, I make the point that the old man is not something internal to us, some part of our sinful human nature, but is instead our status in Adam. This runs contrary to much popular teaching that tries to pin that label on some entity residing within us. I believe the pages of my book soundly refute this idea, and the writings of Stott, Baxter, and many other scholars confirm this approach. But what about "the flesh"? Paul, in Galatians 5:16–25, speaks about the works of the flesh and says that we are not to walk in the flesh and that the flesh wars against the Spirit. In Romans 8, Paul speaks about the mind set on the flesh and that those in the flesh cannot please God. What is "the flesh" in the believer?

Commentators have normally taken two paths trying to explain the meaning of "the flesh" in the believer. One path is to interpret it internally, much like their interpretation of the old man. The other is to speak of it solely in terms of our body, making the outrageous claim (see quotes by Gillham and McVey in the book) that our spirit/soul is completely free of sin because our old man is dead but that sin still resides in and makes its presence known in our flesh. I believe both of these approaches to be incorrect.

The New Testament uses the word, flesh, in three ways:

1. The flesh is a synonym for our physical body – "I have been crucified with Christ and it is no longer I who live, but Christ lives in me. And *the life which I now live in the flesh* I live by faith in the Son of God, who loved me and gave Himself up for me" (Galatians 2:20, italics mine). "For to me, to live is Christ and to die is gain. But *if I am to live on in the flesh*, this will mean fruitful labor for me. And I do not know which to choose…yet *to remain on in the flesh* is more necessary for your sake" (Philippians 1:21–22, 24, italics mine).

2. The flesh refers to our status as sinners under the judgment of God. "For while we were in the flesh, the sinful passions, which were aroused by

the Law, were at work in the members of our body to bear fruit for death" (Romans 7:5). Three points strike me about this verse:

- Paul says we *were* in the flesh, with the implication being that we no longer *are* in the flesh. Paul explicitly says this at the beginning of 8:9: "You are not in the flesh but in the Spirit."

- Paul speaks about the sinful passions being aroused *by the Law*, not being aroused by "the flesh." The external Law caused sinful desires to rise up within us. He does not try to isolate part of our human nature and label it "the flesh."
- Paul says the sinful passions were at work in our physical body, not in "our flesh." Again, Paul does not attempt to isolate something inside us.

Thus, the flesh, in 7:5 and 8:9, at least, refer to "the status of the sinner in solidarity with Adam" and not to something internal to us.

3. The flesh refers to our sinful behavior and habits that our fallen human nature engages in. Galatians 5:16 would fall into this category, "Walk by the Spirit and you will not carry out the desire of the flesh." In this third usage, Paul is not trying to isolate and identify some part of our human nature, which some call the "old man," others "the body of sin," and still others "the flesh." He is simply referring to our behavior that is contrary to God's holy and loving character. Sometimes it manifests in deeds of the body like immorality or murder. Sometimes it manifests in deeds of the heart like envy, jealousy, or coveting. An unbeliever, one who is outside Christ, has the status of "flesh," and his behavior is controlled by this status and his behavior is consistent with this status. A believer, one who is in Christ, has the status of "Spirit" as Paul says in Galatians 5:25, "If we live by the Spirit, let us also walk in the Spirit," and in Romans 8:9, "You are not in the flesh but in the Spirit." The believer must therefore learn to walk according to his new status in Christ and exhibit behavior and strength of character consistent with the likeness of Christ.

Paul tells us in Galatians 5:24 that those who belong to Christ Jesus have crucified the flesh with its passions and desires. He cannot be referring to some internal entity because believers still have sinful passions and desires and some-times give in to them. Paul also tells us not to walk in the flesh in Galatians 5:16. This would be a strange command if the flesh referred to an entity inside us. If it did refer to this, in what way was it crucified? And if it was crucified, why do sinful passions and desires still exist? In 5:24, Paul must be referring to our status in Adam as in Romans 7:5 and 8:9. Those of us who belong to Christ Jesus have crucified the fleshly status with all its sinful practices, passions, desires, judgments, and condemnation. That person no longer lives in the judicial reckoning of God. He was crucified.

Some have tried to make an issue of the fact that Paul says *believers* have crucified the flesh. But I don't think this wording points to a different experience. All believers "crucified their old status in Adam" when they submitted to Christ in faith/baptism.

The flesh will be a major topic in the subsequent volume to *Dead Men Rising* when we take a close look at Romans 6:15—8:13.

Neil T. Anderson, *The Bondage Breaker* (Eugene, Oregon: Harvest House, 1990)

Neil T. Anderson, *Victory Over the Darkness* (Ventura, California: Regal Books, 1990)

William F. Arndt & F. Wilbur Gingrich, *A Greek English Lexicon of the New Testament* (Chicago: University of Chicago Press, 1963)

Steven Barabas, *So Great Salvation* (Eugene, Oregon: Wipf and Stock Publishers, 2005)

J. Sidlow Baxter, *A New Call to Holiness* (Grand Rapids, Michigan: Zondervan, 1973)

G.K. Beale, editor, *The Right Doctrine from the Wrong Texts?* C.H. Dodd, "The Old Testament in the New" (Grand Rapids, Michigan: Baker Academic, 1994)

Manfred T. Brauch, *Hard Sayings of Paul* (Downers Grove, Illinois: IVP, 1989)

Jerry Bridges, *The Pursuit of Holiness* (Colorado Springs, Colorado: NavPress, 2003)

F.F. Bruce, *The Epistle of Paul to the Romans* (Grand Rapids, Michigan: Eerdmans, 1963)

John Calvin, *Commentaries on the Epistle of St. Paul to the Romans* (Grand Rapids, Michigan: Eerdmans, 1947)

Alan Cole, *The Epistle of Paul to the Galatians* (Grand Rapids, Michigan: IVP, 1972)

James D.G. Dunn, *Word Biblical Commentary, Vol. 38A, Romans 1–8* (Nashville, Tennessee: Thomas Nelson Publishers, 1988)

Sinclair Ferguson, *Know Your Christian Life* (Downers Grove, Illinois: IVP, 1981)

Joseph A. Fitzmeyer, *The Anchor Bible: Romans* (New York: Doubleday, 1992)

Gerhard Friedrich, editor, *Kittle's Theological Dictionary of the New Testament* (Grand Rapids, Michigan: Eerdmans, 1971), Gerhard Delling, Volume VII, "Body-Soma"

Bill Gillham, *Lifetime Guarantee* (Eugene, Oregon: Harvest House, 1993)

F. Godet, *Commentary on St. Paul's Epistle to the Romans* (New York: T & T Clark, 1883)

Robert Govett, M.A., *Is Sanctification Perfect Here Below?* (Miami Springs, Florida: Conley & Schoettle Publishing, 1985)

Gary Haugen, *Good News About Injustice* (Downers Grove, Illinois: IVP, 2009)

Charles Hodge, *Commentary on the Epistle to the Romans* (Grand Rapids, Michigan: Eerdmans, 1976)

R.C.H. Lenski, *St. Paul's Epistle to the Romans* (Minneapolis, Minnesota: Augsburg Publishing House, 1961)

R.C.H. Lenski, *The Interpretation of St. Paul's First and Second Epistles to the Corinthians* (Minneapolis, Minnesota: Augsburg Publishing House, 1961)

H.P. Liddon, D.D., D.C.L., LL.D., *Explanatory Analysis of St. Paul's Epistle to the Romans* (Grand Rapids, Michigan: Zondervan, 1961)

Martin Luther, *Commentary to the Epistle of the Romans* (Grand Rapids, Michigan: Kregel, 1976)

Leon Morris, *The Epistle to the Romans* (Grand Rapids, Michigan: Eerdmans, 1988)

Douglas Moo, *The Epistle to the Romans* (Grand Rapids, Michigan: Eerdmans, 1996)

Steve McVey, *Grace Walk* (Eugene, Oregon: Harvest House, 1995)

John Murray, *The Epistle to the Romans* (Grand Rapids, Michigan: Eerdmans, 1965)

Watchman Nee, *The Normal Christian Life* (Wheaton, Illinois: Tyndale House, 1979)

William R. Newell, *Romans Verse by Verse* (Chicago: Grace Publications, 1943)

Barclay M. Newman and Eugene A. Nida, *A Translator's Handbook on Paul's Letter to the Romans* (London: United Bible Societies, 1973)

Peter T. O'Brien, *Word Biblical Commentary, Volume 44, Colossians and Philemon* (Waco, Texas: Word Books, 1982)

William S. Plumer, *Commentary on Romans* (Grand Rapids, Michigan: Kregel, 1971)

Mike Quarles, *The Strange Odyssey Of a Legalistic Preacher Who Became a Drunk, Discovered Grace And Was Set Free*, http://www.ficm.org.uk/deeperissues/miketestimony.html.

A.T. Robertson, *Word Pictures in the New Testament, Volume IV, Epistles of Paul* (Nashville, Tennessee: Broadman, 1931)

Sorin Sabou, *Between Horror and Hope* (Waynesboro, Georgia: Paternoster Biblical Monographs, 2005)

William Sanday and Arthur Headlam, *The Epistle to the Romans* (New York: Scribners, 1906)

John Stott, *The Message of Romans: God's Good News for the World* (Downers Grove, Illinois: IVP, 1994)

John Stott, *Men Made New* (Grand Rapids, Michigan: Baker Book House, 1988)

Tipton & Waddington, editors, *Resurrection and Eschatology, Theology in Service of the Church*, (Philipsburg, New Jersey: P&R Publishing, 2008), Dennis E. Johnson, *The Function of Romans 7:13–25 in Paul's Argument for the Law's Impotence and the Spirit's Power, and Its Bearing on the Identity of the Schizophrenic "I"*

Stephen Westerholm, *Understanding Paul* (Grand Rapids, Michigan: Baker Academic, 2004)

Ben Witherington III, *Paul's Letter to the Romans, A Socio-Rhetorical Commentary* (Grand Rapids, Michigan: Eerdmans, 2004)

N.T. Wright, *The New Interpreter's Bible Commentary, Volume X, Romans* (Nashville, Tennessee: Abingdon, 2002)

N.T. Wright, *Justification* (Downers Grove, Illinois: IVP Academic, 2009